THE VOICE OF THE BARD

*LIVING POETS and ANCIENT TRADITION
in the HIGHLANDS and ISLANDS of SCOTLAND*

THE VOICE OF THE BARD

Living Poets and Ancient Tradition in the Highlands and Islands of Scotland

TIMOTHY NEAT
with JOHN MacINNES

CANONGATE

DEDICATION

To Muriel Kate Thomas

First published in 1999 by
CANONGATE
Unit 8, Canongate Venture
New Street
Edinburgh EH8 8BH
Scotland

Previous page:
Bard Duncan Williamson singing
'Jock O' Monymusk, Fife, 1998.
(TN)

ISBN 0 86241 842 9

British Library Cataloguing-in-Publication Data
A catalogue record for this book is available
on request from the British Library.

The publisher gratefully acknowledges subsidy of
the Scottish Arts Council
for publication of this book.

Chuidich Comhairle nan Leabhraichean am foillsichear le
tabhartas barantais airson cosgaisean-siubhail an leabhair seo

Text and layout designed by Mark Blackadder

Printed by The Bath Press, Glasgow

CONTENTS

ACKNOWLEDGEMENTS

It has been an honour to write this book. It owes an absolute debt to the bards who are its subject, to their families, and to the communities of which they are so vitally a part. Without exception they have offered hospitality and friendship. I am deeply grateful to them. I hope *The Voice of the Bard* gives these contemporary exponents of a great and ancient Gaelic literary tradition a little more of the recognition they deserve.

I would not and could not have embarked on this project without the collaboration of the Gaelic scholar Dr John MacInnes. I thank him. His transcripts and range of reference were a privilege to receive. As always, it has been a pleasure to work with my editors Stephanie Wolfe Murray and Liz Short. Heartfelt thanks also go to Vivian Roden, Margaret Begg, Hamish Henderson, John Berger, Hugh Andrew, Ian Hamilton Finlay, the late Sorley MacLean, John Purser, Peter Adamson, Howard Jones, Lila Rawlings, Angus Ease MacLeod, John Murdo Morrison, Johan MacLeod, Ian Morrison, Willie Morrison, Donnie MacIntosh, Lal O'Brian, Christie Campbell, Francis Neat, Clare Tye, Caroline Neat, Angie Dunbar, Lal MacDonald, Lorna MacAskill, Will MacLean, Dr MacCrae of Uig, Dr Julian Toms of Portree, Norman Johnston, Jim Johnston (headmaster of Farr School), Mary MacCorquodale, Carcanet Press, Polygon Press, Mary Beith, Iain Fraser, Alice Grandison, Ross Carstairs and many others.

The Michaelis Jena Ratcliffe Prize, awarded to my book *The Summer Walkers* in June 1997, provided crucial financial support; as did funds from the Europa Prize, Festival de Cinema de Barcelona, awarded to the Neat/Berger

Bard Murdo MacAskill of Strathdearn (four years a Japanese prisoner-of-war in Burma and Thailand) with Barby his wife, Inverness, c. 1950. (VR)

film *Play Me Something* in 1989. In addition, a Travel Grant from the Gaelic Books Council (1997) enabled Dr MacInnes and me to extend our travels in the Highlands and the Hebrides.

Photographs are used with the permission of the bards, their families and the various photographers. I extend thanks to all who have collaborated and made loans. Photo codes are as follows: Timothy Neat (TN), Francis Neat (FN), Donald MacDonald (DM), Margaret Begg (MB), Vivian Roden (VR), Mary MacLean (MM), Murdani Kennedy (MK), Kenneth Smith (KS), Donnie MacIntosh/Lal O'Brian (Don), Skipper Nicolson (SN), Johnny MacAskill (JM), Norman MacLean (NM), Glasgow Herald (GH), School of Scottish Studies (SSS), Imperial War Museum (IM), an unknown Benbecula airman (BA), unknown sources (UK), Austen Murray (AM), Willie MacPhee (WM), Hamish Henderson (HH), Charlotte Munro and Jessie Smith (JS).

The Poetry. English texts taken directly from authors' manuscripts are codified with the authors' initials. English versions of Gaelic originals, translated as poems and songs by Timothy Neat (working on transcriptions made by John MacInnes), are codified (TN/Mac). Those translated by Timothy Neat from transcriptions made by the authors are codified (TN/Aut). (Timothy Neat's aim as a translator has been not literal accuracy but a literary equivalence which emphasises narrative flow and attempts to create on the page a pleasure which directly compliments the poems and songs as sung and spoken.) Gaelic texts transcribed from the author's own hand or published texts are codified with the author's initials. Gaelic texts transcribed, from the spoken word or recording tapes, by John MacInnes, are codified with the authors' initials and the name MacInnes.

Copyright. Book text is copyright to Timothy Neat. All poetry, songs and diary extracts are copyright to the original authors (both in Gaelic and in English translation). The text of Part 4 is copyright to John MacInnes.

The Voice of the Bard is the second of what will be a quartet of books on Highland life in the 20th century. *The Summer Walkers; Travelling People and Pearl-Fishers in the Highlands of Scotland* was published by Canongate in 1996. *When I was Young; Voices from Lost Communities in Northern Scotland*, will be published in spring 2000. *The Horse's Word; Blacksmithing and Horsemanship in Twentieth Century Scotland* will be published in autumn 2000.

TIMOTHY NEAT
Wormit, Fife, July 1999

PREFACE

The living continuance of ancient bardic tradition in Scotland is a thrilling thought. That such a tradition is not only alive but still widespread across the whole of the Islands and Highlands is, fortunately, still a fact. As Scotland moves into the third millennium, dozens of bards, many almost unknown, are creating vital poetry and song from within a tradition that goes back, unbroken, to the pre-Christian Gaidhealtachd. These poets create poetry that is made to be uttered, to be sung, to be heard.

The Voice of the Bard presents biographical portraits of fourteen 20th-century makars, each of whom has made a distinctive literary contribution to their various communities. Ten of these bards are still alive. The youngest is 59, the oldest is 98. Dozens of other bards might have been chosen. It was a mixture of chance and design that led to the selection of these fourteen, but they stand as fair representatives, geographically and culturally, of the quality and range of bardic composition in modern Scotland. These bards are, at once, tradition bearers and original poets and the tradition they perpetuate has been a crucial factor in the preservation of both the Gaelic language and the peerless song culture of the Scottish Gaidhealtachd.

It is not easy to present the rich reality of Gaelic bardachd in a book in the English language. The bulk of these poems were conceived in Gaelic and made not to be read but heard — usually as unaccompanied song. In the best songs, ordinary words fuse physical and spiritual responses to engender transcendent, visceral and aesthetic responses. Very ordinary lyrics can, given an appropriate melody and authentic rendition, take on, in song, the magnetic resonance of great poetry. Perhaps Scotland has an advantage over most folk literatures in that the music of the Gael seems to possess unrivalled access to the subconscious.

All art exists within a social and public framework: this fact is of particular importance in estimating the poetic achievements of the Gaelic bards. Their work is rooted within a historical continuum that still informs all aspects of their lives. Despite modern forms of travel and communication, despite tourism, the majority of the indigenous people of the Highlands and Islands still live isolated lives in contact with the same natural, social and religious forces that shaped their forbears for generations.

In 1912, the Italian Futurist, Boccioni, painted a suite of three paintings entitled 'The Departure, Those Who Go, Those Who Stay'. Although many of the bards profiled here have travelled widely and experienced extraordinary things in far-flung corners of the world, these bards returned home and their poetry powerfully represents the culture of the people who stayed. These bards, emotionally and historically, represent deep attachment to a native place and the form of this book reflects their feeling of geographical, social and psychological belonging. The poetry and song presented is best 'read' within the context of individual lives lived in particular continuing communities. Thus a series of life-stories are described and these help reveal the particular vitality of the bardachd these poets have produced. The writer J. B. Pick once stated that 'the greatest work of art the Highlanders have produced is themselves' and in the Gaidhealtachd 'the medium' remains very much part of 'the message'. All the bards featured have produced bardachd of high quality – but the overall importance of their work is much greater than any purely academic assessment might suggest re individual 'literary' merit because this bardachd is so integrally part of a living culture that cannot be divided, a culture that has been a source and measure for all Europe since writing began.

In Gaelic the term 'bard' describes makers of all kinds of song and poetry, from the praise-poets of the Heroic Age to the saint-poets of the Medieval period, from travelling minstrels to village bards, from versifiers like William McGonagall to art poets like Duncan Ban Macintyre and Sorley MacLean. The 14 bards featured here were selected because they are closely associated with traditional practice in traditional communities, because their inspiration and achievement is oral rather than literary, their audience local and specific rather than specialist or widespread. Contemporary Gaelic art poets of undeniable literary stature like Sorley MacLean, Derick Thomson and Iain

Crichton Smith have been excluded, as have the younger generation of poets shaped by Higher Education and Arts Council Support, like Aonghas MacNeacail and Meg Bateman. These 14 have all had some work published or broadcast but they are, in general, unknown as Scottish poets, they are as a group 'under-educated', unsubsidised and publicly neglected. They can best be described as 'village bards' but they are much more than this; the totality of their experience provides us with a mini history of the Highlands in the 20th century and the range of their poetic achievement exemplifies most aspects of the long history of Gaelic bardachd.

In Gaelic tribal society, recognised bards enjoyed considerable dynastic or local status and 'bardic immunity' from charges of poetic slander or libel. Such bards usually enjoyed reasonable material rewards from the communities they served and a certain bardic 'idleness' was accepted. The twentieth century bards profiled in this book have enjoyed, with one exception, very low economic status and lifetimes of hard physical labour. This, in an age when stable access to money is so crucial to well being and happiness, must be seen as an injustice but also recognised as a key to the nature and quality of their poetry. It is a social currency, not private property or a financial commodity. It is a gift that is nurtured and passed round. And, because it is a gift, it continues to bestow mystical powers and authority – aesthetic, moral, social and personal. Within monied and institutionalised societies the custodians of such gifts are largely ignored. The remarkable thing about the Highlands is that enough of the old values remain to have ensured that the millennial tradition of bonded giving and receiving continues, a cultural reality, in our time. The deeply human instinct that art is service has helped maintain the innocence of vision, the Medieval 'belief', that underpins and illuminates the production of these unsung makars, these saintly poets of Europe's western edge.

It is generosity, not a sense of grievance that dominates the work of these poets. 'The Clearances', which are the staple diet of too much second rate Scottish art, feature infrequently. These bards know that the 18th century was one of the great ages of Gaelic poetry, song and pipe music and don't pretend otherwise. They recognise that the 19th century's exploitation of 'tartanry' formalised much genuine tradition and is a prime reason for the world's high opinion of Scotland today. They themselves have witnessed the 20th century exodus from the Highlands and played their part in that heroic bleeding that has seen Nazi barbarism defeated, the Gaelification of Scottish culture and the Gael imprint his genes and values around the globe. They recognise that the story of Gaelic exploitation and failure can also be told as a story of success and of life. These bards have not industrialised sentiment; they have lived and fought as frontline troops not staff-room careerists. They, in their lives, represent traditions of soldiering, seamanship and service, traditions, of religious and intellectual enthusiasm that go back, not just to the Reformation but into prehistory.

It is easy to blame the old aristocratic elite for the problems of the Highlands in our commercial age but the problems are historical and economic beyond class. It is, however, true that the high artistic traditions of the Gaidhealtachd have been maintained largely because the pyramid of cultural responsibility has, in recent centuries, been turned on its head. The standard of an ancient culture, which was left at the back door of the castle to rot, has been taken up by the poorest of the poor, by black-house crofters, seaweed-gatherers, shepherds, weavers, roadmen, fishermen, masons, by soldier-pipers and travelling tinkers, and it is from amongst these people that the bards, to whom this book pays tribute, have recurrently risen.

History suggests that there are cultural 'laws' at work in most societies that make it highly unlikely that artistic pre-eminence will pass down generations buttressed by comfort, power and success. There is truth in the folklore that family businesses 'rise, prosper and decay within three generations'. Today's cultural elite, ensconced within institutional Higher Education, seems to be displaying all the symptoms of a similar sclerosis. In modern universities the great ideals of educational and cultural 'service' have been too much replaced by careerism, self-satisfaction and narrow specialism – just as surely as it was in Renaissance Monasticism. This makes contemporary bards not only important as creative 'critics of life' but symbols of renewal. Their achievements, against the odds, are exemplary and democratic. They are living representatives of a dynasty founded on poverty and the recognised value of the word.

Education has long been highly valued in the Gaidhealtachd but of the poets profiled in this book, three left school at thirteen, six at fourteen, two had very little school at all and only one, Norman MacLean, went to university. Lack of formal education has been a handicap to some but it nurtured character and stimulated intellectual ambition without separating these poets from their communities or numbing their oral and musical capacities. Seven of these poets are seriously religious and see their bardachd as part of their spiritual life in communities still close to God. All are linked by geographical isolation and immersion in Gaelic rural environments. Most of these bards have experienced shocking personal loss – the early death of parents, the sudden loss of brothers and sisters, comrades and relatives killed in war. They tend to be introverted and display a personal shyness, yet all honour the idea and practice of martial service. Several have suffered recurrent or sustained ill-health. All have what T. S. Eliot described as 'a unified cultural sensibility', which directly reflects the physical, intellectual and spiritual unity of their lives. All of them have reinforced first-hand knowledge of traditional bardachd with school or book study of English Romantic literature, particularly the poetry of Wordsworth (a man whose 'bardic voice' has been less than fully studied). All but one of them has 'a good ear' and most have astounding aural memories. They continue an essentially Celtic tradition.

The late Poet Laureate, Ted Hughes, described in his last book, *Winter Pollen*, how the old linguistic forms and subjects of poetry continued in Celtic tradition long after they were Latinised and regularised in the English tradition. 'As Chaucer's rhymed iambics displaced the Germanic alliterative sprung rhyme, so that long clangorous line had in turn displaced the verse forms of the indigenous Celtic peoples, who held in common one of the most evolved and sophisticated traditions in world history…(but) the older Celtic traditions survived intact and resilient: for one thing the actual nations survived, separate but attached, concentrated in isolation, like powerful active glands, secreting the genetic remnants of a poetic caste selectively bred perhaps through millennia. The different languages also survived, with the relics of their unique poetic traditions still sacred … The notoriously arduous poetic colleges of the old Celtic world were still active well into the 17th century. The last fully-trained "fili" died as recently as the 1720's, one in South Uist, another in Skye…without this enveloping, nurturing, Celtic matrix, English poetry would be unrecognisably different and vastly deprived.'

If, as Hughes suggested, this Celtic/Gaelic continuance is crucial to the nature of modern English poetry, how much more crucial it must be for poetry produced by tradition bearers on Uist and Skye. The old 'colleges' went but the tradition continued, thriving in the pulpits of the Presbyterian Churches, in the bow-tents of the tinkers, in ancient lullabies sung by mothers and maidservants, in talk at the sheep fank and cuidhe, in the precenting and singing of the great Gaelic psalms. How could such a strong and deep-rooted tradition be lost in such an isolated, resilient, intelligent and educated community? It has not been. In form, style and content the poetry presented here has direct links with very ancient traditions — as John MacInnes explains in his historical survey in part four of this book.

John Keats, paying tribute to Homeric Greek poetry in his sonnet 'On first looking into Chapman's Homer', honoured first the bardic tradition of the Hebrides.

Much have I travell'd in the realms of gold,
And many goodly states and kingdoms seen;
Round many western islands have I been
Which bards in fealty to Apollo hold...

It is a song of praise to the classical sources of European poetry — but Keats acknowledges the Western Isles as the 'living' bastion of that great tradition. And a century later the Scots poet, Hugh MacDiarmid, honoured the same living Gaelic tradition in his poem 'Island Funeral'.

In all the faces gathered round
There is a strange remoteness.
They are weather-beaten people with eyes grown clear
Like the eyes of travellers and seamen,
From always watching far horizons.
But there is another legend written on these faces,
A shadow — or a light — of spiritual vision...

There are fewer and fewer people
On the islands nowadays,
And there are more ruins of old cottages
Than occupied homes.
I love to go into these little houses
And see and touch the pieces of furniture...

I know them also in their origin
Which is the Gaelic way of life
And can speak with equal authority
About a people one of whose proverbs
Is the remarkable sentence:
'Every force evolves a form.'
While this thing lasted
It was pure and very strong.
In an old island room the sense is still strong
Of being above and beyond the familiar,
The world as we know it,
In an atmosphere purified,
As it were, from the non-essentials of living
— an intangible feeling,

Difficult to describe,
But easy to recall to anyone
Who has stood in such a room
And been disturbed by the certainty
That those who once inhabited it
Were sure of every thought they had...

'There is a great beauty in harmony.'
They lived as much like one another as possible,
And they kept as free as they could of the world
at large...They were all
Poor people – whose notions of form
Were both ancient and modern...
The cornet solo of our Gaelic islands
Will sound out every now and again
Through all eternity.

The vulnerable but still-vital society that MacDiarmid eulogised lives on. In
Sorley MacLean it has produced the greatest poet in its history, in our time.
And it remains a society shaped by the poetic genius of people to whom
bardachd has been important, and natural, for thousands of years. (There seem
to be increasingly good musicological reasons to believe that only the musical
forms of certain Native American tribes have older historical continuity than
the waulking songs of the Hebrides.) Prime amongst the custodians and
creators of Gaelic culture today are the singers and poets profiled as bards in
this book.

Part One

Hebridean Tradition

Donald MacDonald

472B SOUTH LOCHBOISDALE, SOUTH UIST

'S e toiseach is deireadh an duine a' bhuachailleachd.'

'The beginning and the end of life is herding.' That's what was said when I was young and it was true in those days. I was a herd from the age of nine till I left school at fourteen. It was the ideal job for old soldiers and boys, taking the cows out, bringing them in for the women to milk. It was my grandmother's cows I herded, over on the west side of the island. Here on Lochboisdale there were always less cattle and today, with big grants for barbed wire and fencing, there's no herding at all. I'm 72. And I think my day will have gone before any herding returns to South Uist.

I've lived alone for 33 years, and for five years before that I nursed my mother. She had a malfunction of the pituitary gland and senile dementia. I was away in Oban, working at the tweed mill, for James MacDonald: my sister had got married, and my two older brothers were away at sea, so it was me that came home to look after her. There was no outside help in those days. The crofting life is a beautiful life but things can be very hard. I've worked this croft for 38 years, alone, eleven years of which I also worked on the alginate, collecting the kelp, the seaweed.

It's a joint tenancy here, that's very unusual these days. My great-grandfather divided the croft. He had two sons and he split eight acres between the two of them. That division stands to this day. Four acres is not much, the rock comes through the surface here, but we used to keep two head of cattle and still had plenty ground for potatoes. In addition, there was common grazing on the hill for the sheep. That's what I've got, four acres plus the hill: a few sheep, no cattle, no path to the door and ten lifetimes of peat just two hundred yards away over the burn. The walls of this crofthouse are more than

Previous page:
The whaling station, South Georgia, where bard Murdani Mast Kennedy spent several winters in the 1950s.
(MK)

Opposite:
The bard Donald MacDonald, South Lochboisdale, South Uist, 1997. (TN)

four feet thick. My neighbour's chicken, Ina, comes across and lays me a few eggs. I'm very fond of her – but poetry is the thing that has given me the greatest pleasure I have known.

I never knew my father. He died when I was seven months old, Donald MacDonald was his name. He suffered from an ulcer of the stomach. That was in 1927. But when I was a boy this was always a happy house and there were always ceilidhs and night-visiting here. My mother had a very good voice and our house was one of the ceilidh houses. I remember singing, talk, stories, from long before I went to school. We children and neighbours and friends all gathered, and I remember falling asleep to the music, or with the singing still loud in one ear. I liked the bagpipes and the accordion, now I listen to the wireless, which is very good. It's company but of a different kind from that we had. One of my poems is called, 'Tales of the Ceilidh House'.

TALES OF THE CEILIDH HOUSE

Though the wind of the wolf-days should blow
With all the keenness of a snell north wind,
Though the snow should stack against wall and the banks,
Though like steel it should lock on the top of the hills –
Nothing will keep us from the Ceilidh House
Where song, tale and rhyme will be heard.

Though rain should come ferociously in squalls,
Though sleet and hail hammer from the skies –
Nothing, not flood, nor deluge will hold me back!
Nor will there be tiredness or gloom about any one of us
When the stories begin – and from the seat by the fire
We hear the rich calm voice of the seanchaidh.

The genealogy of our people will be uttered,
The history of clan and family recited.
There will be debate about the places and process
Of fishing, about the hardship and skill
Of the fisherman's art on the water –
Talk about mishaps and drownings at sea –
And remembrance of friends who the seas took from us.

And talk there would be of the Great War of the Kaiser.
The violence, the cruelty, the organised chaos
that left hundreds of thousands in the cold sacrifice of death.
Such talk would re-open wounds in the listeners,
often bringing tears to all eyes in the company —
each remembering kinsmen and friends who took
their last breath on the battlefield.

And strange tales would come from sailors home back
From the sea — of braving the tops of mountainous waves:
Of cold wind and ice and treacherous weather
Of shinning up masts and climbing the rigging
With the ship pounding hard in the teeth of a gale
Whipping waves to a spume of wild water below them.

And then we'd hear of MacDonald, great chieftain,
Putting his longships with high sails to sea,
Leaving Loch Aoineartor in the first light of the morning
And sailing out through the Sound of Islay in style:
Of how they cut through storm and harsh dangerous weather
To shelter at Carrickfergus as told in the song.

Donald MacDonald and
John MacInnes walking to the peat
cuttings, South Lochboisdale.
The crofthouse can be seen far left.
(TN)

While out on the heights of the wild Irish Sea
MacNeil of Barra would be hoisting more sail!
Ploughing through waves that explode into cloud,
No weather on earth would keep Ruairi in port!
He was a 'Tartar' to the men hard-tying the ropes
The one who raised sail in the face of a gale!

Also we'd be told of spectres and ghosties
And other strange creatures that lived on the banks:
Many was the tale I heard of these beings
And the strivings of those who at last drove them out.
Great distress did they cause to children and mothers
Lying in wait with their evil and spells.

But better to me were the tales of the shielings
Where the young men and women learned music and song;
Where the cattle were tended on the summertime grasses
And herding was easy for the young as of old:
Unfenced was the sward where freedom was ours
And timeless the peace as we walked home to the fold.

But those days and the Ceilidh House are now in the past
New fashions and habits have forced change on the glens:
The old folk who sang in the houses I knew
Now moulder in earth they once trod so lightly.
New ways and new merriments have replaced the old ceilidh
And the houses of youth have long shut their doors. (TN/Mac)

No 472 B, South Lochboisdale,
Uist, 1997. (TN)

SGEULACHDAN NAN TAIGHEAN-CÈILIDH

Ged a shèideadh Faoilteach oirnn is faobhar nan gaoth tuath,
Ged bhiodh an sneachd' a' taosgadh 's na stac ri taobh nam bruach,
Ged reothadh i mar stàilinn gu mullach àrd nan cruach,
Cha chumadh siud bhon chèilidh sinn, far 'n cluinnte sgeul is duan.

Ged shileadh i gu dìorrasach le frasan fiadhaich fuar
'S clach-mheallain tighinn bhon iarmailt ga siabadh oirnn mun cuairt,
Cha chumadh tuil no dìle sinn 's cha bhiodh oirnn sgìths no gruaim,
'S na h-eachdraidhean gam mìneachadh le seanchaidh sìtheil suairc'.

Bhiodh sloinneadh air ar sinnsearachd ga mhìneachadh 's ga luaidh,
Bhiodh deasbad air an iasgach ann, 's gach deacair bha na ruaig;
Bhiodh tubaistean is bàthadh, is gàbhaidhean a' chuain,
'S bhiodh ionndrain air na càirdean ann thug tuinn an t-sàile bhuainn.

Bhiodh Cogadh Mòr a' Cheusair le chuid chreuchdan is mì-stàth,
A dh'fhàg na ceudan mìle ann an ìobradh fuar a' bhàis;
Na sheanchas dh'fhàgadh leònte sinn 's bu tric thug deòir nar pàirt,
A' cuimhneachadh a' chòmhlain sin a thrèig an deò sna blàir.

Chluinnte sgeul bhiodh sònraicht' aig seòladair a' chuain,
A-muigh air bhàrr nam bòc-thonnan ri aimsir reòthta 's fhuar,
A' dìreadh do na h-àrd-chroinn 's a' tèarnadh asta nuas,
'S an iùbhrach dol gu dùbhlan ann an dùrantachd nan stuagh.

Bhiodh birlinnean MhicDhòmhnaill len cuid sheòl a' dol gu sàil,
A' fàgail bun Loch Aoineart le soills' na madainn thràth,
A' seòladh tro Chaol Ile ri aimsir iorghaill gràic
Gu fasgadh Carraig Fhearghais, mar chaidh ainmeachas san dàn.

A-muigh air bhàrr Cuan Eirinn 's muir ag èirigh do na neòil,
Bhiodh MacNèill cuir bhrèid rith' gu reubadh nan tonn mòr:
Cha chumadh aimsir Ruairidh an àm ceangal cruaidh nan ròp —
Bu Tartar anns a' chruadal e an àm cur suas nan seòl.

Bhiodh bòcain agus sìthich a' tuineadh cinnteach feadh nam bruach —
Bha iomadh sgeul ri inns' orra san tìm a chaidh air ruaig;
Bhiodh iad tric ri fàth-fheith 's nan aincheist don an t-sluagh,
A' cur geas air pàisdean 's a' cur mhàthraichean fo ghruaim.

Chluinnte sgeul mun àirigh is mun mhànran is an ceòl
A bha cho tric a' tàrmachadh am measg nan àlach òg;
Bhiodh tàin ann air am buachailleachd a-muigh feadh chluaintean feòir,
Bha saors' is sìth neo-bhuaireasach a' cuartachadh nan crò.

Dh'fhalbh na taighean càirdeil ud, 's nan ait' tha gnàthach ùr,
'S tha mhuinntir bha gam pàirteachadh an-diugh a' cnàmh san ùir;
Tha dòighean eil' air tàrmachadh 's tha 'n abhcaideachd air chùl,
'S tha fàrdaichean an t-sòlais ud 's an còmhlaichean 's iad dùint'. (DM)

There were four children in our family. My eldest brother was Ewan, he went to sea and lived in Glasgow. He died a year ago. My second brother, Donald John, was a good singer, he used to make songs and he had a good mind for remembering songs. When he came home from sea he would be full of singing and, because he was often along with the Lewismen, he would come home with the Lewis songs. He never wrote any of them down, so all his own songs will be lost now unless the Lewis men took them on. He was drowned in the Runcorn canal at the age of 51. He'd just phoned home to his wife and was returning to his ship when he slipped on some oil and went into the water. He was brought home to be buried here in Uist. My sister's still alive. She lives across the way. Each night she gives me a phone before retiring to bed. Just to say everything's all right.

It was December 1926 when I was born. I knew no English at the age of five, when I started school. After the First World War there were plenty of children here in South Lochboisdale. Two or three new families had come across from Eriskay, so they built a school at Glendale at the back of the hill. It was just a tin shed on the moor, all by itself. It was there from 1922 to 1937. The roof and the walls are long gone and made use of, but the concrete foundations are still there to be seen. Glendale school served three townships with a footpath wending from each one. It's about two miles from here. A lot of teachers passed through that school, Miss Kerr, Miss MacPhee, Miss MacMillan, Donald John MacLean from Barra, Miss MacQueen, and Katie Ann Nicolson from Skye – she was a singer. My first memory is of her coming to this house when I was three years old. She had dark hair and I remember her voice by the fireside. She had an amputation and died about two years ago.

It didn't take us long to get a grasp of English and I liked English. We studied the sonnets of Shakespeare, Wordsworth, Shelley and Byron, Sir Walter Scott and Thomas Campbell. I especially liked Wordsworth and Byron. We learned 'The Lady of the Lake' and 'The Burial of Sir Thomas Moore' by heart.

There were plenty of bards here when I was young. A new song by one of the bards was a big event. There were the two John Campbells, and Roddy Campbell and Donald John MacDonald. They all made good songs when the inspiration took them. Roddy Campbell was a great bard and a great singer; he died in 1947. It's a pity the tape-recorder was not going when he was alive. If I was to say I had a master, it was Roddy Campbell. I myself was never a singer but I first started to make poems when I was at school or out at the herding. I liked to make up rhymes and stories, but I was very shy and in those days I always kept them to myself. I used to think that with so many real bards, good bards, my own work would be the subject of ridicule. And this was partly because most of the bards wrote about local events or sang songs which told stories, whereas I always liked to write about the hills and lochs and the sea. I've always liked descriptive poetry. I recently finished a long poem about the months of the calendar. It was a poem by Longfellow which inspired me to write it. I have always loved nature. My poem 'Catriona' is about a girl and about nature and I've added two verses about mortality.

CATRIONA

It was by the ocean you grew as a child,
Close to the waves and the line of the shore;
There you played happy in innocent glee
And danced where the eye spies the Kyle of Barra.

Uist is green to the edge of the sea
And here you were raised on a meadow-like machair,
Nursed and brought up a maid who embroidered
Love song and music deep down in my mind.

You are as the moon in the Heavens,
You guide me yet like the Morning Star,
You are the diamond in the ring,
The tallship on the sea's horizon.

It was the soft wind of the ocean
Put the bloom in your cheeks:
The sound of its waves gave you lightness of being,
Grace and strength to a body that endured like the tide.

And when I walk to Borrodale as often I do,
I still see a glimpse of your face in the distance,
Two gentle eyes beneath two slender brows,
Eyes alight with beauty and the joy of living.

May such meetings go on forever,
I bless the ground where e'er you stand:
May your step be light and careless,
May each day bring health and happiness...

Death cut you down in the gold green meadow,
A rose of fourteen is now buried in earth.
Never again will a comb trace your hair
And broken the heart paints this picture of you.

Dark is the world your leaving has left me
But green is the light to the harbour from storms
And shining above both harbour and ocean
Are stars that illumine the height of the Heavens. (TN/Mac)

CATRIONA

Ri taobh a' chuain chaidh d' arach suas
An cois nan stuagh 's a' chladaich;
Gun chluich thu saor nad phàisde maoth
Am fianais Chaolas Bharraigh.

An Uibhist uain' ri iomall chuan
Far 'm faic sin cluaintean maiseach
A thogadh suas an rìbhinn òg
Chuir fonn is ceòl air m'aire.

Tha thu mar ghealach anns an speur,
Tha thu mar reul na madainn,
Tha thu mar dhaoimean ann am fàinn'
No long air bàrr na mara.

'S i ghaoth tha sèideadh far a' chuain
Chuir dreach nad ghruaidh is maise;
Thug gàir nan tonn dhut sunnd is fonn
'S chuir neart nad chom bhios maireann.

Nuair thèid mi Bhòrradal air chuairt,
Gum faic mi bhuam ort sealladh —
Na sùilean caoin fo mhala chaol
Le mais' is aoidh a sheallas.

Mo shoraidh slàn-sa bhith gu bràth
Gach àit an dèan thu fantainn,
Do cheum bhith sunndach air a' bhlàr
'S dhut saoghal slàn is fada...

Thug a cèitein dhuinn air ais nam flùran
'S thug e bhuain an ùr-bhlath bheir nan ròsan
aig ceithir deag a bhliadhachan a dh ùine.
Gur duilich leam an ùir a bhith ga d' còmhdach.

'S duilich leam do chuailean dualach rìomach
A bhith 'san ionad far nach cuir gluais a chìr e 'n ordugh an còr e
Ni mi dealbh na h-àilleachd ann an uir dhiot
Ged nach faca mi le m' shùilean ann an fheòl thu (DM)

Donald MacDonald's mother,
Catherine, her eldest son, Ewan,
Mary Flora Campbell and postman
Donald MacRae, c. 1960. (DM)

The bard's father,
Angus MacDonald (right) with
his friend Angus MacQuarrie,
c. 1920. (DM)

No 472 B, South Lochboisdale, Uist, 1997. Donald MacDonald with Dr John MacInnes. (TN)

Some people can put beautiful tunes to bardachd, bean Eàirdsidh Maghnaill (Mrs MacDonald) was like that; she had all the old songs and she would know just the right tune to give to a new poem, but I have no gift for singing or for music. I am a bard who has always made poems, not songs. I get an idea, or a number of lines and I write them down. Things come slowly to me. I might write two verses and then a fortnight will pass and then two more will form themselves in my mind. I need to write things down. I remember the last verse of a poem coming to me one night in bed, I was half awake and half sleeping, and I knew I must jump up and scribble it down, which I did. And in the morning I was pleased with what had come.

One day I came home from church on a Sunday and, as I sat down waiting for my dinner, a whole poem came to me before my mother brought in the plates. It was a poem about a place out in the hills and I wrote it down before rising to eat at the table. I go to church but I don't consider my poetry religious; you don't get much of that amongst my crowd at all. On Mondays I go to the Post Office to get my pension but that doesn't mean I write about money.

Many people say that heredity is very important in poetry and I think this is true. All our family was keen on poetry, even if they didn't sing or make bardachd. My mother sang, my sister was always fond of poetry, Donald John made songs. My grandmother, Kirstie Fraser, liked bardachd; she came from North Uist and I think she may have been some kind of relation to the bard, Donald of Corunna. My other grandmother was a MacKay and came from Sutherland. That is the land of Rob Donn MacKay. He was a great bard of the 18th century. Rob Donn used to sing all his bardachd. It was not him that wrote his songs down, it was somebody else. He was a cattle drover. Very few

No 472 B, South Lochboisdale, Uist, 1997. (TN)

people could write Gaelic in those days, or in my day, and bardachd was only kept, if somebody liked a song or poem so much that they learned it and made it part of their own repertoire and passed it on to others. I like to work on paper. After the Apollo space mission landed on the moon I wrote a poem for children. It's called 'The Rocket':

THE ROCKET

I sit in the cone
On the top of a rocket
Two companions beside me
'With ears on fire!'

Ten, Nine, Eight,
The countdown continues!
Seven, Six, Five!

Three hearts thumping as the moments pass,
My mind leaps faster than light
To our target, the Moon!
I am leaving the world but I hope to return.

Four, Three, Two, One —
Ignition!
We have lift-off!

We part from the earth —
Power that man has taken out of the earth
Has lifted me free of the earth.

My face is distorted with the force of gravity:
The world is not wanting its people to go!
But the invention of man triumphs
Over the great forces of Nature
And out of the window I see earth falling away,
As swiftly we hurtle through the silence of space.

I sleep and am awakened.
I seem to grow younger!
I float weightless in space.
I eat tablets of food.
I glide through our chamber
Like a bird on the wing.

We circle the moon
And draw down towards it,
Seeing that side no man saw before!
Undocking we leave one crewman to circle
Whilst I with the other
Head down to the zone.

Like an eagle we landed!
That's what we both said,
Then we step down alive
Into the dead dust of the planet
And we bounce as we walk
And seem to be floating.
And there is the earth
Like a great moon rising
Enveloped in a blue no mind can imagine,
Save the man who, like us, was there and who saw.

But of course I know that you will have seen us
Despite all the darkness and distance between,
On TV you'll watch us with oxygen packs
Tread through the moon-dust that never was trod.

But now, high above
The Mothership is calling
And a vertical take-off
Through the skies of the Moon
Sees the three of us safe
In our rocket once more.

Homeward we pass into radio blackout
Where a measureless heat burns the skin of the cone,
Then gently we parachute into the cool blue of the ocean
And are back in the element where all life began;
Back on the earth where everything started
Back on the earth with everything changed. (TN/Mac)

AN ROCAID

Na mo shuidhe ann an cùil chumhaing
aig mullach rocaid,
dithis chompanach còmhla rium
ag èisdeachd, cunntais —
deich, naoi, h-ochd —
mo chridhe plapadaich ag èisdeachd —
seachd, sia, còig —
m'inntinn a shiùbh'leas nas luaithe na solas
air a' ghealaich romham,
mi fàgail an t-saoghail is mi 'n dùil ri tilleadh —
ceithir, tri, dhà, aon —
lasadh:
dhealaich mi ris an talamh,
cumhachd a thugadh às an t-saoghal
gam thogail bhon t-saoghal.

Cruth m'aodainn ag atharrachadh,
an saoghal ga mo tharraing air n-ais thuige,
ach thug cumhachd beag ann an acfhainn
buaidh air cumhachd mòr a bha sgao... (? end of word cut off on ms)
dhealaich mi gu tur ris an talamh,
tha mi siubhal luath agus a' fàs beagan nas òige.
Tha mi a' cadal agus a' dùsgadh,

ithidh mi biadh agus chan eil cuideam annam,
seòlaidh mi na mo sheòmar
mar fhaoileag air sgèith,
tha mi a' cuartachadh na gealaich
's air mo tharraing ga h-ionnsaigh;
chì mi taobh dhith nach fhaca mi riamh.

Fàgaidh sinn companaich ga cuartachadh,
tha mi fhìn agus fear eile dol sìos;
laigh sinn mar iolaire
agus 's e sin a thubhairt sinn:
"Tha sinn ann an seo, dithis bhèo
ann am fàsach mòr marbh";
tha sinn a' bocadaich mun cuairt
eadar bhith coiseachd 's a bhith seòladh,
tha 'n saoghal mar ghealaich mhòir liath
ag èirigh suas,
sealladh nach tuig inntinn
ach am fear a bh' ann
's a chunnaic.

Anail na beatha air mo dhruim,
's chì mi liath i air astar,
cluinnidh sibh agus chì sibh mi
le innleachd dhaoine,
's mi ag èirigh tro speuran na gealaich.
Tha an triùir againn còmhla gu dòigheil a-rithist,
a' feuchainn dhachaigh
's a' dol tron chachaileith chumhaing;
tha sinn innte, cha chluinn sinn dad
agus cha chluinn duine sinne,
teas mòr thar tomhais a' leaghadh
taobh a-muigh ar taigh-còmhnaidh,
ach tha e nis air fuarachadh sa chuan.

Tha sinn air tilleadh air n-ais,
tha sinn gu math,
ach cha bhi sinn tuilleadh mar a bha sinn. (DM)

They talk about the young ones being wild today but so were we. We would cut the tongues out of old boots and use the tongues to make a sling with leather straps. All the boys here made slings. Very dangerous they were. They could throw a stone about a mile. You could kill a man with a sling stone. I've seen birds taken down and targets hit at 300 yards. The tongue would be the last thing to wear out on a boot. The soles would go, the uppers would go, but the tongues stayed good, shiny and supple till the end. There was an art to good slinging but that's another of the things you don't see any more.

Halloween was an important time with us. You didn't work. There was very little work to be done in November. That was the month we honoured the dead. The weather would often be very bad. We'd start preparing months before. Slaughtering the sheep, drying the skins. For dressing up, our faces would go through the back end of the sheep. And the faceskins, the masks, would be made from the belly of another sheep. They would be like a hood with two slits for the eyes. Halloween was a big night. We'd start at the end of the township and move down collecting bread and tea and having a feast. Everybody would wear their sheepskin. Wool on our backs and skin on our faces and wearing our most unidentifiable clothes, no one knew who anybody was. The point of it was to go from house to house dressed-up and unknown. The test was, would they recognise us, by our voice, our hands, or a strand of hair?

There was no mischief at Halloween in those days. People up to 50 years of age would join in, and older. There was none of this 'trick or treat!' that the children get from the television. You entered a house and walked around and stayed silent. Or, perhaps, you'd make noises like a sheep, or a baby. The people inside the house might touch you or chase you. You might be offered a dram and a cake or a scone. Of course, if you raised your false face you risked exposing yourself. The bigger the sheepskin the better it was, the whole fleece hanging down from your shoulders. You could get very warm. If a man drank too much he might just fall asleep in a chair. The children might get a sweet but they would keep them in their hands until they got outside the house, so as not to show their face. It was just local people guising here when I was a boy. There was no one else, there was no road for miles, but just before the war, people started coming from the west side of Uist in cars. Driving out in big cars, all covered in sheepskins! But many we wouldn't have known if they'd come naked as babies. The road to South Lochboisdale got finished in 1934. That's how Halloween was in the old days. People tried very hard to keep themselves unknown and many people never knew who it was who visited them. But before the night was out, I expect there would be some would take down their masks just to prove people right or wrong. Hogmanay was another big night. Going into the house we would recite this rhyme:

I come to you tonight
To renew your Hogmanay.
No need to tell you the origin of it,
It goes back well before my grandfather's time.

Sunwise I turn before your lintel
And knock a welcome at your door:
Reciting my rhyme with the knowledge of ages
I stand in the mid-winter dark.

My Hogmanay breastwool is safe here in my pocket
And blue is the smoke I will waft from it.
Round each child, I will waft it —
Nor forget for a moment the woman of the house.

Woman of the house — it's you are most worthy!
For it's your hand dispenses the good Hogmanay —
That honey sweet fruit of the summertime
That tastes so good on your barley bread. (TN / Mac)

We ate every part of a sheep here. Sheep's head was a big delicacy. We severed the head, leaving the wool on the face. The whole thing would then be singed in a fire. The skull would be split in two with a blow from an axe, the brain taken out and some of the brain smeared on the cheeks, on the wool, to reduce the taste of the singeing. The whole lot was then slow-boiled, so there'd be a soup as well as the meat for eating. On the table, the head would steam on a white plate and we'd cut the flesh away and eat it with potatoes, oatmeal and maybe neeps or kale.

I've heard it said that the custom of the sheep-masking is very old. That it goes back to the time of the Greeks and that theatre had its origin in ancient practices like our Halloween. Some say that Halloween would be a time when the younger men and women could let their hair down, but I have to say that I didn't see anything like that here. I enjoy the company of women, but I'm not a man was ever wildly in love, not like Byron, not like the poets you read about. I have written poems for women but it's not love poetry that I write. My poem, 'The Girl of Loch a' Mhuilinn' is more a praise poem than a love poem:

THE GIRL OF LOCH A' MHUILINN

The bard, 1997. (TN)

If my ship was rigged and ready to plough the seas
I would make use of this keen wind from the north,
I would steer her towards Oban
Through the weight and high crests of the waves
To a girl with the colour of gold in her hair.

You lighted the darkness of the isle of my youth
You scattered and banished the cold violence of March,
You, the first daisy to come back to the machair
You illuminated the fields in the warm softness of May
When the breeze was as gentle as the welcoming flowers.

High fortune shines forth in the light of your eyes
And it was kindness that kindled my joy in your face,
Loyalty and charm were just part of your nature
And honour was given because high honour was due:
In frost-clear night-sky you were the jewel and a star.

May sweet lovage long grow in that garden of thine
May the cornflower, so lovely in form and in hue
Spring-up to enswathe your fields in plenty:
May date-palm and apple and sharp herb give you pleasure
And silk clothe your body from gold lock to black heel.

O lovely as the rubbing of the ocean in bays
Is the sound of your voice and the frost coming down,
And lovely the murmur of the cold mountain burn
As it thrills to the sea like hands to the harp —
And the call of the wild swan comes up from the creek.

Now my picture is painted, may providence steer you
Through bright happy days and those days without sun,
For on the street of life's pleasures
You must be your own guide — but know I salute you
And will always enjoy your feast in the garden of life. (TN/Mac)

MAIGHDEAN LOCH A' MHUILEANN

Nam biodh mo long fo h-èideadh
'S i deas gu reubadh cuain,
A soibhrich bhith dha rèir sin
Le oiteig ghèir bhon tuath,
Stiùirinn air an Oban i
Tro chudthrom cròiceach stuagh
Far bheil a' mhaighdean bhòidheach
Le dath an òir na gruaig.

Shamhlaich mi ri neònean thu
Nì an eilean m' òige fàs
Nuair theicheas tìmean reòthta bhuainn
Is fòirneadh a' mhìos Mhàirt:
Air machraichean is raointean,
Fo oiteig chaoin na Màigh,
Tha fàilteachadh nan dìtheanan
Gu dàimh na sìde bhlàth.

Tha àrd-rath an aoibhneis
A' boillsgeadh na do shuil;
Tha cridhealas a' choibhneis
A' soillseachadh nad ghnùis;
Tha dòighealachd nad nàdar
Dh'fhàg àrd thu anns a' chùirt,
Mar neamhnaid oidhche reòthta
Bhios an còmhnaidh na cairt-iùil.

Gum bu fad bhios sunais
Nad ghàrradh suas a' fàs,
Gum bu phailt nad chluaintean
An gorman uain' is àill,
Pailm agus craobh ùbhlan
'S gach lus bheir sunnd do d' chàil,
'S an sioda bhith gad chòmhdach
O d' chuailean òir gu d'shàil.

Laigh mo shùil Didòmhnaich ort
Sa chòmhlan am measg chàich,
Is rinn mi dealbh cho bòidheach dhiot
Ri tè chuir bròg mu sàil;
Ghlac mi peann nam mheòirean
'S chuir mi 'n còmhradh seo an dàn
A bhios na lòchran iùil dhut
Air a' chùrsa nach tèid ceàrr.

Mar fhuaim an taibh sna bàghan
Air oidhche shàmail reòtht',
Mar ghuileag eala bàine
A' snàmh air feadh nan òb,
Mar chrònan uillt nam fuar-bheann
A' triall gu cuan le deòin,
Tha teud cheòl-phong na gruagaich,
A sheudaich snuadh bu bhòidhch'.

Am freasdal bhith gad stiùireadh
'S a' cumail sunnd nad cheum
Tro làithean soilleir sùrdail
'S tro aimsir ghnùig gun ghrèin;
Air cabhsairean an t-sùgraidh
Gur ceann-iùil thu air gach rèis,
'S an gàrraidhean na fialachd
Gur brèagha leam bhios d' fhèisd. (DM)

There was a wildness in the life of the great love poets but the crofting life nurtures tranquillity and kinship. Passionate love, I would say, is a product of war, of licence, of division of race and class. I believe it is found amongst the tinkers here. I heard a story about a young tinker man who travelled from Uist over to Eriskay and there he went up to a house to ask for a drink. He had fair hair and was handsome. A young woman came to the door and she told the young man she would get him a cup of water. When she returned, she stood before him; then, suddenly, she flung the water in his face. He went back down the path, looking back once. She went inside, into the kitchen, where her mother and father were sitting and she said, 'I'm going away with that man.' And her father said, 'You can't go with him, he's not one of our people.' And the girl replied 'I have to go.' And the two of them went away from Eriskay and got married and had a family. And in later years when the Travelling People came back to Uist, it was often remarked how the children of that marriage looked like the Eriskay people.

There is a power in the stranger. Many novels depend on the coming of a stranger. I heard another story concerning a tinker man and a girl. He was in her house and he took a fancy to her and he asked if she would give him a hair from her head. Now, the girl could feel the power of this man and she knew the power of the tinkers, so she refused to give him a hair. When he asked for a third time, she went outside and climbed a hillside above the track to the house to a place where a cow had died that morning and she plucked a hair from the forehead of the dead beast. Then she returned to the kitchen where the tinker was rising from the table and she gave him the hair. He left the house and she watched from the dark of the window. As he passed the spot where the dead cow was, she saw the body move, then it rolled over and over and crashed into the sea just behind him. And that tinker man walked on without looking back.

And here is a story I witnessed myself, here at the back of this house, when I was seven years of age. One summer the daughter of a fisherman from Fraserburgh, over on the east coast, fell in love with a tinker man and she went away with him and they got married in the tinker fashion. Her parents had tried very hard to dissuade her but she was determined and for a while it seems she was happy. But she was too proud to beg and she didn't like selling round the houses, and maybe her husband was rough with her, we don't know. But before long she knew she'd made a mistake. She wanted away, she wanted to go home. So secretly she sent a letter to her father asking him to rescue her and take her home. And after that, wherever he fished around the coast of Scotland, he would ask after the daughter he had lost. Well, it was here in Lochboisdale he found her.

The tinkers were camped at the back of this house when her father, with a dozen fishermen, came upon them. The travellers tried to make a run for the hill with the girl but she fought and struggled and the fishermen came up to them. A big crowd of crofters had gathered and we heard the father say he had come for his daughter and he would take her home. There was plenty of shouting. Fights broke out, but in the end the girl was given over to the fishermen and they walked back to the boats with her. She was walking in the middle of a big gang of fishermen, and they sailed away to Fraserburgh. Later, we used to call that 'the battle of South Lochboisdale'.

There are some beautiful girls amongst the travelling people but they seem to lose their looks whilst still young women. It's the poor conditions they live in, they hit the bottle, they smoke and that dries and wrinkles the skin. They have handsome men amongst the tinker people. And there's a gift for fighting amongst the men. Often we'd see them fighting amongst themselves over in the camp but, it's a strange thing, in the morning they'd be the best of friends. That saying, that you should 'never let the sun go down on your wrath', was the natural way of life for them. We were always pleased to see them, though none have been here for many years now. I've listened to that storyteller, Duncan Williamson, on the wireless. He's quite famous now. I hear he married a young woman from America. She came to visit him, to hear his stories, and they got married.

I think the happiest days of my life came in 1961. For eleven years I had suffered from a stomach ulcer. I was continuously ill, often in great pain. Every day I was vomiting and for weeks I could eat no solids at all. At last I was operated on. It was a very big ulcer, right at the back of my stomach, and when it was gone, I suddenly felt so well, life came back into me. I was euphoric. It must have been poisoning me for years. Lying there in the hospital, I was so happy. The nurses, the view from the window, the white sheets on the bed, everything was so beautiful. That ulcer would have killed me as it killed my father before me. The pain I suffered had forced me to drink and if I drank too much the following day I would be so depressed, deeply, deeply depressed. I'd be feeling as if everybody in the world had gone away and left me on my own. I'd feel betrayed, feel that everything was against me and I'd think that the only cure was another glass of whisky. And I smoked twist in a pipe, and cigarettes by the dozen and all this was making me worse and worse. No one knew it was an ulcer. I used to suffer from thirst. In bed I'd be desperate for beer or water, I'd be up three or four times in the night. It was after I collapsed that Dr Alistair MacLean sent me up to Stornoway and at last they saw this ulcer on the X-ray – and I entered a new world. Man does not live by bread alone, but we depend on our bodies like nothing else.

After the operation was a good time for poems. Poems come to me when I'm in a happy mood, when the earth seems young and fresh and full of joy. I enjoy the struggle of trying to get a poem right. I have to be very pleased with a poem before I consider it finished. I have to be sure it won't hurt or upset anybody, or cause annoyance. I wrote a poem about one of my nurses but it hasn't been published. When I wrote my poem about the Calvay Lighthouse, I worried that Lachie MacKenzie, the lighthouse man, might be offended but, in fact, when he heard it he was most terribly pleased and proud.

In this poem the old lighthouse at Calvay in South Uist offers counsel and advice to the new lighthouse that is about to replace it.

THE OLD LIGHTHOUSE OF CALVAY

A thousand welcomes to you, friend
Coming to a rock like this
But be warned
Should you ever be tempted into foolishness
Your end might well be nigh.

But take due note and care
And you will stand a hundred years:
You will grow grey
As well befits one made to serve the waves
Of this grey Minch –
And they will let you know
That it is not without some hardship
You will earn your livelihood.

You may see yourself as young and strong
With many kinsmen up and down the coast —
But I warn you of the many days
And of the many nights
When the very elements will explode
And you will stand in dire straits
Amidst a raging torrent of white sea foam
That will give you good cause to remember me
And the hardships I have suffered.

Many a winter's night I've stood here
Giving promise and hope to mariners,
Men safely sailing the green of the ocean
Suddenly exposed to a Sou-westerly gale,
Ferocious squalls giving them a hammering
A relentless blasting without mercy.
O many's the time my light has guided them
And brought them safe to port.

And well it was I knew the fisher folk —
Good men from hereabouts
And this my neighbourhood
And their's from long ago:
Very well it was I knew Ronald, son of Iagan,
Ah what a boat he had St Patrick,
So beautiful it was coming round Rubha na h-Ordaig,
A perfect picture on the brine:
Not once in a long life have I seen a boat so splendid.

Such men and boats!
I knew each one of them so well
But those days are all now past and gone:
There is a great comradeship across the perils of the sea
And sad I am that of my oldest friends
Not one will see me now depart;
Their sun has gone down beyond the horizon
Their evening has dimmed and they sleep now
Lulled by the waves of Western Ocean for all eternity.

And often enough I watched others going,
Stout, resolute, strong lads
Maidens and young matrons,
Going into that exile beyond the sea…
Sad was I and sorrowful
And how I have missed them since they went away:
Of course, I was still here when many came back,
Even if it was only the smallest part of them
That was returned to this, their native shore.

My story is long as the beam that I throw
And if set down in print,
I can say without doubt,
All those who can read would learn more than they know.
I've stood many years on this rock of earth
And my recollections are far from lightweight!
I have, what are known as special powers
And the endless anger of the sea has taught me much.

I have witnessed elemental combat and tumult
As year follows year;
I have experienced two World Wars
And played my part in both:
My commitment was tested, my sense of duty was proven
And no imperfection ever seen in my rays!
So with pride I state, no fault can be laid
Or piled at the door where I stand.

And now a thousand blessings on each friend
Who stood so bold, so firm inside me,
Especially Big Lachlan MacKenzie!
A man as fine as any ever walked the land:
Over the years he proved an excellent keeper,
Conscious of security, safety in every particular;
I wish him good health and great success
In you — new master of this place.

For the time of change has come
And I must move aside for you:
I've got my hard-won freedom
And an old-age pension too!
I'll take a trip and be once more amongst
The good folks that I knew:
A grand welcome I will give to each
And none will find me lacking
In that gift for the lighted word —
'Be our meeting humble', or at the table of a lord. (TN / Mac)

SEANN TAIGH-SOLAIS CHALBHAIGH

Mìle beannachd dhut, a charaid, tighinn gu carraig air nach eòl thu,
'S ma tha amaideas nad ghiùlain, cuiridh ùine sin air fògair;
Ma nì thu seasamh ann ceud bliadhna nì thu liathadh mar as còir dhut,
Is nochdaidh tonnan a' Chuain Sgìth dhut nach ann gun strì gheibh thu do bheòshlaint.

Ged a tha thu òg is làidir 's mòran chàirdean air do chùlaibh,
Is iomadh oidhch' is là thig èiginn nuair bhios sèideadh air na dùilean;
Nuair a chopas tuinn na mara tighinn nan steallan geala tuillich,
Cuimhnichidh tu orm an uair sin 's air gach cruas a bha nam dhunach.

'S iomadh oidhche ghruamach geamhraidh thug mi gealltainn agus dòchas
Do mharaiche nan tonnan uaine bhiodh air bhàrr a' chuain a' seòladh;
An uair a shèideadh i bhon iar-dheas le frasan dìorrais air bheag tròcair,
'S tric a rinn mo sholas iùl dhaibh 's e toirt an cùrsaireachd gu òrdagh.

Na dìochuimhnich a' ghruagach air a bheil an cuailean òr-bhuidh' —
'S tric a smaointean is a bruadar air na tonnan uaine cròiceach;
'S tric bhios iomchair na gluasad nuair thig sèideadh cruaidh bho Aeòlas —
'S e dh'fhàg na h-aonar anns an uair i gun tug i luaidh do dh'fhear an t-seòlaidh.

B' eòlach mi air luchd an iasgaich — bha iad riamh an seo nam nàbachd:
B' eòlach mi air Raghnall Mac Iagain 's am bata brèagh' aige, Naomh Pàdraig;
Nuair nochdadh i thar Rubh' na h-Ordaig 's i bha bòidheach air an t-sàile —
Chan fhaca mi rè mo shaoghail dol tro chaolas tè cho àlainn.

Bha mi eòlach air na daoin' ud: bhiodh iad daonnan tighinn nam chàirdeas —
'S duilich leam a bhith smaointinn nach fhaic a h-aon aca mi fàgail;
Rinn am feasgar aca ciaradh, chaidh an grian-san sìos air fàire,
Tha iad ann an suain nan sìorraidh, is tuinn a' Chuain an Iar gan tàladh.

Chunnaic mi tric a' falbh iad, gillean calma, smiorail, làidir,
Maighdeanan is mnathan òg a' dol air fògairt thar an t-sàile;
'S mi bhiodh muladach gan ionndrain agus tùrsach gun do dh'fhàg iad,
'S bha mi ann an seo nuair thill iad, ged, mo chreach, nach d' thill ach pàirt dhiubh.

Nam biodh m'eachdraidh air a h-innse ann am mìneachadh clò-bhualaidh,
Bhiodh luchd aithris agus sgrìobhaidh ann an iomartais na buanachd;
Tha mi ùine mhòr san t-saoghal, 's cha ann aotrom bhios mo chnuasachd:
Tha mo chomasan cho àraid - dh'ionnsaich farpaisean a' chuain mi.

Chunnaic mi ri ruith nam bliadhna iomadh iorghaill agus còmhrag;
Dh'fhiosraich mi dà Chogadh an t-Saoghail 's anns gach aon dhiubh ghabh
        mi cò-phàirt;
Chaidh mo dhleasnais a dhearbhadh, cha robh cearbaiche nam dhòighean,
Chan eil aibisean rim fàgail no rin càrnadh aig mo chòmhlaidh.

Mìle beannachd le gach caraid bha cho daingeann air mo chùlaibh,
Gu h-àraid Lachlainn Mòr MacCoinnich, fear cho sgoinneil 's tha san dùthaich:
Bha e math dhomh 'n rèis nam bliadhna ann an tèarainteachd is cùram —
Gum bu fada fallain slàn e tighinn don àite seo ga d' ionnsaigh.

Ach a-nis bhon thàinig caochladh, nì mi saod air a bhith gluasad,
Fhuair mi airgead na h-aoise 's tha mo shaorsa air a buannachd;
Thèid mi cuairt am measg nan còmhlan 's fàiltichidh mi le deòin is suairc' iad,
'S cha lorg iad aineolas nam chòmhradh ged a ruiginn bòrd nan uaislean. (DM)

When I first left school I went fishing out of Lochboisdale, so when the SS *Politician* went down off Eriskay, I was one of the first on the scene. Whisky Galore! Of course, the news got round and everybody went over. We never knew who was who because everybody was covered in black oil. It was just as well. There were many cases brought in here. I kept two or three myself. We buried them in holes in the ground. The police and customs men came looking for things but how would they find cases on an island this size? They had to go by the letter of the law but we found them less than zealous in their duty. There was a war to fight. But the whisky didn't do us much good, first of all because

people were not used to much whisky. There are no distilleries on the Outer
Isles, and in the thirties very little whisky was drunk, because people were
poor and whisky expensive. Then when the war came there was none at all. So
with all that whisky floating ashore, some people got hooked and it brought in
roughnecks from all over, wanting cheap deals. There's no silver lining in a
whisky bottle. Our case lasted years. My mother would take a dram, she'd take
a drop on her porridge, and she liked to 'whisk an egg wi' a drap o' the cratur'.

I've written about 100 poems. Some have been published in the
Stornoway Gazette and other newspapers and magazines but many are just here
in the house, written out on paper. One of the last I wrote is called 'Camilla's
Picture', and it's about Lady Camilla Parker Bowles. Many, many thousands of
poems have been written about Princess Diana but I think I must be one of the
first to write about Camilla. I wrote this in March 1996, long before the death
of Diana:

I saw your picture like a golden jewel
In that paper the Sunday Post
And it came welcome as a guiding star
To the mariner on a voyage far from land.

I saw a photograph of Beauty,
A lovely lady astride a splendid steed
In a green field, a kiss-curl at her temple,
An image of welcome, peace and calm serenity.

Your complexion like an apple in a garden,
Your face offering happiness and friendship.
Teeth white as snow on a distant hilltop,
Your smile breaking like a lighted ocean wave.

Your eyes beautiful
As the dew on a daisy.
Your shapely calf elegant
As any slid inside a riding boot.

You have mounted and sped over many pastures;
Knowledge and experience have opened before you
But I doubt in your youth you thought for a moment
Your picture would light these thoughts in a glen.

Nor once did you dream as you slept on your pillow
(I'm certain it never once entered your mind!)
That your image one day would be treasured by a man
Deep in the heather of this far distant glen. (TN/Aut)

A school teacher saw that poem when it was published in Am Pàipear (*The News of the Isles*) and she decided to translate it and send it on to Prince Charles. And he wrote me back a very nice letter. I had it, framed, up on the wall. The priest took it away. He said he wanted to make a photocopy of it but he hasn't brought it back. That was months ago. It came on 1st November. 'His Highness the Prince of Wales recently got a poem from Miss Jacqueline Marsh, which you wrote. His Highness has asked me to thank you most sincerely for the bother that you took.' It was signed by the Prince but the name of the writer was Claire Southwell.

I get the *Sunday Post* every week, and sometimes I get given the *Sunday Sport*. I saw this photograph of Camilla on horseback. She looked beautiful and a poem started forming in my mind. It was her birthday, she was 49. The article stated she ate meat-burgers for her birthday tea and the next week the *Sunday Post* had a cartoon being sarcastic about her eating meat-burgers, but she was raising money for charity and she has a certain beauty. I don't like contempt. The eye of the beholder is king.

There is a story told that when the bard, Alasdair MacDonald, met the Mairi to whom Duncan Ban Macintyre composed his great love song, 'Màiri Bhàn Og', Alasdair told Duncan Ban that Mairi was much less beautiful in reality than she appears to be in the song. To this remark Duncan Ban replied, 'Say what you will, but you do not see her with my eyes.' And it could be that Alasdair was jealous of Duncan Ban for, whereas Alasdair was well-connected and well-educated, Duncan Ban could neither read nor write. Duncan Ban's gift for bardachd was purely natural. I've heard it said that Duncan Ban was a man on whom gloom never descended and that happiness followed him as it shone from his face.

Ina and Donald's kitten by the front door. South Lochboisdale, Uist, 1997. (TN)

Mary MacLean

YELLOW POINT, GRIMSAY, NORTH UIST

I wanted to go to Africa when I was young. I had been reading and I got a prize at Sunday School. It was a book, Mary Slessor, all about her life and work in Africa and I thought – that's what I would like to do. Be a missionary. And we had a missionary here at Carinish, a Mr MacKay, and he used to visit us. And he asked me, 'Mary, what are you going to be when you grow up?' So I said very brightly, 'I want to go to Africa and be a missionary.' And he turned, very pleased, to my granny and said, 'Mrs Cameron, I think she will make a good missionary.' But it happened that he came on a day when granny thought I'd been behaving very badly and she looked at him darkly and said, 'I think she'd make a much better heathen!' And she wasn't far wrong! Over the years that notion passed and when I left school at the age of fourteen I knew I wanted to become a bard.

I wrote my first poem in class. I would have been about twelve and I got the strap for it. You see, I should have been paying attention to my geography lesson and I wasn't. We had been given the map of Poland to study but my mind was on something else. The day before, a lady had come over from the Isle of Harris to visit, and the word got round that this lady was young, so all the boys in the village gathered outside the house where she was staying, all hoping to see this young and very beautiful woman. And when she emerged she turned out to be 60! And not beautiful at all! So all those boys, who so often made fun of me, had made fools of themselves. I was in my glory. And next day, as I sat looking at the map of Poland, a poem came into my head. And underneath the atlas I secretly wrote out the poem, getting my own back on them. Suddenly I heard a great shout: 'Mary MacLean! Come out here! And bring that piece of paper with you!'

Opposite:
The bard Mary MacLean,
North Uist, 1997. (TN)

Mary MacLean with the
Cassillis Cup, Inverness Mod,
1950. (MM)

I remember walking out, and my face growing terribly hot, and standing at the teacher's desk very humbly. And when she saw it was a poem I had written, she threw it in her desk and gave me two of the best with a leather strap. But the story does not end there. When we went out at three o'clock for our ten minutes' play I noticed the lid of her desk was raised, and there she was reading the poem and laughing. Miss MacDonald was her name. Later on she married Murdo MacKinnon. They had several children and one day she was listening with one of her daughters to the wireless, to the ceremony of the Crowning of the Bard at the Mod. It was a live broadcast from the Usher Hall in Edinburgh, and it was me that was about to be awarded the crown, for my poem 'Beinn Eubhal'. Well, this is a very moving ceremony. Everybody stands to sing the evocation, a noble and beautiful song, and the commentator described me walking up the aisle, 'looking straight ahead, as if her eyes beheld her beloved mountain'. And as the crown was being raised above my head the tears began to run down Mrs MacKinnon's face and a great sob broke from her and her daughter asked, 'Mother, what's the matter?' and she replied that nothing was the matter, but she was remembering the time when she beat me for writing my first poem and now 'she is crowned bard of all Scotland'. She was very proud of me and when I got home to Uist, Mrs MacKinnon was one of the first to congratulate me. And she told me how sorry she was to have beaten a bard for writing a poem! She delivered two blows on the same hand and, as the second came down, I instinctively moved my hand a little to the side and I can still feel that belt come down on my thumb full pelt! It made the blow very, very painful.

That first poem was a humorous poem, with a short punchline at the end of each verse. Some people say that the structure comes from the song tradition but, as far as I know, I never knew any such songs, I just wrote that poem down as it came to me. I still have it in my head. It pokes fun at my stepbrother, he was a leader of those who rushed to gaze on this beauty from across the sea, the woman from Harris. He was about 17 then and full of the joys of spring. Two years later he was killed at St. Valery in France. He was with the Highland Division and ten years later I wrote my poem, 'The Battlefield', in which I imagine what it would be like to be in a modern battle.

THE BATTLEFIELD

The disruption and barbarism of war.
Deadly guns, harsh metal, outcry,
Lamentation and the gasping of men:
Wounded and groaning they drift into darkness.

Flame, smoke and noise engulf
Each bank and trench, each rock and glen:
Hateful, terrifying, awful, a tumultuous
Drumming thunders forth and back in the hills.

The utter devastation of what once was a field
Is the unquiet grave for which these men are destined:
Earth itself has forsaken all leave of its senses,
Cruel battle triumphantly bellows its rage.

Is this your doing, Great King of the Universe?
Destruction, ill-will, oppression and pain!
The great mass of people swept up in hatred;
Bloody in thought, in word and foul deed.

This — despite the growing blue of the watch,
This despite the evening prayers of the poet,
For even now as she evokes peace and tranquillity,
The cries, the moans, the death and slaughter continue —

And fresh warriors fall with their backs to the ground
And stare at the sun — locked in the iron shackles
Of the everlasting sleep of death — glimpsing light
For that moment before darkness dims the Heavens forever.

I am with them. And upon my looking round,
Hard is the sight; so many wounded, so many
Suffering, broken, weak, filthy, defiled;
Lying cold on the earth, alone.

And there — slumped against a tree stump
At the base of a wall — rests a man.
His eye catches mine and draws me towards him,
Recognition flickers over his countenance. He's alive.

But already a cloud of unknowing is coming
Down on his eye, like a film,
And the sheen on his brow is not sweat
But the dew, the unhealthy ooze, of death.

The sharp pains of death are tearing his soul:
But even now — as Death takes him into its clutches —
His senses grow sharp before fading forever,
His breast rises with the injustice he feels so keenly.

Mary MacLean's stepbrother,
killed at St Valery, June 1940.
(MM)

And very slowly he speaks, saying, 'Friend,
Listen for a moment, I soon sleep forever,
The light of the sun is going down for me
And my star stoops low in the west.

'It was a slender black rifle
That made rubble of my dwelling
And a shell has reduced it to ash,
My lease here is ended, Death now takes my rent,

But – if fate provides you with means of deliverance
Out of the hands of the enemy,
And if, one day, you should pass by the home of my people,
I ask you to bear my final farewell.

Tell my folk of my love;
Tell those I love, whom I left,
At home back in Uist that...' (TN/Mac)

There, I can't go on, it's a very emotional poem for me. And it's quite a long
poem so I'll just leave it there.

AM BLÀR-CATH

Feuch, trilleach ro gharbh is borbachd cogaidh,
Le marbhteachd gunn' agus lann;
Cluinn gearain is caoidh is daoin' a' plosgail
Le osnaich ghuineach 's iad fann:
Tha 'n lasair le fuaim a' ruagadh thairis
Air bruaich is carraig is gleann -
Gur gairisneach, uamhalt' 'm bruaillean sgreamhail,
'S gur cruaidh mac-talla nam beann.

Tha lèirsgrios an t-slèibh neo-shèimh mar ghailleann –
Ghrad-thrèig an talamh a chiall;
Tha 'n cruaidh-chath le reubainn, sèisd is creachadh
A' beucadh thairis, gach iall:

An e seo da-rìribh brìgh na cruinne —
Sgrios, mì-rùn, ainneart is pian?
A bheil mòr-roinn an t-sluaigh air ghluasad uile
Le fuath is fuileachd gun rian?

Ged bha 'n òg-mhadainn chaoin a' sgaoileadh thairis
('S bu chaomh i sgaradh nan tràth),
Bha cneatraich is gaoir, bha aog is casgradh
Air raointean coimheach a' bhlàir:
Bha ceatharnaich ùr 's an cùl ri talamh
Fo chuibhreach daingeann an sàs
Bhiodh, mus tuiteadh an duibhr' o chùirt nam flaitheas,
An dùsal maireann a' bhàis.

Air dhomh amharc mun cuairt, bu chruaidh an sealladh:
Gach truaghan lag agus leònt'
Nan sìneadh cho fuar, grad-bhuailt' ri talamh,
'S iad truaillte, salach gu leòr;
An taice ri craoibh ri m' thaobh bha balach
Le chiorraman lag agus breòit' —
Bha athchuing na ghnùis 's a shùil gam tharraing
'S gam ghairm gu fantainn na chòir.

Bha sgleò air a shùil, 's a' taomadh tro mhalaidh
Bha driùchd neo-fhallain a' bhàis;
Bha acaid a chreuchd a' reubadh anam,
An t-eug ga tharraing an sàs:
Bha luasgan a chlèibh gu geur a' casadh —
A mheud chan aithris mo dhàn —
Ach bha bhuadhan gu lèir gun ghèilleadh fhathast,
'S rium féin gun d'labhair e, 'g ràdh:

"A charaid, dèan èisdeachd rium car tamaill
Mus tèid mi don chadal bhios sìor;
Tha solas na grèin' dhomh féin a' laighe,
Mo reult a' cromadh san iar;
'S e 'n gunna dubh caol rinn smùr de m'aitreabh —
Tha 'm ball' air a leagadh na smàl,
'N taigh talmhaidh ag aom', tha 'n aonta seachad,
'S bidh 'n t-aog a' togail a' mhàil.

"*Ach ma tha e an dàn gun tàrr thu fhathast*
A làmhan frioghail luchd-fuath,
'S gun tèid thu ri d'bheò an còir mo dhachaigh,
Thoir an t-soraidh mu dheireadh seo uam:
Dèan inns' do m'luchd-gràidh a dh'fhàg mi 'n Uibhist
Gu robh iad gu tairis nam smuain,
'S ged tha mi 'n seo brùit' is ciùrrte buileach,
Tha rùintean m'anam gan luaidh.

" '*S ma bhios iad fo ghruaim le smuairean aithnicht'*
'S na deòir a' frasadh on sùil,
Dèan aithris gu luath gun d'fhuair mi cobhair —
Gun d'bhuannaich m'anam cairt-iùil;
'S nuair dh'fhuasglar an snaidhm tha daingnicht' fhathast,
Gu tairis gan ceangal san t-saogh'l,
Gun coinnich sinn shuas, gach buaireas thairis,
An comann neo-sgaraicht' nach sgaoil."

Le cromadh na grèine thrèig an anail
'S bha chèis ud falamh gun dàil,
'S chaidh a chàradh leis fhèin san rèidhleig thana
Gun bhrèid no anart no càil;
'S bidh 'm preasarnach uain' air uaigh mar phlaide,
Le suain gun airsneal na blàths,
'S cha dèan buaireas an t-sluaigh no fuaim a' bhatail
A shuaimhneas bhriseadh gu bràth. (MM)

No one poet or tradition has shaped my poetry but Donald John MacDonald was very important to me. He was a marvellous bard from South Uist and he and I were engaged for five years. He later married another woman. She was an excellent housekeeper for him and she did a great deal of work around the croft but she never had any interest in his work as a bard. She was older than he was. A book has recently been published, setting out all his poems, and the editor of the book, Bill Innes, has been here to see me to check various facts.

Donald John MacDonald influenced my life very much and he influenced my poetry. We discussed many things and I used to send him my poems for his judgement. I was young then. The essence of his criticism was this, that my ideas and thoughts were being clearly expressed, that my use of Gaelic was sound, that image and imagination were there but that my poetry was being hemmed in by use of a too clipped metre. He wrote me long letters

Mary MacLean's crofthouse, at Yellowpoint, Grimsay, Uist. (TN)

about this. I think his judgement was correct and I slowed my metre down. He used longer lines than I did, with a slower rhythm. For example, one of his most famous poems was composed when he was a prisoner-of-war in Germany, 'Moladh Uibhist' – 'n praise of Uist'. He was captured in the battle in which my brother was killed. It is a beautiful poem, written to a slow, steady, rhythm, and that became the metre I used in many of my poems. I found it much easier. It gave me room to manoeuvre and my work, which had often been frivolous, became more serious. It was always in me to make fun and prick pretension, but that is only one of the roles of a poet.

We got engaged on 7th October 1949, in Glasgow. It was a Monday and we got the ring in a jewellers called Fred Hill's and then we went for a meal at the Wheatsheaf Rooms. Afterwards Donald John would often come down from South Uist to visit us here. It was a very difficult journey. Grimsay was a little like the dark side of the moon to outsiders in those days. I believe the coastline of Uist is almost as long as the coastline of France. He used to come north by bus to Gramsdale, then, if the tide was out, he would walk the ford. If it was in, we sometimes sent a motorboat across to meet him. On other occasions I would go down to the shore and wait for the tide to drop and I would be able to just see him on the far side. There are cairns set out to mark the passage over the safe sand.

Intellectually, and as friends, we got on very well, but as time passed differences came between us. He was a Roman Catholic, I was a Church of Scotland Presbyterian. That is a simple difference that speaks for itself. Although I could not have become a Roman Catholic, I know that Donald John might have become a Presbyterian. What was it, then, that came between us – we two, who loved each other very much? It was me. I am a very strange creature.

Donald John was such a good man. I never heard him say a harsh or unkind thing about anyone. Even those German guards who treated him roughly during his five years as a prisoner escaped his wrath and were never decried. If we had married and there had been rows, I can say with certitude they would not have been his fault but mine. There is something fierce and deeply solitary in my character. It's still there today, I bridle at other opinions, I won't let anyone go for my messages, or take me by car to the church. I walk. In those days I could not stand the idea of being tied down. Now I see that I was very wrong. I was stupid. Why, we'll never know. Not a day goes by but I think of him, and regret the loss of all that might have been.

In some ways, I suppose, I was very modern but at that time I was also obsessed with the idea of the dissolution of the body and had become very religious. Even if Donald John had been an elder in the Free Church, I would have had second thoughts about marriage. It is a great commitment to promise to share your life. Marriage, in those days, was an absolute giving of one's life and I, in all honesty, felt unable to give my life to a single man. I wanted to write great poetry. I am very independent. I get criticised for it yet. I can't help it. I felt I had a vision of the world which I had a duty to express through my poetry. So I decided that the relationship would end.

Of course, things have changed much since those days. The churches have all changed. Divorce has become much more common. In those days the priests kept people down. We were both shaped by our times and I was full of contradictions. When I got the news of his death, I wept all day. It was the bard, Donald MacDonald of South Lochboisdale, who phoned to tell me. It was so unexpected. Donald John died in Glasgow, in hospital. We had laughed together so often. We had shared triumphs at the Mod. We wrote humorous poems about each other. When he came here, he liked to visit a very old lady who had no English at all. He was very fond of her, so I wrote this poem, suggesting he would leave me for her!

It was chance and poetry brought us together; then we parted and made our two separate lives. One of the last poems he composed is a beautiful poem that tells of how he saw death approaching:

I see yonder the boundary wall
And gate of Tir nan Og:
I am tired of this long journey,
My vigour not as it was,
My step not so light and quick,
Nor my appearance so lively.

I see yonder the boundary wall
And gate of Tir nan Og:
Journey's start went well —
Fair wind in my ship's sails,
New lands and Eden's apple
Sating my desires.

I see yonder the boundary wall
And gate of Tir nan Og:
I await the flooding tide
And the ferry coming for me —
Oh, may eternal light shine
On me beyond life's end.

(from 'Gate to the Land of the Young')

… Chì mi bhuam an gàrradh-crìche
'S geata Tìr nan Og:
Tha mi sgìth san t-slighe bhuan sa,
Gun mo chlì mar bha i uairean,
Gun mo cheum cho ealamh, uallach,
No mo shnuadh cho beò.

Chì mi bhuam an gàrradh-crìche
'S geata Tìr nan Og:
Tùs an turais bha nam fhàbhar,
Soirbheas-cùil an siùil mo bhàta,
Fearainn ùra 's ubh'l a' ghàrraidh
Sàsachadh mo dheòin.

Chì mi bhuam an gàrradh-crìche
'S geata Tìr nan Og:
Tha mi feitheamh sruth an lìonaidh,
'S am bàt'-aiseig tighinn gam iarraidh —
O, gum boillsgeadh soillse shìorraidh
Dhomh thar crìoch nam beò.

(from 'Geata Tìr nan Og')

Echoes of our relationship keep coming through in that poem. There is an element of tragedy in so many lives. How well I remember the day in 1954 when I parcelled up the engagement ring Donald John had given me in Glasgow. I was across there in my granny's cottage and the tears were coming down my face, but I had to do it. I had to be free. I was thinking how dismayed I would have been if he had suddenly said he would adapt to my religion. I knew that he loved me but I didn't want to force him to give up his faith. I admired him so much I didn't want to do that. Such an act would have taken the wind out of my sails. So the parcel was posted and after that I never saw Donald John again.

His sisters used to come and visit me here, and once I was travelling home from Glasgow, on the old Lochmor, from Mallaig to Lochboisdale, and Donald John's sister, Anne, arranged that I should call at her house whilst I waited for the bus. She met me at the pier and she told me that Donald John was there at the house. He had arrived with a load of peat on his tractor and, knowing that I was coming on the steamer, she persuaded him to

Mary MacLean with Lettie,
c. 1954. (MM)

wait and see me. But the Lochmor was late and, with no lights on his tractor, he drove home before I arrived. He left a message saying how sad he was that he was unable to see me — and so was I.

Often I used to think how much I would like to meet with him again but that was the closest we came after the engagement was broken. I heard that he took the break very, very badly. And that bothered me deeply. We had no telephone in those days, and I felt it wrong to write once my mind was made up. Of course, I heard his poems on Gaelic radio sometimes and he would have heard my poems and short stories. After his death, the commentators spoke very well of him and of his poetry. In his later years he turned to God – not so much to religion as to God. This is very evident in his writings. His marriage was made on the rebound but I always wished him and his wife all the happiness on earth.

1954, the year of the break, was also the year in which I moved from the Church of Scotland into the Free Church. The previous Christmas, I had gone to a house to celebrate the festivities but I was suffering a great darkness of the soul. I couldn't eat and I was thinking, 'How can I eat when I am not at peace with God?' I told the host that my stomach was upset and excused myself. After that I began to give myself more and more to things of the spirit, and very slowly that dark cloud began to lift. A strange peace came on me. I began going to the Free Church here in Grimsay. I found clarity of thought and commitment; I found the psalms majestic and uplifting. Here, I felt, is true worship. This singing is an unqualified celebration of the glory of God.

I had always liked to hear the psalms of David. Hearing them at a distance, out of doors, can be magical. When I was a young girl, the communion services were usually held outside. And it was wonderful to walk towards such a gathering, hidden in a hollow at the foot of the hills, and to hear the psalms sung by a large crowd coming towards you on the breeze. The sound would seem to well out of the very ground and fill the sky. Coming towards those ancient places resonant with praise was a very beautiful experience. Now that I am old, I think of it more straightforwardly as the sound of a people in communion with God. Then, I felt I'd become part of the holiness of nature, like Wordsworth's Lucy: 'Whirled round in earth's diurnal course, with rocks and stones and trees'. We still have our communion gatherings. Here we meet in June and people come from all over Uist, from Harris and Lewis, even from Skye. They can still be great events, with people visiting each other's houses and great questions being raised, and the services can be marvellous. They are like a spiritual Gathering of the Clans.

In committing myself to Christianity, I experienced no moment of revelation; it was the result of a long process. I had begun by seeking something better, something clearer than that which we were being offered in the Church of Scotland. One never gains absolute certitude but I have faith: in the midst of a committed congregation, responding to the lead of a good precentor, a sense of spiritual ecstasy can come, at once overwhelming and sublime, yet totally within one's comprehension and control. So it was, in March 1954, I broke my engagement and went into the Free Church. One of my poems tries to express the kind of very powerful emotions I felt then. It's called 'Glory or Agony'. It's my own vision of The Last Day, the Day of Judgement. I originally wrote it for a competition organised by the Church of Scotland, and I won first prize.

GLORY OR AGONY

The night is nigh
The wind blows high
The ocean bellows roar;
I hear their sullen, angry cry
Against the darkening shore —
This is grim Jordan's fearful brink
And I must journey o'er.
My race is run,
My sun does sink,
To rise on earth no more;
The starless, midnight hour is near
And Charon waits for me
The murky messenger of fear
The King of Terror's here.
Beside the swiftly warring flow
I see his sable pall
Above the rushing winds that blow
I hear his mournful call:
Behold, my soul, the amber west
The herald of the storm;
Behold each fateful snowy crest
Upon each wave's dark form.

Think'st thou thy barque
Will surely ride
That dark tempestuous foam?
Hast thou a pilot who will guide
Thy frail craft safely home?

The world's confines are fleeing fast,
Their beauties fade from view;
All charms and triumphs now are past
Nor will they bloom anew.
Was I given this fleeting breath
For this dread hour alone —
To slumber evermore in death
When the quick'ning germ has flown?
From Calvary's Isle
Comes a beacon light
The Heavenly waters o'er:
The howling chaos now grows bright —
I see the golden shore;
The Star of Hope shines through the gloom
Dispersing fears and foes,
And soon my desert place shall bloom
As fair as Sharon's rose. (MM)

When I was a child we said prayers morning and evening, all in Gaelic. Out in the fields and by the hearth, everything was Gaelic. Our entire intellectual and spiritual life was explored via the Gaelic language and the Church. I still read the Bible every day in Gaelic and, though I know many speak against the influence of the church, it cannot be denied that the church has been very important to the Gaelic language and to Gaelic culture. I also have a daily readings book by the eminent preacher, Spurgeon. There's a great simplicity in his writings, yet the thought is highly exalted. He writes in English and there is much poetry in his writing. It is the New Testament I like. If I was to choose one chapter from one Gospel, it would be St John, chapter 14, where Christ says, 'You believe in God, believe also in me. In my father's house are many mansions...' The Old Testament is, for me, too bloodthirsty. In the New Testament, with the advent of the Saviour, we are given hope. I feel that the Old Testament takes away my hope.

Although I have made songs, most of my work is written, literary poetry in the modern European tradition, and I do not see myself as a religious poet. I have a natural bent towards irony and satire, my range was always wide, but despite that I have never had any complaints from the church. Our Minister here, James Morrison, was very strict but he encouraged my writing. We were great friends. I have his photograph upon my desk. His wife was also a great friend of mine and after he died, when she, like me, was alone in the world, I visited her every week till the day of her death.

It is from the Old Testament that the Sabbath prohibitions come. It is a book of doom and gloom; it is the New Testament that nourishes the soul. As children we observed the Sabbath, we went to Sunday School, but we were also allowed to play – quietly. Things were never taken too seriously by our family. I still observe the Sabbath but I also enjoy my Sunday walk. In my father's house are many mansions. I like to put a little rouge upon my cheeks. Why not? The Book of Revelation has always excited me even though I find it very difficult to understand. The imagery is awesome. I read it aloud because I know it to be sheer poetry of the highest order. Amongst the poets, Wordsworth has always been my favourite. I like Tennyson. John Cowper is a man I have long found interesting, partly because he was a poet who suffered black despair not unlike my own. I read John Bunyan in Gaelic.

The older I get, the more I think of the days of my childhood: I hear my grandfather's voice telling every word of a story but I can't remember where I put the shovel this morning! My very first memory is of going to a wedding. Grandfather was very much in demand at weddings because he had a gun. And the custom was, in those days, that as soon as the minister pronounced a couple man and wife, a gun was fired. Well, I remember my grandfather polishing his gun, and I remember the precentor singing, giving

Above left:
Mary Maclean at Arrochar,
c. 1950. (MM)

Above right:
Mary MacLean, c.1956. (MM)

out the line, as we say, and this precentor had a lovely way of swaying with his book. And the singing was wonderful and I was so happy, then, suddenly, the gun fired a volley into the sky. My grandfather had crept outside and just at the right moment, fired the gun! I remember the ladies putting their hands to their ears and holding onto their hats. Everybody was laughing and afterwards there was a great procession and we went to a room where a feast was set out, all organised by my step-grandmother. She had been a cook in England in her young days. And there it was, the table-cloth so white and beautiful, the trifles with their jellies shining red and green, and the cake. I had never seen such things at home.

Both my grandparents knew English very well but in our house everything was Gaelic unless they didn't want me to know what they were talking about, then into an unknown tongue they went! I knew no English until I went to school at the age of five. I was brought up very, very close to my grandfather. When I first began to weave stories, I would tell them to him. Walking out to the sheep, he would hold my hand and I would tell him a story, and the next day I would tell him another; I was full of stories. And one day I heard him saying to my grandmother 'that child's going to be an awfully good liar when she grows up!', and he roared with laughter. They used to stick up for their contrary grand-daughter. One day the Sunday School teacher, the mother of the teacher who beat me at school, came visiting our house and she said to my grandmother, 'It's so nice to know that Mary enjoys Sunday School so much', to which I was very pleased to hear my grandmother say, 'I don't know why you say that, she grumbles a lot about having to go, she says five days a week is quite enough without Sundays!' 'Oh dear, we'll have to see about that', replied the teacher and after that, she tried to make Sunday School more interesting and would give us an apple, or an orange, or a sweetie to eat on the road home. She was a very good woman and she tried very hard to answer all my questions.

Grandfather had left home when he was seventeen and spent half his life at sea. His was the age of the great sailing ships. He liked to talk about the River Plate and about the Argentine. He took part in the great sea race home from China between the tea clippers, *Taeping* and *Ariel*. He was on the Ariel, but it was the *Taeping* that won. He said he took some comfort from the fact that the skipper of the *Taeping* was a Donald MacKinnon from Tiree. And many was the time he spoke of the glories of the *Ariel* in full sail, and often he would sing 'The *Ariel*' for me, or at ceilidhs in the house. It's a beautiful Gaelic song.

My mother was Catherine Cameron from Cnoc Cuidhein and my father was William MacLean from Carinish. He had a business at Carinish. A

grocery business. He would come to visit us on the croft. He was very good to me. He was a strong character and people tell me it was his nature that I inherited. When I was being contrary my mother used to say, 'You're so fancy! And we all know where you got that from!', meaning my father. I had one adopted brother, John. His father was killed in the First World War, and he was killed in the Second. He and I lived with my mother, my grandfather and grandmother, she being his second wife.

When my grandfather left the sea, he came home to a croft of nine or ten acres. That was the average size around here. He was a craftsman in the old tradition. He made horse-collars out of the bent grass. And he made rugs out of *marram*, the long grass by the shore. He would braid the fresh grass into ropes, strands like raffia, then weave the ropes into rugs. They looked like coconut mats and they were used for the same purposes – at the door, in the kitchen and by the fire. He made all our own carpeting, right up to the Second World War. And he got orders for rugs from as far away as Skye. He would dye them a beautiful gold or crimson. He also made furniture, we called them 'sorna', chairs with grass seats and sometimes grass backs.

Mary MacLean with her mother at Black Point, c. 1956. (MM)

Those were very happy days. Everything was done by hand. From the time when the wool was taken off the sheep's backs to the time we wore it as jumpers and socks, everything would be done by ourselves. The tweed would be waulked in our house twice a year. The waulkings were great times for singing. It was a time for the women. The men would feel it was bad manners to be around at the waulking. They would be working, or take themselves off ceilidhing somewhere. The women from miles around would come and special teas would be made for afterwards. And beforehand there would be a bucket outside for them to gather the urine for shrinking the tweed. Everybody made their contribution. Later the men would appear to take their womenfolk home. One night I remember a young man coming to meet his girlfriend who was in the party of waulkers. He leaned in the doorway and he sang a beautiful song that I've never heard since. John Wilson was his name, a tall handsome young man. He sang that song just once but I can still remember his voice, the melody and fragments of verses.

Mary MacLean in Glasgow c. 1960. (MM)

I still make all my own butter, once every week. I whip it from single cream I buy from the van but in those days we made everything – butter, cream , crowdie, whey –we baked scones and oatcakes, we trod the bay for flounders, we salted fish and mutton, we killed our own sheep. We collected crotal from the rocks for dyeing the wool, and carrot tops; and the roots of the iris. So many things were wonderful when I was young. Going into our small shop was like entering Aladdin's Cave. Going to school, I would go up to the globe and spin it with my little finger and thrill in wonder at the thought of countless lives being lived in far-off lands – the sun rising on domes and long robed mullahs crying the people to their morning prayers. Even yet, I have no electricity here. My television's driven by a battery. I still like to learn about Africa and Mongolia, but it's a strange thing, all those things which once seemed so close to me now seem far, very far away.

I was born in Cnoc Cuidhein on 3rd June 1921 and I went to school at Claddach Càirinis. In 1935 my family removed here to Grimsay about five miles away. At that time I had no wish to go away to High School and I started work on the croft. I liked the cattle very much. I took them out to the moor and brought them back for milking. Our cattle were very tame. They would be waiting at the dyke. I took a stick but never needed to use it. Often I would take a book to read and just glance at the cattle every now and then to see they were not eating the corn.

Leaving school so early was a foolish decision. I immediately began to yearn for education, and through advertisements in the newspapers, I started various correspondence courses. The most important of these was with The Writing School in Shropshire, in England. It's said that a writer is

born, not made, and that is true, but I found the teachers in Shropshire very helpful. What I wrote in those days tended to be long and rambling and they taught me to be concise, to describe a person in just a few words. My father paid for these courses and all my family encouraged me, because they wanted me to do something out of the ordinary.

I'd write in the evenings. My grandparents' crofthouse was very small and very dark but we had candles and oil-lamps. They give a very friendly light. My mother would be carding and spinning and I would be reading or writing. How pleased I would be to take my work down to the post office and post it to England. And how my heart would leap when I saw the postman coming with a letter for me. And all the time I was studying, I was also writing poems. My memory was so good that I could make a poem and hold it in my head with no fear of losing it. I cannot do that today. Now I need to sit down at a desk with pen and paper and get everything down in writing as soon as it comes to me. In those days I would go to dig peats, or bring the peats home, and lines and fragments of poems would come into my mind and I would sit down and form them into verses. Later I would sit at the table and draw the whole poem together. If the weather looked good, I might take a notebook and pencil out with me and compose on the spot. It was about the pleasures of life that I wrote.

The tinkers were always very welcome with us. They came around in May and by then granny would always be needing new pails for the milking, skimmets. And the tinkers brought all the things the shops didn't have, hairpins, talcum powder, hairbows, shoe-laces. When they went away in September I used to miss them. And we children would go up to their camping site and search it to see if they had left anything behind that we might have. A broken mirror we found, and an old shiny pot. That was at Carinish. They always had most beautifully decorated plates set down in their tents.

I continued with my correspondence courses till the war broke out in 1939, when I was eighteen. I was keen to do war work, so I joined the ATS, the women's Auxiliary Territorial Service. I served in Wick, Thurso, Inverness, Edinburgh Castle and, for a short time, Orkney. I enjoyed the life, meeting many people. The discipline was hard but it gives shape to one's life, it knocks the awkward corners off. After the war, I worked for five years as a wages clerk in Oban, and just came home to Uist for holidays. In 1949 I got engaged to Donald John. In 1950 I gave up my work and came back to Grimsay to look after my grandmother who was getting old and infirm, and I stayed with her till her death in 1963.

My first success as a writer was in 1948, at the Glasgow Mod in St Andrew's Halls. I won the Glasgow Skye Gold Medal for the highest aggregate marks in the oral section. We had to read an unseen piece of prose in

Mary Maclean's grandfather bringing home the peats, c. 1930. (MM)

Gaelic, give a speech which we had composed ourselves, speak a piece of bardachd we had written and recite one piece by another writer. That year it was 'An Cuilthionn' by Donald MacLean of Skye, who was a Crowned Bard himself. In Inverness the following year I won a whole series of prizes. At Dunoon in 1950 I only won small prizes but in 1951, at the Usher Hall in Edinburgh, I won the Bardic Crown with my poem 'Beinn Eubhal'.

Eaval is the most beautiful almost pyramid-shaped mountain you can see from all parts of North Uist. I remember, when I was a girl, one day after school, going out and up Eaval with the shepherd. A storm was gathering and he had to bring down the sheep and he took me with him, but the gale got so bad he had to leave me sheltered behind a rock whilst he rounded up the last of the sheep. For an hour I watched him working the sheep whilst the storm raged around me. Coming down, we could see his wife in the doorway of the tiny cottage below us. She was looking up with her arm shading her eyes. She didn't know I was up there and, when we got back, she told us she'd thought I was a stray dog coming down at his heel! I was so small on the mountain. That experience helped inspire me to write 'Beinn Eubhal'; it's a mountain whose presence is always with me.

BEN EUBHAL

It is the all powerful spirit of Poetry
Compels me to set my thoughts down in verse,
Lighted by Gaelic so dark, rich and warm,
And my subject will be the high mountain
That coloured the years of my childhood
With its ramparted face, its ridge
Like a henchbone, its green patchwork and mist;
A mountain rough-hewn, unadorned and morose,
Which stands hard in the blast of the elements,
Amidst the mid winters' ice, so wild and ferocious,
Which in spite of the beating, the baiting,
The mauling, the mangling that nature has flung
Each drenching year since the beginning of time —
Still stands where it did above the coast and the sea.
Precipitous, corrugated, dangerous and high,
You stand water-loud where you did —
With your fast flowing streams
Coming down from the summit,
They churn through the gaps and descend
Gentle voiced to the quiet bevelled edge of the shore.
Wide and solid your escarpment towers over the island,
The beautiful island, that rouses music in me,
And despite the darkness and hardship of winter
May returns like the dew, bringing flowers into bloom
And sweet breezes that crown you in cloud.

What if history and lore were not gathered, all proven?
What might we learn from the ages of yore?
What Eaval: if you, like mankind of the earth,
Were fortunate enough — to hear and converse?
Were you ever as you are, have you risen, or shrunk
Since the Lord of Graces created you in your youth?
And what have you witnessed of Man since that dawn
When God put a form around Adam and breathed
Him into being from the dust and the stone?

Beinn Eubhal, North Uist. (TN)

You were there on the day,
It will be deep etched in your memory,
When they crucified our Lord:
When — after the scourging, humiliation, exhaustion,
He gave up His life and black gloom descended
Over mountain and moorland and darkness covered
Both your face and the earth.
Was your sense of resentment and justice sharpened
By the sight of those shallow, arrogant people
Mocking our Glorious Saviour?
And did you hear the cry?
Did you hear the joy of the peoples of the world
When He rose in the holiness of His majesty?

Was it then, that the thunderbolt,
In a splintering shower of bright white and blue,
Came down from the firmament and plunged into your side,
Breaking and tearing the sheer steeps of your rockface —
Pitting and scrapping the brindled flank of your torso?
It is a wound planted for eternity.

Since the origination of the earth,
Time and people have come and have gone
But your beauty is changeless,
Your beauty endures:
No one can deny you.
Until time is drawn back to the heights
And the bright sun is dimmed —
You will stand in the place where you are... (TN/Mac)

Evening, Yellow Point,
Grimsay, 1997 (TN)

DO BHEINN EUBHAL

A spioraid bhuadhmhoir na Bàrdachd,
Nach tig thu nuas leam an dràsta
Is leig leam duanag a thàthadh gu deònach
Is ni mi luaidh air an àrd-bheinn
A rinn mo bhuaireadh 'nam phàisde
Le h-aghaidh chruachanach, chàireanach, cheothar;
Le h-aghaidh chiar-chorrach, ùdlaidh
Mum bidh na siantan a' bùirich
Nuair thig i fiadhaich sna Dùdlachdan reothte;
'S a dh'aindeoin riasladh gach drùdhaidh
A chuir gach bliadhna bho thùs ort,
Tha thu stéidhichte dluth air a' chòrsa.

Gur corrach, cas-leacach, ard thu,
Le d' shruthan bras-sligheach, gàir-uisgeach,
'S iad air taisdeal o d'bhàrr chun a' chomhnaird;
Air am maistreadh tro bheàrnan

'S iad le tais-ghuth a' teàrnadh
Gu 'n tig iad faisg air an tràigh a tha fòdhpa;
Gur leathann, tàbhachach, dùr thu,
Nad shuidhe sàmhach air ùrlar
An eilean àlainn a dhùisgeas gu ceòl mi,
'S nuair thilleas Màigh-mhios an driùchda
'S a bheir i fàs air gach flùran,
Gun dean i fàbhar 's gun crùn i le ceo thu.

'N e bheithir lasrachail liath-gheal
A rinn le fras tigh'nn on iarmailt
'S a rinn do chas-chreagan riabhach a sgrìobadh
'S a rinn do bhreacadh 's do stialladh
'S a chuir an sracadh nad chliathaich
A bhios ri fhaicinn gu siorraidh mar leon ort?
'N e buillean goirte na h-aoise
A thug na nochdaidhean braoisgeach
A tha cho nochdte 'nad aodaonn tron cheo ort
'S a rinn do lotadh 's do mhaoladh
'S a chuir a' chroit air do chaol-druim
'S a rinn do bhoghtaichean fraochail a shroiceadh?

Ach on thùsaich an saoghal
Ged shiubhail ùine agus daoine
Cha tainig mùthadh no caochladh nad chòrsa
'S a dh'aindeoin bùirein nan gaothan,
Cha dean thu crùbadh no caoineadh
'S cha chuir am Faoilleach na 'n Dùdlachd gu bròn thu
Tha thus', Eubhal, an dràsta
Sa chruinne-chè seo san làrach
San deach do steidheachadh tràth ann ad òige
'S gu 'n tig a' chrioch as na h-àrdaibh
'S an téid a' ghrian gheal a smàladh,
Bidh thu fianais san àite sam b'eòl thu. (MM)

Those are just extracts. 'Ben Eubhal' is a long poem and it won me the Bardic Crown.

I was young and I was a woman and the papers made a lot of that in those days. I was cross-eyed for a week. You didn't know where the next flash was coming from. There were photographers everywhere. From that time on I

Above:
Window-sill, Yellow Point,
1997. (TN)

was almost a full-time writer. I had to work on the croft but always wrote a good deal, stories for magazines, many short stories for the Gaelic Department of the BBC. I wrote novels. Although the BBC now does a great deal for the Gaelic language, it does very little for me. Since 1976, when they took off *Sgeul na h-Aon Oidhche*, they have bought nothing and asked me for but one interview in 22 years. It can't be that I'm too religious or serious; much of my poetry has always been frivolous. I enjoy the ridiculous and always enjoyed writing to make people laugh – although in a small community you have to be careful, you can have people at each other's throats in no time. The poet has a certain power and for this reason a bard must either seek protection under the ancient laws of 'Bardic Immunity', or be very careful. A bard, by nature, is not born to be careful; his art depends on the uncensored truth. So, by tradition, a named bard, a recognised makar, has special rights in law. I don't know the detail of this but it is a very old tradition enshrined in statute. However, although I'm a registered author and a recognised bard I've always taken care not to offend people and I make sure certain poems never reach the ears of those who might be offended.

Soon after I wrote my first poem, about the woman from Harris, I wrote another about some potatoes that got stolen in the village. To this day it remains unpublished. I recited it to my family but they got very nervous and said such a poem should never pass beyond our walls. But that didn't stop me writing. My next poem was inspired by a young girl who went to work in the post office in Solas and got married there. This encouraged her mother to speak very loudly,

all over Grimsay, of how 'My daughter has not married to a crofter! My daughter has married a shopkeeper with something behind him!' Pretension is a thing that makes my hackles rise; so I wrote a poem that starts like this:

> *Thousands wish to marry you*
> *You refused them with disdain*
> *You refused a nobleman from India*
> *And refused the King of Spain!*

The last poem I wrote was for the Clan MacLean Society. Since Sorley MacLean died in 1996, I am the clan bard. It is an honour but these days it doesn't seem to mean a great deal. My name appears on the menu sheet of their grand annual gathering in Glasgow. They write to me when they want something and that's about it. I grumble. I have reason to grumble and I know a certain dissatisfaction is good for an artist!

When granny died I was left the croft at Blackpoint. And after my mother and step-father died, I was left Yellow Point as well. I live alone but do not feel lonely. These days I'm too stiff to work outside the house. I had a slight stroke two years ago. I have my two dogs. I still write a little. I listen to the radio. For years and years I've listened to *The Archers*; I follow it every day. It paints such a good picture of life. Everyone is so gentle and kind and hospitable and genuine. My favourite character is Mrs Archer, Jill Archer. There are one or two likeable rogues but it's very real and the life is like our life here, with the cattle and going to church. I didn't always listen to it but one day, about 30 years ago, I was walking home from the School Library with a friend and she asked me what my favourite wireless programme was. I said I had several, *The Three o'clock Play*, the Gaelic, of course, *Twenty Questions*. And she said, 'Don't you listen to *The Archers*?' and I had to confess that I didn't. She said I most certainly should, so I started to listen to it, and got hooked. Working out on the moor at the peats, I always used to make sure I was home by quarter past one for *The Archers* and I would listen to the repeat at seven o'clock, I never missed either of them.

In the fifties I also used to listen to *Journey into Space*, about the planet Hescus. That programme was written by Angus MacVicar, a second cousin of mine. I knew his sister well. In 1950 she won the Mod Gold Medal for singing, when I got the second prize for bardachd – for 'The Battlefield'. She was a beautiful singer. She seemed to have a slight cold that year but her voice was so beautiful and she won. The newspapers carried the headline *The Girl with the Golden Voice*, but before the next Mod she was dead. It was not a cold she had, it was cancer. I still remember the two minutes' silence in her honour at the start of the Mod that year. Her voice was so beautiful and her life was so short.

Looking back, the happiest day of my life would be when I received word from An Comunn Gaidhealach that I had won the Bardic Crown, because not only was that the fulfilment of my great ambition as a bard but also it meant a visit to Glasgow, which I loved in those days. I stood and I thought of the Clyde flowing, the sounds of the city. Almost 50 years have passed; and the Clydesdale Bank has a new ten pound note with the head of Mary Slessor on one side and a map on the other. You see the sailing steamer in which she sailed, her nursing the children, her reading a book. A white rose is pinned to her breast. Her life was given to poetry, as I have given mine. It's the way I was born.

Murdani Mast

13 MARVIG, SOUTH LOCHS, ISLE OF LEWIS

I got the name Murdani Mast because of my father. He was very tall, very thin and very strong and he stood on a fishing boat most of his life. He was like a mast. Mast was his nickname. All our family, even the girls, are now known as Mast, Ailidh Mast, Johnny Mast, Catriona Mast and so on. My own name is Murdoch Daniel Kennedy, so since I was a boy I've been known as Murdani Mast.

I was born in 1926. My parents were both local to Lochs, here in Lewis. Like many others I went away to the Merchant Navy. I'm a crofter, a fisherman, a weaver, and for some years I was a whaler down in South Georgia. Over-wintering in the Antarctic you got plenty of time to think about songs. I'd say I've composed close on a hundred. Most of them never written down.

When I'm composing a new song, I need to be on my own — coming home from the fishing, at the weaving, or on watch. At sea, we'd all take turns to be 'farmer', that was the name for the lookout in the forecastle. You'd be up there for two hours. You didn't have to steer the ship, you just had to be there and keep a lookout. That was a very good place for making songs. The rise and fall of the ship, the rhythm of the waves, the porpoises jumping, the night sky, remembrances of home — any of these might bring a tune to my mind and whole verses would suddenly come in with a rush. Every now and then I'd ring a brass bell to show them, up on the bridge, that I hadn't fallen asleep! Then back to the song. In those days I never wrote anything down. Every song I made in my head, and I've kept them there for 50 years.

I still compose in my head, but nowadays I usually write a song down as soon as I've finished it, because I'm beginning to get to that stage

Opposite:
The bard Murdani Mast Kennedy,
Marvig, Isle of Lewis,
c. 1960. (MK)

where you forget, or you think you might. I wrote my first song when I was seventeen and the most recent came last year, when I was 73. Sometimes months will pass and I have no inspiration, no wish even to try to make a song, then suddenly something starts inside me and the whole thing comes very fast – a bit like a big woman having a baby! And when a song does come, it's amazing, you just wonder where it's coming from. When I get a song like that, I think, 'Anybody could do this – it's easy!' But the strange thing is, they can't, and most of the time nor can I. For me the words come with the music. I have a tune in my head, it goes round and round and the words and the story just come.

My tunes I pinch from other songs. I pick up a tune very easily but I don't write music. I know many hundreds of songs and melodies and when I'm thinking about a new song, a particular tune and rhythm just locks in my head. Once I've finished a song, I never forget it. So far anyway! I have a very good memory - I can't help it, as they say! I don't think I could forget a song even if I wanted to. They imprinted themselves into my brain like fingerprints. I hate writing things down. I always have.

Singing has always been part of my life. We sang the psalms morning and evening. I used to sing on board ship, in pubs, at parties, now it's mostly just ceilidhs and weddings. I like an occasion, an event. It's something unusual, a surprise, that triggers the idea for a song. Once I had a bad night out poaching and I turned that into a song. Most of my songs have got a touch of humour in them – they're entertainment. My poaching song still goes down very well: it starts with a refrain and it's called 'The Deer Song'. Because my songs are very local and Gaelic, the translations have to be very free.

THE DEER SONG

I'll rove no more, nor hunt the deer,
I'll row across the kyle no more,
I'll rove no more, nor hunt the deer –
Not even a royal stood proud on the shore!

O come ye and listen to this my sweet song
And I'll tell you a tale of a man who did wrong,
Of how I lay in the Park, cold, wet and alone,
With the rain dancing down on my back from a cloud
And the moon hid dark in a black, black shroud.

REFRAIN.

At Cro Allt nam Bearnach we landed in silence,
A good friend at my shoulder and a gun on my back.
We trod lightly the shore and my hope was sky high,
A grand night before us, no worries or cares —
But the Enemy was watching, 'night sight' to his eye!

Up the mountain we climbed, my good friend and me
On the lookout for stags or hind running free
But nothing we saw till coming over a hill
We met face to face the gamekeeper himself!
We asked for a light — and then ran like hell!

He bent down to unleash a huge brute of a dog,
With teeth would cut through a bloody great log!
I hoped he would go for my friend before me —
But alas I was the man was meat for the chase
And leaping the river I fell, shearing my knee.

Lost in the mountains, up hill and down glen
I struggled like a stupid, bedraggled wet hen!
What folly, I thought — what a great fool I am!
Tramping the moor, like a thief in the night
Whilst everyone else snores safe out of sight.

O I wished and wished I was home in my bed
And not like a fool out walking the moor
And I said to myself, 'You've half gone to pot!
To Cro Allt nam Bearnach I'll never return —
Though the red stag himself stands up to be shot!' (TN / Mac)

I don't call myself a poacher. I'm too old for the deer but the salmon is a sea fish and I've been known to catch a salmon. I'm a fisherman and I set nets in the sea and if I catch a salmon, too bad for the salmon. I'm not going to throw it back, dead or alive. The Fishery Protection crews have been after me for years. They take on average two nets a season from me — out of the sea, or out of my boat. I don't think it's right. I don't set the nets near any of the rivers but out along the coast. What I catch we eat, or I give away to friends. I've ended up in the Police cells once or twice but whilst I live I won't stop setting a net every now and then. It's in my blood.

A few years back I made a song about the BCCI scandal, when the Western Isles Council lost millions, speculating on interest rates in that Arab Bank in Abu Dhabi. I sang it at the old folks' party at Christmas time and they enjoyed it very much. They're the only ones who've heard it so far. I call it 'The BCCI Song':

THE BCCI SONG

Ho ro there's news coming through
Would make a man sad and turn his face blue —
BCCI have crashed through the floor
And Abu Dhabi is laughing all the way to the bank!

Melancholy should smite every one of us here
Sixty three million lost in one year!
The Council know nothing — their head's in a fank
And Abu Dhabi laughing all the way to the bank!

Who started this trouble, who gave us this prang?
Was it Maggie, or Major or the great Tarzan?
Or is it the Council we have to thank
As we watch Abu Dhabi laugh all the way to the bank?

Just one thing is certain, MacBrayne's fares will go up
And the rates keep on rising like a big horny tup!
All the Home-help's been cut and the old women are ill —
But in Abu Dhabi they're building a house on the hill!

The new bridge to Scalpay shines bright as a trout
With money from Europe that'll never run out!
There's a causeway to Berneray for planting potatoes
And Prince Charles is laughing all the way to Barbados! (TN/Mac)

Opposite:
The bard Murdani Mast,
October 1997. (TN)

Ho rò, tha mi duilich is gur mise tha tinn,
Ri 'g èisdeachd na naidheachd th' air aithris mun chall:
BCCI air a dhol far an cinn –
Abu Dhabi gu chùl a' gàireachdainn.

Gur duilich an naidheachd a thàinig oirnn fhìn,
Le còrr agus (?) trì fichead 's a trì
Dh'fhalbh air a' Chomhairl' 's gun fhios ac' air nì –
Abu Dhabi gu chùl a' gàireachdainn.

Cò dh'adhbhraich an trioblaid 's a thòisich an call –
'N e Magaidh no Major no 'n e Tarzan a bh' ann?
'N e pàirt dhan a' Chomhairl' nach do thuig ann an àm?
Abu Dhabi gu chùl a' gàireachdainn.

'S tha aon nì tha fios air nach tèid às ar cuimhn':
Na rates dol an àirde, na fares *aig* MacBrayne;
Home help *air a ghearradh is cailleachan 'nan teinn –*
'S Abu Dhabi gu chùl a' gàireachdainn.

Fhuair droicheid gu Sgalpaigh a nise na cars
Le airgead Roinn-Eòrpa nach teirig gu bràth;
Gu bheil causeway gu Beàrnaraigh son cur a' bhuntàt –
Prionnsa Teàrlach gu chùl a' gàireachdainn. (MK)

It goes on and on. I'm getting on myself, but I still work 48 creels every day, lobsters and velvet crabs. My heart's not good. I took a turn coming back the other day in the boat but I like to keep going, and it's best to keep going. I was born here in Marvig and it's here I'll die. There were ten in our family and there's nine of us alive. I was number five. Neither my father nor my mother was a bard but they both had good voices. Everybody in our family has a good voice. Many of our people were precentors in the church. I'm a precentor myself, even though I'm not an adherent or an elder: they call on me when there's no one else! There's a crazy thing in the Free Church here, if you're a non-communicant you're not allowed to precent. How could I become a communicant, me a whaler down there in the Antarctic! Fortunately, at the local church, often enough there's no one can do it – so they ask me to do it anyway. And I enjoy it. I've two brothers who also precent regularly. It's a singing family, right out to the cousins and the nephews and nieces and great uncles and so on. And my brother John is a bard, like myself, over in Elgin, in Morayshire.

I grew up in a tradition where family worship, Bible reading, psalm singing was the regular thing. The habit of singing, the joy of singing, is natural to me. If I had a master, outside the family, it was Murdo MacFarlane, he was a great bard in Lewis. He died seventeen years ago. I didn't know him well but I knew his songs and one day my mother asked me to take him up some messages. I was very shy about going up to the bard but he asked me in and what a night we had. Entertainment? I could be there still. Murdo MacFarlane always composed to set tunes but because he liked to write in five line, or six line verses, the traditional four line tunes wouldn't fit, so he added tunes of his own, or he sewed together a patchwork of different melodies. He was very creative and very original. His work was modern as well as traditional. I sing many of his songs myself.

I went to school here in Marvig. There were 60 or 70 of us, including the children from Calbost, where today there are none. The headmaster was Mr MacArthur and he had two teachers. I didn't learn a lot at school. Fishing was so much in the core of us that going to school didn't seem quite real. At home it was all Gaelic, at school it was all English. We were practical, working people – boats, gear, weather, engines, fish, tides, currents, markets, they were all real. Sitting in rows in a school saying the tables was a bit like a joke for us.

My father fished all his life. He got married in 1914 but had to go straight off to what we call 'The Big War' and he didn't start a family till after he returned. Then, he made up for lost time, and my mother had ten children. All the relationships within our family were very, very happy, and it's still the same today. Closer than thieves! We don't need to try to get on – we just do. We've got seven children ourselves and I'm very proud of them all.

My brothers and I left school as soon as we could. We went to work, so that we could give money to our parents and help out with the younger children. They were very poor. I went out as a cook on the *Lady Margery*. She was known as 'The Training Ship' because all the young lads in Marvig took their first jobs on her. I got £9 for a season of four months. All we cooked was herring, so the cooking was easy – but the work was hard. It was wartime and there was very strict rationing. No butter, no cheese. Just one day a week we had meat. I gave £8 to my mother and kept £1 for myself.

In those days I suffered from sea-sickness. I'd even get sea-sick going over to Stornoway in the bus. The next year I went out on the *Lewis Castle* with skipper Andy Nicholson. There were eight of a crew. I was boiling herring in the morning, then going down for four hours into a very dark hold, coiling a very tarry rope, and it was down in the bowels of the *Lewis Castle* I composed my first song. I was seventeen and the skipper fell over the side! The words just

Lemreway, Lewis, looking south to the Shiant Islands. (TN)

seemed to come to me and, when the rest of the crew heard the song, they were thrilled with it. And they got me to compose more and more verses. That's how I got started as a bard.

After that I was on the *Speedwell*, then the *Coronata* with Finlay Campbell — she had ten of a crew. It was all drift-netting. During the war the fishing was good. The best shots might bring in well over a hundred crans, there being four hundredweights in a cran. Today we have radar and echo-sounders and you can actually 'see' the herring, but in the old days you depended on your own eyes and on the seagull — what kind of turn she had up in the air. And you kept your eye on the gannets and especially the black-backed seagull. If you saw a gannet or a black-back sitting in the water, you knew there were herring in that area. So round we'd go and throw the nets out. You'd shoot with the wind and drift for about four hours through the night. Then you'd start hauling the nets on this big tarry rope. And there was the capstan, a winch, and I'd be down in the wee hole below, coiling this rope off the winch all the time. And if there was a riding turn, or if you fell asleep, there'd be a good deal of shouting came down on top of you!

During the war there were hundreds of herring boats drift-netting from Lewis. You could stand here at Marvig and look out onto the Minch and all the lights would be there, beautiful in the distance, like a great city. All the boats would start fishing and stop fishing at much the same time and steam back to Stornoway. Dawn was the Rush Hour. Ashore, they'd put samples of herring to the market and the crew might go to bed for an hour before the market bell rang at nine o'clock. Busy days they were in Stornoway – barrels, horses, carts, all over the quay, thousands and thousands of barrels. And the herring would be salted, what we called 'rousing the herring', then sent off in big boats to the mainland in barrels, filled very full and capped down. There was no ice used in those days. Beautiful, tasty herring. The biggest and best came from around the Shiant Isles. Today there are very very few herring in the Minch.

Youngsters would get ragged, but most of the crews got on well and nicknames got attached to just about everybody. I remember the *Bucach* – a man who'd spent several seasons at the herring in Buckie. The Gauld from Carbost. He was so-called because a gauld is a stormy petrel, a wee seabird like a swallow. It never settles on the water and it feeds by scooping fish oils off the surface of the water. It's a bird very 'economical' in its eating habits, and this man was called 'the Gauld' because he was so tight with his money, never spent anything nor gave anything away.

Almost all the lads played the melodeon here, and it was very important for weddings and dances. They used to play 'Ceanag Mòr', 'Tha Mi Sgìth' – 'I'm Tired', the same tunes over and over again, until five or six o'clock in the morning. Sometimes the dances would be in a barn or the school but often they would be on the road, a road dance. At a crossroads. Our place was halfway between Marvig and Calbost, and maybe there'd be no instruments, just mouth-music to keep the dances going. That took some doing – a night of mouth-music – just two or three of the men.

In 1946 I joined the Merchant Navy. I went out on a tanker, the *British Swordfish*, to Abadan in the Persian Gulf. I'd had one or two girlfriends and I made up a song for my mates at sea. It's just a bit of fun, it's two thirds in English and one third in Gaelic and I called it 'Mary, Dear Mary'.

Once I had a girlfriend that came from Cromore,
She was a school teacher with money galore,
She was a darling like Marilyn Monroe,
– But she gave me the bachle
to come back no more.

On the first time I met her it was on the bus
Coming from Stornoway Saturday night
When I sat beside her and I gave her a light,
She said to me, *Darling, will you please hold me tight.*

On reaching that night I didn't sleep well,
Waiting for Sunday to come and to pass.
Off on my bike I spent the night courting
And she whispered, *Darling, I'll always be thine.*

On the night I proposed she was all dressed in silk
Beside the peat stack behind Angus Dick's house.
Her lips were like roses, her eyes were so blue.
What she said was, *You're charming and I've always been true.*

Then I went away sailing to get her some cash.
So that I could buy her *engagement* ring when I got back.
I brought her some nylons over from Bombay.
When I got back she said, *You'll do as I say!*

O, Mary, dear Mary, Oh, what have you done?
You've gone and refused such a wonderful man.
He's gone to the whalers, he'll soon be back home
But watch yourself, *or he'll make you a Song!*

Now, all you young sailors, will you bear this in mind,
That the love of a school teacher is very hard to find —
They sing your high praises in English so fine
But when it comes to the morning you'll find them unkind!
(MK/TN/Mac)

I worked on tankers and sugar boats and brought woodpulp from Norway. I
was out there with a neighbour, James MacKenzie, and we met very nice girls
– to whom we taught Gaelic! Years passed in the night. Then in London I joined
the Union Castle Line. Big ships. And just before I went away, I met this lovely
young woman, Louisa MacLeod. I met her at a Whist-drive-Dance at Cromore
and I didn't recognise the girl who'd for years been my next door neighbour in
Marvig! She being young and me being away from home so much. Somebody
introduced her to me and I thought she looked beautiful. I took her home that
night and she's still here with me after 38 years. But straight away I had to leave

her to join the *Elesia* a ship then known as 'The Terror of the Clyde': she had seven holds and 28 derricks. She looked like a monster. We sailed out to Bombay, Karachi, Aden. It was a four or five month trip. One of my jobs was to put new wires on all those derricks. I had Louisa's photograph and I was writing her letters. When I got paid off, we got engaged. I had £54. I bought her a ring and I wrote her a song. That was in December 1957 and we planned to get married in the following June after one last deep water voyage, to save money for the wedding.

Now, when you signed on in those days you had to sign two-year articles and they could hold you for two years if they needed you. So I checked that we would be back and paid off before June. I said, 'I'm not here to be shanghaied, I'm to be married in June.' 'Kennedy,' the captain said, 'it doesn't pay this company to keep the ships out too long. I guarantee this, if you've got the same girlfriend in June, you'll be married.' So I signed on and I made an allotment of £15 a month to my father and £9 a month for myself. We loaded cars and whisky and set sail for Durban. After that it was Lorenzo Marques, Trinidad, New Orleans. And that ship was slow. I began to suspect I was on a slow boat to China! You remember the song!

New Orleans was very beautiful. I was writing letters to Louisa, looking forward to being home, and she was planning the wedding. Then we went up the Mississippi and the six months went by. I didn't ask her to look for another fellow but, when I was at the wheel, coming back down the river one morning, I noticed there were trees growing very close to the banks with great branches sticking out over the river and I was so fed up that, coming into a bend, I gave the wheel a really big hard-over and she didn't come back. She cut right through the trees. I can hear the anti-pilot now, shouting out in his Southern drawl, 'Call the Captain! Draw up the hook! Hard a-starboard!' And I can still hear the trees snapping like matchsticks! I did that deliberately. A tug had to pull us out, whilst we watched the alligators thrashing about in the mud. Everybody thought it was the tide pulled us in!

After that it was across the Pacific to Cuba, Japan, and on to – wait for it – China! Communist China! We got orders to throw overboard all magazines, papers and books. Anything about politics, all and everything with pictures of the Western world – overboard. And where did we land – Shanghai! I remember saying to the captain as he came down from the wheel, 'What's the name of this place?' 'Shanghai' he said, and then he remembered. 'Well, Kennedy, I'm no more pleased to be here, than you are! But that girl must be a very nice girl if she's still waiting for you!' And she was and she is.

In harbour we weren't allowed to even look over the side of the ship. The only place we could visit ashore was the Seamen's Mission. We were escorted there with sten guns on each side of us. And the ship went on fire! They'd given us the wrong bunkers. They blew back. There was £30,000 of damage, and the Chinese wouldn't let us leave until they had every penny owed paid into their hand. That's Communist China for you. From Shanghai we took coals up to the far north of China and it was very, very cold. Then south to Hong Kong, to Borneo, down to Fremantle in Australia and home via Honolulu, where we broke down again and were stuck for three months! We got paid off in Hamburg. And 'The Terror of the Clyde' was a rusty, poor looking thing by that time. And it was from Hamburg that I phoned home to Louisa, eighteen months after setting sail. So we got married one year late, in Stornoway, June 1959.

I'd brought home £545, so we took a room and kitchen at Charing Cross in Glasgow, and next month I signed on to a coaster, the *St Ronan*, one thousand tons – so that I could spend weekends at home. Our first cargo was iron bars, steel bars, very heavy, for Rotterdam. I joined the *St Ronan* at Workington in Cumberland. In the English Channel we went into fog. I was on watch on the forecastle. I could hear the ships blowing their horns. Dead slow. I was shouting back to the skipper where the ships were – how many degrees to port, how many degrees to starboard – when suddenly I saw this ship coming straight at us. It was like Mount Everest coming out of the fog. Full speed, ten thousand tons, square on from the side. I shouted a warning. I waited. No orders came for me to leave the forecastle. She was coming straight for me, so, at the last moment, I ran for my life.

She went right through us. Cut us clean in two, in less than two seconds. The skipper jumped over the side. But I'd been studying the safety raft the night before, reading the instructions, so I went straight for it and buggered it over the side and, soon as it hit the water it inflated, perfect. There was an Irishman. He rushed below to get the men who'd been sleeping. It was impossible. He had to come back. The front half of the ship had now sunk and our half was turning over as she went under. I clambered up the high side and jumped off thinking, if I went on the low side, she'd come over on top of me. I was a strong swimmer then. Under the water I took my shoes off. And when I came up the only thing I saw was the white rim of the funnel disappearing under the waves. I heard the Irishman shouting, Hughie Farrell was his name, 'I can't swim!' But by now the hatchdoors from the *St Ronan* were bursting up all round us. I told him to grab one and hold on till I got to him. He says that I saved his life.

The three men sleeping never got off the boat and they were drowned. But the skipper, the mate, the engineer and two crew were now in the life raft. The skipper had lost his hand to his own propeller. The chief engineer hadn't stopped the engine. They were both in too much of a rush.

Hughie and I were an hour in the water before we got onto the raft. I remember how heavy I felt as they took me aboard. I was wearing a jerkin that my sister, Catriona, had made for me, it was full of oil and water. I went into that raft like a dead seal. That was 11th July. Finally we got picked up by the same ship that had run us down – a Greek tanker. We were treated very well. Then the Dover lifeboat came out and brought us ashore. When we landed we were met by the television people, but the mate told us to say nothing at all. Seven men were saved and three were drowned.

The Shipwrecked Mariners Society took us up to a shop to get new clothes. There were a couple of Glasgow fellows amongst us and they suddenly realised they were onto a good thing. They got themselves kitted out with the best of suits. But I didn't have the patience to hang about choosing clothes; I wanted to speak to Louisa, my bride of just a few days. I thought she must have heard about the sinking on the radio, so I walked out of the shop and into a bar, in my bare feet. The barmaid came up and she asked me what I wanted. I said I just needed to make a phone-call. She looked at my feet and asked what was wrong. I said, 'I was on the ship that went down this morning' and she took me upstairs and gave me a brandy, and she phoned the number I gave her and Louisa was there. I told her I was safe – with a brandy in hand. And the *Daily Record* took a photograph of her receiving the call – and the next day she was there on the front page – my beautiful bride.

We lived several years in Glasgow and I found work at the Albion Rover Works. Working nights, I could make £14 a week. That was a decent wage in those days, the early sixties. But when my father got left on his own, I decided to come back to Lewis. Louisa was sorry to leave Glasgow, we had a nice house in Whiteinch, but things were changing for the better up here with the weaving and fishing so we came back with our wee daughter, Catriona. I built this new house and learned how to weave, and went fishing for a season with my father-in-law, for herring. And I was at the weaving for seven years. And I made some of my best songs weaving, or tying, the tweed. One of those songs was called 'The Song of the Loom'. It's quite famous now: it's sung by the Lochies and various others.

In the middle sixties, the sale of Harris tweed suddenly went down, completely. There was no point in weaving tweed if you couldn't sell it. I couldn't make a living from the crofting so I went to work for the County – cleaning drains, working the roads. Then I was laid off and went to Greenock to work on the Defence boat, the *Sucker* and I wrote a song about her. After that, for seven years, I fished on my brother Iain's boat, *The Resolve*, out of Stornoway, until I started having trouble with my ticker. Then I went back to the loom for another six years, taking my pills every day – till my son, Duncan,

Murdani Mast with fellow
seamen, c. 1952. (MK)

*Louisa Kennedy receiving the
news that Murdani is safe
after the sinking of the St Ronan,
1959. (The Herald)*

gave me a thousand pounds' worth of fishing gear and said, 'You'd be better making your living out of that,' so that's what I did. I started fishing with creels. It was a nice new boat and I'm still at it. I've done trawling, I've done drift-netting, I've done whaling, but creels are the best thing for a man of my age.

It was pure chance that took me out to the whaling. I'd come back from New Zealand on the *Dominion Monarch* and I was having a drink in this bar in Glasgow before coming home when I got talking with these men going out to the whaling. And they said, 'What about coming over to Leith with us?' And instead of going home, I went to Leith and signed on with Salveson's. It's not the kind of thing I'd do today. That was 1955.

We sailed from Southampton on the *Southern Garden*. In South Georgia our job was to clean huge tanks which had carried down diesel oil, to make them spotless so they could be used to bring whale oil home. It was scraping hour after hour, scraping and scrubbing, high up in bosun's chairs. Then we'd be swung down, get dressed up, and set to with the Butterworth high-pressure hoses. Butterworth was a Geordie who couldn't sell his invention here, so he took it to the Americans and it was them that developed it. It was a very powerful three-nozzled hose. Afterwards, the mate would check the tank with a white handkerchief and, if he picked up a stain or a mark we had to do the whole tank again. There were no detergents in those days. If the tank was clean, he'd give us a tot of rum. Pepper was added to the tot and black tea! Very nice but sometimes there was very little rum there at all! Then it was straight on to the next tank. It was a hard old life. On the way down I wrote this song, 'Turas a South Georgia':

VOYAGE TO SOUTH GEORGIA

Tonight I am lonely,
Full sad did I leave —
Expecting to meet
With my father and mother.

When I signed on with Salveson
I'd just left the Saville Line!
It was Captain Smith who told me —
The Southern Garden sails on time!

As I signed up the articles
My Chargebook he did case —
He looked at me and shook his head,
'There's no beer in that place!'

I asked if there was anyone
From Lewis on the ship?
He told me 'the Spatcher' was aboard —
And the carpenter from Habost.

The Allotment note he gave me then,
I signed it on the spot,
'I'll post it on without delay —
But we sail on the dot!'

The following day I boarded her,
A chariot rusting red!
The doctor was a Harris man
And the skipper Peterhead!

That day we turned our backs on land
And bade farewell to Leith.
In putting off the pilot boy,
We saw he had no teeth!

First port of call was Naruba,
A Gazette there from Mhairi!
Telling of a great Land Raid
Upon the house of Gladie.

South Georgia at last
Was full o' well kent folk!
And every man a beard wore —
Like the stags up in the Park.

Whether I'll last the winter here
Is now my only worry!
When summer comes, I tell you this —
I'll get a licence for a lorry! (TN/Mac)

The Ice Barrier, 1950's. (AM)

TURAS A SOUTH GEORGIA

Sèist

> 'S gur mise nochd tha muladach,
> Gur duilich rinn mi fàgail
> San uair bha dùil gun coinnichinn
> Ri m' athair is mo mhàthair.

'S nuair thòisich mi aig Salveson,
An dèidh Shaw Saville fhàgail,
'S e Captain Smith a dh'fhaighnich,
"'N tèid thu null air an Southern Garden?"

'S nuair shoighnig mi na h-Articles
'S a dh'iarr e a' mo Dhischarge Book,
'S gun chrath e rium a cheann — 's e thuirt —
"Chan eil lionn san àit ud."

'S gun d'rinn mi dhàsan faighneachd
An robh mòran às ar n-àit ann;
'S e thuirt e rium, bha Spaidsear ann
'S an Carpantair à Tàbost.

'S nuair thug e dhomh — Allotment Note
'S a shoighnig mi gun dàil e,
'S e thuirt e, "Na biodh maill ann —
'S biodh e anns a' phost a-màireach."

'S nuair bhòrdaig sinn a' charbaid sin
Sa mhadainn làrna-mhàireach,
Bha doctair às Na Hearadh innt'
'S an sgiobair à Ceann Phàdraig.

'S 'n ath mhadainn chuir sinn cùlaibh,
Leig sinn soraidh leis an àite;
Nuair chuir e dhith am paidhleat,
Liege 'n ceann aic' Leith Harbour

'S nuair ràinig sinn Naruba,
Bha Gasait an sin bho Màiri,
'S cha chreid mi nach do leugh mi ann
Man a reudaig iad Taigh Glàdaidh.

'S nuair ràinig sinn South Georgia,
Bha eòlaich às an àit ann
'S a h-uile fear le feusag air
Man fiadh bhiodh anns a' Phàiric.

'S ma nì mi fhìn an geamhradh seo,
A chaoidh cha dèan mi dhà ann:
Thig mi air ais as t-samhradh —
Gheibh mi laidhseans airson làraidh. (MK)

Well, there we were down at the Ice Barrier. From ship to ship we'd pass in a basket. Dead whales were laid as fenders between the ships. It wasn't pleasant work, but I never found a lorry! And next season I went down there again! This time I worked in a factory which rendered the bones of the whales into fertiliser. Everything got used — the guts, the speck, the bones — all stuffed into packs weighing 170lbs. We had to sew them, lift them, stack them and be ready for the next one coming down. There was no clock, no bosun to watch over you, every man just got on with the job, but if any man slowed he choked the whole machine and it was endless hard fast work, hour after hour. The speck is the skin of a whale. It's very thick and used to get torn off with a big hook.

Top:
'Buoy boats' returning, 1950's. (AM)

Below:
Work on a factory ship, 1950's. (AM)

Sometimes the speck would rip and the hook come away. I was hit by a hook, a glancing blow to the head, but a man from Bragar was hit full in the face and killed instantly. He's buried in the cemetery in South Georgia.

I was down on the Ice Barrier when the New Year came in – with three pals from Lewis. But there were no drams down there, no alcohol allowed on the Ice Barrier. The only treat we could find between us was an apple. So as midnight approached, I cut the apple in four, and when the New Year came in we raised the pieces, toasted 'Slàinte Mhòr', and very good that apple tasted. And very sad I am when I think of those three mates today. All three were killed before reaching home.

One day, heaving sacks, I slipped a disc. I went into the hospital. I couldn't move, I was in agony. They decided to send me back on the first ship, a tanker, the *Southern Satellite*. I wasn't the only invalid. There was a man who'd gone berserk, a man from Edinburgh called Craig. Very big and immensely strong. One day, down on the Ice Barrier, he'd started to throw his clothes out of the porthole and he turned on his cabin mates. He suddenly screamed, 'I'll give youse boys one tenth of a second to get out of this cabin – NOW!' Well, they reckoned they got out with time to spare. He'd gone mad and he shouted, 'I'm going to dive into the ice!' But he couldn't get through the porthole! When he came through the door about ten of them managed to grab him. He was brought to the small hospital at Leith harbour and placed in the bed next to me. He had to be tied down. The doctor ordered him home on the same ship as me. He had a big Norwegian guard but I didn't look forward to that voyage at all.

However, it turned out that Craig was very, very friendly. He told me that in real life he was a masseur and he asked me if I would let him massage my back. He said, 'That's what you need.' He was such a huge strong man that I didn't want to go against him in any way. So I said, 'I'll volunteer.' And he was very good and very gentle, and each evening gave me a massage like the best of the professionals. We got to be firm friends. My back started to improve and when we got to the tropics we started to sunbathe out on the deck. Off Trinidad Island, I heard Craig ask his Norwegian escort, 'How far is that island?' Then he started stripping down to his jockey-pants. 'Craig, what are you doing?' I shouted. 'Stornoway,' he said – that's what he called me – 'I'm going to leave you,' and with a run he went straight over the side. The lunatic just dived straight over the side! And as soon as he came up through the water he started swimming for Trinidad. It was about four miles away, but he was strong with a beautiful style.

Now the *Southern Satellite* was a big ship and she was doing fifteen knots. It took the skipper more than two miles to turn her round. Then straight back along the wake we went, with everybody on the rails on the lookout. And there he was still swimming at a good speed towards Trinidad and there were four or five sharks circling round him! And there were more coming in. The skipper ordered the mate into a lifeboat, and they went out after him, rowing. As they got close, the mate took the tiller off the rudder – to keep back the sharks and to club the man. But there was no need for the tiller! As the boat came alongside, Craig made a grab for the gunnel and jumped into the boat. He was so strong! And he just sat in the prow – very pleased with himself. And when the lifeboat got back to the *Southern Satellite*, he came up the ladder like an ape, 'Stornoway,' he said 'you'll be ready for a massage tonight?' 'No way, Craig!,' I said 'I'll give you a rest!'

Now, it's a strange thing, those sharks circling round, not going for the man like that. Perhaps they were just about to, or perhaps they could see this thing was mad! Or perhaps they could see he was very, very strong and not to be meddled with! Anyway, they didn't touch him and some of the boys got photographs of the whole thing. After that he calmed down but, when we got close to Las Palmas, he started to get excited again and he said, 'I'll make it this time, there are no sharks on this side.' I told the mate, but no one wanted to tackle him! No four men would hold him. So the mate said, 'Craig – if you want to go, go quietly, no one's going to miss you.' And he walked off. Well, that did it. Nothing happened. We sailed straight through the Azores with Craig sunbathing like the rest of us and, when we got back, the police took him away. The *Liverpool Echo* printed the photos of Craig swimming with the shark fins cutting through the water all round him. It was a big story.

Looking back, I was lucky slipping my disc and coming home with the berserker because my three Lewis mates, with whom I shared that New Year apple, never got home. They followed us north just a few weeks behind and all three were gassed in a hold. Bone-meal had been sealed up for weeks in the heat of the tropics and poisonous gases had built up. They must have been ordered in to work too soon. That was a great tragedy for me and many people in Lewis. The oldest of them was 'the Spatcher', from Shawbost, Kenneth Finlayson. He was a great entertainer, a real comedian. Then there was Alasdair MacDonald, from Achmore. He was just 28. And Angus MacLeod, from Ranish. He was 29, the same age as myself. When the crew saw what was happening, they rushed in to try to save them but it was no use – four or five of them fell unconscious and the rescuers themselves were lucky to escape with their lives.

Life on Lewis sometimes looks like a catalogue of disasters. Accidents, war, TB, the *Iolaire*. We had a tragedy here in Marvig just a year ago. A father and a son were lost. The boat was lifted and broken on the rocks in a sudden swell. Two years ago at Oransay there were two sinkings within seven weeks and seven men were lost. These things affect the community in a very deep way – but the call of the sea remains. I love the sea. My own two sons have their own boats, and though I have no need to go out I like to get out every day that I can. The salt's there in my blood. And it's coming home with the creels that the songs still flood into my mind – old songs and new songs.

It's hardship – the sea, the mountains, the desert – that has made people religious through history and we have all three of them here. They are part of life and they bring acceptance of hardship and death.

As I said, at family worship my father used to precent the psalms of David; and it was direct from my father and from my mother that I picked up my way of precenting – both at home and for the church. Like me, my father was not a member of the church but when there was no one else, he would be called to be the precentor and many people liked to be there when he was precentor. He had a great voice. And when he grew too old to do the job well, I took his place. I still do it and I like it. I love the psalms and the psalm tunes, 'Torwood' and 'Moravia', all those.

You have to have a good pitch to start off with – you send out the line and the congregation sings it back. And then you start the new line before they've finished the old, so the whole thing takes off, like a big orchestra of voices. My voice used to be very strong and I commanded the congregation with my voice. I very seldom went wrong, in fact I think I have never gone wrong when precenting.

And it was not just us. All the homes here on Lewis would start the day with prayers and psalms – and it must have had a big influence on the children. Worship and the family were two sides to one coin. At sea I stopped daily prayers but, after we got married, I felt the need to start up the practice once more. Even in Glasgow it was prayer set the day. It was good discipline. It united the family. The singing would always lift the spirit. It was the same with my brother Alex, the sea captain, down in Wallasey. He led the worship in his family, and when I went to visit him, I would join in. I always admired him very much and when he died we were deeply upset. One day I was coming back in to Marvig in the boat from fishing when a song, a lament, began to come to me. And I went up to the weaving shed and started tying the tweed, and I stayed there till the whole song was finished and clear in my mind.

LAMENT FOR AILIDH MAST KENNEDY

O, that was a blow both heavy and cruel,
A double blow for us expecting you home;
It was not your face but your death
Brought our family together.

It was on a Saturday we heard the news
That you were low and hope was small;
We prayed that you would survive and our hope
Grew strong that we'd see you alive.

When I climb the shieling knoll
And see the land of our youth,
When I see that tree on the heather clett —
Willingly I still shed tears.

And when I go out fishing,
Sorrow is with me and alone at the helm
I see your face before me and great is the pain
Of knowing you are not with me.

When I go to the window and look out at the sea
I view waters you knew like the back of your hand,
When I see the strait of the heather-clad skerry
I think of the work you did there in your youth.

Often are my thoughts with the one gave you love
And today is alone with deep-wounded heart;
With you at her shoulder she lived in contentment
And great was the treasure she gave from her store.

By nature warm-hearted and compassionate you were,
You nurtured us youngsters till knowledge came to us;
It was your hand that steered us out to the world,
It was you set the course on which we have sailed. (TN/Mac)

Captain Alexander Kennedy
(Ailidh Mast), c. 1965. (MK)

DO DH'AILIG A BHRÀTHAIR A BHÀSAICH AIG AOIS DÀ FHICHEAD 'S A NAODH

O siuthadaibh, dhaoine, gur trom a' bhuille —
Gum bu chruaidh a' bhuille a thàinig oirnne,
'S an uair bha dùil againn riutsa dhachaigh,
Gur h-e do bhàs a thug sinn uile còmhla.

'S ann Disathairne a fhuair sinn sgeula
Gur h-ann ìosal is gur beag do dhòchas;
Bha sinn ag ùrnaigh is gun deigheadh do chùmhnadh
Ach is beag bha dhùil a'm-s' nach fhaicte beò thu.

Is nuair a dhìreas mi Cnoc na h-Airigh
'S a chì mi 'n t-àite sna thogadh òg sinn,
Nuair chì mi chraobh ud sa Chleite Fhraoiche,
Gur mi bhios deònach a' sileadh dheòirean.

Nuair a thèid mise a-mach a dh'iasgach,
Is mi bhios cianail is mi nam ònar —
Saoilidh mise gu faic mi d'ìomhaigh,
'S gur mòr am pian dhomh nach eil thu còmh' rium.

Nuair a thèid mi chon na h-uinneig
'S a chì mi 'm muir air an robh thu eòlach,
Nuair chì mi Caolas na Sgeire Fraoiche —
Gur h-iomadh saothair rinn thu ann bho d'òige.

'S gur tric mo smaointean air an tè thug gaol dhut
Tha an-diugh na h-aonar 's a cridhe leònte;
Fhad 's bha thu ri gualainn bha i gun uallach,
'S gur mòr am buannachd a bha na stòr dhi.

'S gur tu bha truasail 's gur tu bha uasal —
'S tu chuidich suas sinn gu 'n d'fhuair sinn eòlas;
Rinn thu ar stiùireadh a-mach dhan t-saoghal
'S gun d'sheat thu cùrs dhuinn air 'm faod sinn seòladh. (Aut)

That's my 'Lament for Alexander Kennedy', Ailidh Mast, he was a very brave man and a very good seaman. He went across to help with the evacuation of the British forces from Dunkirk in June 1940 – and his own words paint a picture of what it was really like to be there:

I'll never forget my first sight as daybreak broke – fourteen bombers plastering the shipping and the beaches and a pall of fuel-oil smoke hanging over Dunkirk, oil tanks blazing to the skies and the water thick with oil and lines and lines of soldiers, like hedges, from the town down to the water's edge and so very few boats taking them off. Dunkirk harbour itself was blocked with ships, decks awash, sunk at the piers, so I made for a spot about two miles north of the breakwater, where a small Dutch schuit was anchored, along with a Lowestoft drifter. Cautiously we approached the shore, sounding with a pole. There was quite a swell running. The soldiers were up to their shoulders in the water and, as soon as we were close enough, we began to take them aboard, most of them clambering over by the grab-lines, as we had no ladder. We had to keep the boat stern to the swell so as not to go aground. Within a few minutes we were almost swamped and backed out, with all who could hang on to the grab-lines clinging on for their lives.

I was glad the Dutch schuit was so near. We were soon alongside and discharging all we had aboard, mostly French and Belgian soldiers. We made that trip time and time again, until the schuit was full. Then we shifted our attention to the drifter, which was commanded by a very keen young RN Sub-lieutenant. During all this time, the beach and the shipping was being both bombed and shelled. The noise was terrible; as if you were in a great engine room or inside a huge drum.

By this time we were beginning to feel hungry and thirsty but we found that most of our food and water had gone – the troops having helped themselves. Their need for water was very great. Most of them had rum but that was no use as a thirst quencher. Towards evening I went towards one of our other boats where I could see a fellow with red hair hanging onto the stern. He was just about finished. Recognising me, he said, 'Give me a hand, Jock,' and we got him on board. There was no sign of any others. We were shipping a good deal of water and I began to wonder how long our engine would last with great dollops of water plastering over it and it suddenly petered out and we were unable to keep her off-shore. As soon as she touched bottom, we knew it was hopeless but it was whilst trying to push off

Dunkirk, June 1940,
British Forces await embarkation
for England. (IM)

with the oars that we realised how weak we now were – and soon enough we were high and dry on the shore, like thousands of others.

After a quick look round, we decided that it would be best for every man to do as he thought best. One of the Leading Seamen, a big powerful chap, decided that the only way we could get away now was to swim for it – and with that he stripped off. We watched him as he struggled out through the swell to the drifter. He made it. Because two of our party were now in very bad shape, we decided to make for the town of Dunkirk. We hadn't gone far when Jerry planes swept in, machine guns pummelling the beach just ahead of us.

We fell in with a party of Royal Engineers. We told them about our boat. They decided it was our best option. When we located it again we found a big hole in its bottom. We stuffed this hole with greatcoats. A Buckie fisherman tried to get the engine started and at last he got a splutter out of it. We then had to get her back into the water and afloat. With men and oars and luck we did it. I stood in the water at the stern of the boat, with my chest against her and my hands cupped behind my back, and in that manner the soldiers climbed up and over my shoulders into the boat. This went on till she was almost gunnels under. As she backed off a big sergeant grabbed hold of my arms and I struggled aboard whilst a dozen more clung to grab-lines. Two dropped off from exhaustion before we got out to a Dutch coaster, with a Naval crew aboard.

There must have been over 100 soldiers in that boat, but only six of the 24 crewmen who'd left Ramsgate with me, in our eight lifeboats, two days before. As they clambered aboard the coaster, I stayed pumping the boat.

I must have fallen asleep, for the next thing I was aware of was seawater up to the gunnels and the coaster banging down on top of me. We were being attacked from the air. The water was boiling and my lifeboat being chopped to pieces by the propeller of the coaster as the skipper violently worked the engine ahead and astern. My rope was caught in the propeller and the lifeboat was being dragged into it. Fortunately, one of the Lewis gunners firing away on deck, caught a glimpse of me from the tail of his eye, and he jumped from the gun and flung the end of a guy-rope towards me – and it fell neatly into the palm of my hand. I hitched a bowline round my body and was hauled aboard just as the lifeboat finally broke up in the thrash of the propellers. If that gunner's rope had missed me, I'm sure I would have been drowned or smashed to pieces. I had no strength left. I owe that sailor my life.

Aboard, some kind person gave me a cup of hot coffee. The first warm drink I had tasted since Ramsgate. It did me the world of good and soon I began to take stock. There was no room to stretch out. There were many wounded. I saw a big burly officer asking for some hot water for a shave. In no time he was quite spruced up, kilt and all the rest of it, ready to go on parade! Most of us were covered from head to foot with oil and there was hardly a boot on the boat. The silence was awful, hundreds of men dead on their feet, too tired to talk.

I can never express what my feelings were when I felt my feet on the solid concrete wall. I could have kissed it, as I followed the Lieutenant Commander ashore. On arriving at the Concert Hall, which was being used as a clearing station, a WVS member handed me a hard-boiled egg. There were mountains of them. The next step was a hot bath and some clothing, followed by a hot bowl of tomato soup. Then we were told to get our heads down anywhere we could, and we threw ourselves on the floor oblivious of all that was round us.

Some time next morning we were told to go back to Lowestoft. I thought I was dreaming as I watched a cricket match through the window of the train. It did not seem to fit in. We were taken before the Commodore to whom we six survivors gave an account of our work on the beaches, pointing out the disadvantages we had been under and how helpful ladders and sea anchors would have been. We were given a fortnight's 'Survivor's Leave' and I set off for Lewis at 2pm on Sunday and arrived home at midnight on Tuesday. It was uncanny to be home – so unreal that I couldn't sleep – and I wandered round the village most of the night A salmon jumping in the harbour brought me to my senses: the din of Dunkirk left my ears and I went back to the house, threw myself on the sofa and fell sound asleep. Next evening I got my recall to Lowestoft – invasion was imminent....'

All that comes from my brother's own hand. Later he was out with the mine-sweepers. He won the DSM, and rose to become a Lt. Commander in the RNR. At 26 he got his skipper's ticket and he served on the Isle of Man boats till his death at the age of 49. His death was untimely, a great tragedy for us, and that Lament is one of my favourite songs.

I have a memory of Ailidh Mast when I was only two. One evening my mother went out and asked Ailidh to look after me. She would have gone to get peats or something like that, but his father had also asked him to get mussels whilst the tide was out and he was wanting to get down to the shore! He was stuck! But he got an idea. In those days there was no electricity here, and the irons people had were big heavy irons heated by a hot stone inside them. So Ailidh thought that the iron would be just the thing to hobble me with. He found a good length of rope and tied one end round my leg and the other end to the iron and he took me out to the front of the house and he left me there on the green. I remember my aunt finding me, and what a fuss she made of me! But I have to say, that hobbling did me no harm. My mother got her peats, and my father said he was proud of us both, and we ate the mussels for supper.

Opposite:
Murdani Mast, fisherman and crofter. (MK)

Left:
Murdani Mast at home with his sheep dogs, 1980s. (MK)

Kenneth Smith

EARSHADER, BY GREAT BERNERA, LEWIS

My father came home on the *Iolaire*, for the New Year, 1919. I don't remember him, being only seven months old. I was born here at Earshader, on the day the Big Push began, 23rd May 1918. That morning in France, British forces launched a great counter attack on the Axis powers. It was a stubborn attack and the German retreat began. That attack continued and, bit by bit, the Germans started losing their nerve and that offensive went on without remit until the Armistice was declared on the 11th November. The same thing happened in the last War. I was in Egypt and I met a minister from Edinburgh by the name of J.B.L. Sloane. He was a brilliant man – he could preach in twelve languages, and he knew Germany and he knew the German character. I remember him saying, just before the Battle of El Alamein, that the Germans were invincible when fighting on their own terms but, once they had a setback, they could be confronted and, once they were confronted, their nerve would first give and then break. And that's what happened after Alamein, and Stalingrad, and that's what began, in the First War, on the day I came into the world.

In 1918 my father was in the Navy down in Portsmouth. In September he got leave and he came home and I was baptised John. After the Armistice the Lewis men began to come back in their thousands. Everybody wanted to be home for the New Year, so many that the *SS Sheila*, which would normally have brought them across from Kyle, was too small by half, and the *Iolaire* was brought into service to bring the men home to Stornoway. Coming into the harbour in the darkness, she struck rocks, the dynamo broke, the lights went out, the weather was very bad. My father, with two men from Uig, was below resting. A man from Ness swam ashore with a rope – he died very

The bard Kenneth Smith of Earshader, Isle of Lewis, 1997. (TN)

Kenneth Smith, father of the bard, who was drowned in the tragic sinking of the SS Iolaire, 1st January, 1919.
(KS)

recently. All those that survived owe their lives to him but almost 200 were drowned that night, my father among them. He was a very strong swimmer and it's thought he was dashed unconscious against the rocks. His body was one of those that were found and my mother was left with my older sister and myself. In July 1919 she received her first payment of a pension, 35 shillings a week it was, and after a year my name was changed from John to Kenneth, in memory of my father. After four years of warfare, that night was a terrible blow from which the island of Lewis has still not recovered. Eight hundred Leòdhasaich had died in the war and another 181 drowned that night.

My father was born Kenneth Smith in 1873. As a young man he started out as a fisherman, then he worked on the crofts, and did nearly 30 years in the Royal Naval Reserve. He was 41 when he married on 1st March 1914. My mother was Christina MacKay from Cruluvig. As a Reservist, my father was called up on 1st August 1914 and when he arrived in London he found that war had been declared. He served at Chatham, with three other Lewismen, one from Bernera, one from Point and one from Uig. Throughout

Christina MacKay Smith, mother of the bard, c. 1914. (KS)

the war he was splicing ropes – it was a specialist's job. 'Bosun sparkies', we used to call them. There were a dozen sparkies in the bunch and there must have been Englishmen among them. Four years of ceaseless work, then he came home on the *Iolaire*.

I was brought up in this house overlooking Great Bernera with my mother and sister, and my father's brother and sister. Mother had her pension and we shared the croft.

Singing and bardachd were always strong in our family. My mother had a beautiful voice and her mother had a beautiful voice. She was the last person to be buried in the cemetery on Bernera. I remember it so clearly. A boat took us out and she was laid to rest in a spot as lovely as any I have seen on this earth. My great uncle was a very good bard. I remember a beautiful lament he wrote for a man in London, who lost three lovely sons in the First World War. He was a MacKay and worked away in a Scotch drapery in Manchester. He wrote a song for my mother, about my father, but I never heard it. Perhaps it made her too sad. She would sing by the fire and doing the washing and going out to the cows. He also wrote a poem about the galvanised wire fence the government commissioned for Bernera. It was very necessary and it was a long time coming and, when it came, it proved extremely useful, so he made a song about it. My mother used to sing it and I'm now very sorry I didn't write it down. I know parts of it but not the whole song. She used also to sing the songs of Peter Grant and Dugald Buchanan, two men famous in the Highlands in their day. She died in 1985, approaching her 93rd birthday. I was with her on the night before she died. I had worship with her and we prayed together. She was a Christian and her face on the bed was radiant. My sadness was thus transfused with the knowledge that she was content and, although I was shocked when the telephone rang to say she had passed away, I knew she had gone to her eternal rest.

I've lived alone here now for more than twelve years. I read the Bible, aloud, each morning on rising and each evening before I retire to bed. I cannot remember my father reading, but my mother was a fine reader. Family worship was very strong here and for me it is the most natural thing in the world to read God's word aloud. It was the late Alexander MacLeod who established family worship in Uig in 1824. He was the first Evangelical minister to come here and he was very keen that people should not only worship, but learn to read and write, in their own language. It was he and the Scottish Society for the Propagation of Christian Knowledge that taught the people here to read Gaelic. His work and his memory remain very precious to us.

The first memory I have is of my grandfather. He died when I was 24 months old and he was 82. I remember the funeral service here in this house. The house was full of people, they were dressed up but so dull and depressed looking. And then the psalms began. And I remember the precentor standing singing, and me lifted up in my mother's arms. This was unusual in our house, to see a man standing up singing, for I had only known singing seated round the fire or by my bed. I must have been very fond of my grandfather. One day he was resting, half-seated on a large stone against the front of the house. It was a beautiful calm day, in April or May, and I was playing with his walking stick when a neighbour arrived. This neighbour grabbed one end of the stick and pretended to wrestle the walking stick from me and I pulled and pulled and really thought he would take grandfather's stick from me. And when at last I got the better part of the walking stick to myself, I rushed in between the two knees of my grandfather and I closed his left hand and right hand round the stick and challenged the neighbour with words along the lines of 'You won't take this stick from Grandad!' I loved him very much.

I went to school in Crulivig, just up the road here. It was not a good school and unfortunately when I was eleven or twelve we got a teacher who belonged to Stornoway and she was useless. She was the worst teacher I've ever heard described. After about four years all the parents sent a petition to the Education Authority and she was removed. But that was too late for me. I'd left at fourteen. It was a one-teacher school. Her system was this: she'd come over from her house, take the register, give us the morning prayers, go back to her house and stay there for the rest of the day. And that went on for four years! Of course we would have a grand old time, chasing one another round and up to every imaginable thing. My sister had gone off to attend the Nicholson Institute in Stornoway. I might have gone, but to go there you had to pass a test and win a bursary and in my time no one from our school was getting anywhere near the standard required. That teacher was the sister of the well-known pianist, 'Major' Duncan Morrison, and her name was Bella Morrison. What was wrong with her I don't know.

I left school in 1932 at the height of the Depression. I had an uncle in Glasgow and my mother asked him if he could get me an apprenticeship but he told us there were thousands on the streets unemployed, there was nothing in Glasgow. And in Stornoway there were just two apprenticeships offered by building contractors. That was all, so I found jobs round the croft, potatoes, sheep, milking. Later I started weaving. I finished my seventh tweed the day I was called away to the war in 1939. It was my mother's war widow pension kept us going.

I had joined the Royal Naval Reserve in 1937. I did training in Portsmouth and Chatham and I was 21 when I was called up on 23rd August 1939. From Scapa Flow I went out on an armed Merchant Cruiser on Northern Patrol looking for contraband. I was at Southsea when the ships started bringing in the evacuees from Dunkirk. I went to Canada to bring over destroyers. I was in Portsmouth on a night when the Germans dropped 20,000 incendiary bombs. It was a beautiful clear night with a full moon when the raid started, by ten o'clock you could see nothing but smoke, the whole city was ablaze. Thirty-five fire engines were pumping water from the harbour. That water played a big part in extinguishing the fires but the salt seemed to increase the stench that rose from all that burned and afterwards the city stank for days, indeed for weeks. Then I went to Beirut for eight months and to Egypt for more than two years. They used able-bodied seamen as camp guards. We were scorched by the sun, no protection for hours and hours, down by the Bitter Lakes. Then, because I'd served seven months more than decreed on duty overseas, I was drafted up to Stornoway and I saw the war out here.

But things had changed before that. As a young man I played the melodeon, I was a member of a band, I went out in company that enjoyed drinking and dancing but in 1937 I was converted, I gave myself to Christ. I put

The bard Angus MacKay, grand-uncle to Kenneth Smith, c. 1910. (KS)

Able Seaman Kenneth Smith (right) in Beirut, 1942. (KS)

the melodeon away and since that time I have only composed spiritual songs. One of my early poems is about a child who was found alone in a field. It is a parable that speaks of the Church of Christ. The story comes from Jeremiah, who compares the church to a baby lying in its own blood in an open field, unable to do anything – unable to feed, or warm or defend itself – and a voice came from Heaven and spake the two words – Be Alive – and the poem goes on to tell how that child was brought into the church. It still speaks to me, for as a young man I suffered a crisis of the soul, and I would like to think it speaks for us in the world today.

A friend who came back on the same boat as me from foreign service in Egypt said he had only one complaint about my poems – that they were too long. He was an excellent Gaelic scholar and knew what he was speaking about. I knew they were long but answered him by saying that I made every effort never to repeat myself and believed none of my poems were longer than their narrative need. He accepted this but stated that the problem was that few modern people would take the trouble to memorise such a long poem – thus there was the danger that my poems might disappear with me. Fifty years later, however, 60 of my poems have been published in newspapers and magazines, so they will live on in some form.

The happiest moment of my life came when I knew I was under

Able Seaman Kenneth Smith (right) in Egypt, 1943. (KS)

the influence of the promise of God; when I recognised the liberty of the Gospel and the text of God's word was applied to my soul and I was taken out of my prison and took possession of liberty. For weeks before that, I was in no man's land. I had left frivolity behind me but I was in a very bad state, deep in a trough close to despair – so when His presence was revealed to me, my joy was very great and days of happiness followed one another.

That happened in October 1937 but my conversion had been set in train by my attendance at a Royal Navy Reserve course at Portsmouth barracks in the January of that year. I returned north by rail with a big contingent of Lewismen and we sailed home overnight from the Kyle of Lochalsh to Stornoway. When we got on board ship, I remember one of my contemporaries gathering us around him and saying that we should be an example to everybody aboard – that no one amongst us should be seen to be drinking or under the influence of drink but that we would have a night-crossing to remember all our lives. There were seventeen of us from Lewis and he was a very wise young fellow. He came from Uig. And he said, 'There's a fellow here with a melodeon,' and he asked if anybody else could play and I said, 'I can play.' And through the night we danced, all the way from Kyle to Stornoway, we two on the melodeon in turns, never stopping but to join in the dancing.

Well, when at last I got home to bed, a thought struck me –

'Kenneth, you were dancing and playing the melodeon over the grave of your father, over the very waters where your father was drowned.' And it went through me like an arrow and before dawn broke I said, 'Never again will I go onto a dance floor or play a melodeon whilst I live.' And I have not done either till this day. And, of course, I was not alone. There was a great revival surging through Lewis and I joined a group of young men. We all started going to prayer meetings and over the following weeks the power of the Gospel was revealed to me and my life was changed. I gained liberty of soul. Before that I had written various frivolous poems; after that serious poems began to come to me. They describe my life in the Navy and sprang from my reading of the Bible. One that I wrote is called 'The Women at the Tomb of Christ'.

THE WOMEN AT THE TOMB OF CHRIST

Our Beloved Saviour lies in the tomb,
Taken down by the power of death,
And no relative there to ease the pain of Mary.
Knowing that her noble son is dead,
She gathers spices to anoint the body of Christ.

At the rising of the sun the women came
In silence to the grave in which He lay:
They entered the tomb and found it cold,
And Lo, the body of our Lord was gone,
For power had come down from on high.

Glorious was the vision the two women then beheld
For as they turned towards the light
They saw a blessed youth in shining raiment clad,
Who said, 'You shall see Him who died
On Calvary alive — for He is risen.'

At this the women went forth from the empty tomb
And out into the garden, where stood a man
Whom Mary did not recognise at first.
He spake: 'Mary go now forth to Galilee,
Where we will meet as once we were.'

And when Mary heard Him speak in His own voice,
She recognised this was her only Son
And great joy replaced the grief that had descended
When she believed that she had lost the subject
Of her love. He stood there by her side.

'Poverty and death shall be no more.'
The illumined truth of all he'd ever said
Cascaded round her from on high
And she felt the power of unconquerable love
Banish all that had put sadness in her step.

He liveth: He had risen from the grave.
He had overcome the dragon of death with Love.
And now he enjoined her to go forth with the news
Of Salvation — to tell the world
That His Love was alive and enduring.

And that morning His light fulfilled the Law of Moses,
The promise of God decreed down the ages,
That His people would know justice
And be delivered from death and all
Be gathered into the bosom of His own people.

He freed them from sin and all wickedness,
Always listening, ever speaking, ever present.
David foretold the fervour of His love in the Psalms:
His raiment was divided on the fall of a dice,
And a crown of thorns was thrust down on His head.

Later He parted from them, and they on the mountain,
Saying, 'Forever I am with you, go forth to every corner
Of the earth with the Gospel of Salvation in your hand,
Revealing the promise I bring from on high —
'I am risen and come amongst you.'

He is still speaking: His word illumines the flesh.
'O, come to me, all you who mourn,
My word will be a blessing to all in trouble
And distress — and on reaching harbour —
My promise to each one of you will be fulfilled. (TN / Mac)

My conversion was just a very small incident in a much greater development. There were several very great preachers in Lewis and it was inspiration from preachers and missionaries that spread the revival across the whole of Lewis. People liable to become converts would feel first a conviction of their own sinfulness. A silence might be noted amongst the men, or weeping amongst the women. In church they might suddenly feel exhilaration in singing the psalms. They might be deeply moved by some truth in the Scriptures, or by the recognition of wrong-doing in themselves. They might hunger for discipline. Then there would be meetings and help given by preachers and elders and their soul would be nurtured. Converts might feel troubled and depressed for four or five weeks – then quite suddenly they would see the light at the end of the tunnel, and great comfort would come to them and they would be embraced into the church.

There was a man in Bernera who was a missionary and also an outstanding bard. His name was Smith but he was no close relation of mine. He wrote some very amusing bardachd when he was young. Apparently a whale came ashore on the west side of Bernera. It had probably been killed by a swordfish. Some of the fishermen here had seen a whale being attacked by a very large swordfish just before this creature was washed ashore dead. Well, the young bard made a poem stating that it was so and so who killed the whale! Now this accused man was mentally and physically backward and it was most unlikely that he would have been able to kill a sheep, let alone a whale, so it was a very funny poem and many people sang it. It became a great favourite. But then the bard Smith got converted and went up to Harris as a missionary, and his attitude to poetry changed. One day he met my grandfather in Stornoway, the man whose walking stick I struggled to defend, and the missionary asked my grandfather about Uig and Bernera. 'Do they still sing the songs I composed when I was young?' And my grandfather said, 'O, yes! I'm afraid they do!', not wanting to upset him. And the missionary said, 'I cannot deny that what you tell me pleases me, for all bards are vain, but I must ask you to ask them not to sing "The Whale Song", for that song is made up of direct lies! My song brought derision on an innocent man and I am ashamed.' Of course, my grandfather took the message back to Bernera but that song is still being sung in Lewis today! The good thing is that, as the years pass, the identity of that backward young man is getting forgotten. Only the song lives on.

Another bard also wrote a song about the herring fishing, a beautiful song that describes the skipper steering his boat under canvas against the wind and the current, like a bullet. A song of his I used to sing myself was called 'The Bachelor'. It was very witty, pointing out that the bachelor, having never married, did not know the joys he was missing and so on. It tells of all the good and useful things a wife provides. I think about that song sometimes because I never married and I think I'm past redemption now! 'Too old!' –

that's the advice I'd give to any lady who would agree to marry me. The bard Smith married three times but was father to no children.

Life, death, destiny, the hope of resurrection, these are things we live with and no one knows how things will be. One of the young men who joined the church at the same time as I did died at the age of 67 in tragic circumstances about twelve years ago. He was putting down food for the cattle and there was a small heifer there with horns and as he bent over to feed her she lifted her head and struck him a sharp blow by the temple. He thought little about the wound but it refused to heal. First he went to Stornoway, then to Raigmore Hospital in Inverness but instead of getting better, he got worse and he died. I never saw the certificate affirming the cause of his death but I believe some poison from the horn of the heifer was lodged in his blood-stream and nothing could be done to save him. His death was untimely but, as a Christian, death would hold no perils for him.

For many years I worked as a gillie on the river here. I gillied for Earl Mountbatten's daughter and her husband, Lord Leyburn. It was his mother that was killed when Earl Mountbatten of Burma was murdered in Ireland. Her twin sons were also on the boat. They were injured but survived and they were brought here for a holiday. I was asked to take them down to the river. The younger one, Timothy, was in a very bad state, almost a nervous wreck, but I set them fishing and within half an hour they caught a sea trout. And the keeper saw this and he said we should stay on the river, even though that was against the rules. After eleven in the morning the river was never fished but we kept at it and they soon caught a small salmon. With that fish they began to recover and at the end of a fortnight they were on top of the world.

In many ways I enjoyed my war service. It was in a strange way an easier life than life at home. When I came back everything was the same, crofting, weaving, very little paid employment, and widespread hardship. From 1951 till 1953 I got a break working on the Bernera Bridge. Then I worked for twelve years as a part-time insurance agent. I had a bubble car and drove all over Lewis. Then I did my twelve seasons as a gillie at Garynahine. Now I'm retired but I still tend the croft, I've still got a dog, I still go to church and I still write poetry - though as I grow older I seem inspired less and less.

Inspiration is important to a bard. I'll tell you a story about that. One day, after I'd written a new poem, I took it up to a minister, Donald Gillies, in Crosbost, and he asked me to read it. When I'd finished he said, 'Kenneth, I want to ask you one question. Did you ever lose a poem? Did you ever experience something that inspired you as a bard but which you didn't get down into a poem?' And I answered, 'Yes.' And he said, 'Tell me about that.' 'Well, – it was about seven o'clock on a beautiful summer's day and, with two neighbours, I was going out to gather our sheep for shearing. As I went out through the door

I was suddenly struck by the beauty of the morning. The loch between here and Bernera was dead calm and the hills and the islets were all reflected with perfect clarity on the surface of the water and deep in the water. I was struck with awe at the beauty before me and a poem began to form straight away in my mind. But suddenly the men who were with me were calling and the spell was broken. I had to go out after the sheep. I climbed the hill thinking of what a song I would make when I got home that evening! All day we worked and, when I came home, the poem was gone and it never returned.' The minister said, 'I thought there would be such occasions.' And he told me, 'Kenneth, some things are more important than work, you are a bard and your inspiration should be honoured – by yourself, as well as by others.' He then suggested that I should always carry a notebook and pencil with me, to respond to the strikes that poetry makes in the mind without fear or favour, and that I should not lose such a moment again. I was in a hurry and I lost the opportunity that morning.

We had a night rainbow here, just recently. There was a full moon, it was a squally night with showers and broken cloud scurrying through at about 2000 feet. The moon was in the east and the rainbow in the west. Two friends have told me how they were down at the Callanish Stone Circle and they saw the rainbow form a perfect hemisphere over the stones. Beneath the bow, the sky took on a paler glow – so there was the dark night sky, the coloured rainbow itself and then a flattened dome of luminous grey light. I don't suppose such a thing has been seen often in 5000 years. But quite recently across in Harris, Murdo Morrison saw a related phenomenon. It was November and, with other crofters from Ardvourlie, he was gathering the sheep, bringing them down off Tomnaval for the winter. He was very high up when, looking down, he saw a rainbow below form itself into a complete circle. It was like a wheel of fire, like a great halo ringing the glen and through the rainbow the sheep were walking, followed by the men with their dogs. It was a sight like something from the Old Testament. And Murdo turned to Campbell and said, 'It's a pity you don't have your camera to catch that.' And Campbell said, 'No, Murdo. This is a moment in time, this is something to be seen and remembered , not to be put down on paper.'

The bard Kenneth Smith of Earshader, Lewis, 1997. (TN)

Nature has always inspired poetry. For me making a song – and all my poems are sung – the experience has to be first-hand and then put into a religious or spiritual context. I'm in my eightieth year. There can be no doubt that my days as a poet are numbered. My faith in the Word of the Lord has been repaid a thousandfold. Although I never knew my father, his life and his memory have been a guide to me, as was the life of my mother. I cannot see an eagle but I think of the *Iolaire*, so deep is that name engraved in the heart of every man and every woman on the Island of Lewis. But even such a tragedy is nought in the balance of the redeeming power of Jesus Christ.

Part Two

Highland History

Hugh MacIntosh

PORT SKERRA, SUTHERLAND, 1901-89

There was no such thing as electricity in my time, no such a thing as bathing in our house, there was no such thing as a water supply, all had to be carried from the well. All the light that we had was a small paraffin lamp on the corner of the mantelpiece; they stood in every house. I remember, once, my mother sent for a hanging lamp, from Thurso. Horse coaches were still coming through Melvich at that time, there were no cars. I went up to Melvich with her and we got this lamp down from the carriage. It was just an ordinary hanging lamp but we thought it was a great light. And the lamp was hanging up there over the table, or in the window shining out into the road. For us boys and my mother, the new light was a wonderful advantage but my grandfather, he didn't like it. He would take the Book down for prayers, every night and morning, and on the evening the lamp arrived one of my brothers took the lamp over and placed it on the edge of the table beside him. I remember his face in the light and the white pages of the Book. He sat silent, then he looked at my brother and asked him to put the lamp back where it came from, and he said, 'No house has need of a light brighter than the sun, a window is enough for me.'

You want to know what life was like in the old days? Picture eight of a family, and picture the father and mother, and picture the grandmother and grandfather, and put all these people into the one house, a three roomed thatched cottage, jam them all in together. Now picture them sitting down for a meal, two sittings to a meal. That was our life. That's what a family up here was.

Every house had a meal-girne, a big wooden chest with three sections, each holding a boll of meal, or maybe more. Oat meal would go in one section, bread meal in one section, and barley meal in one section. Then there was the barrel of herring and your tatties. That was us for the winter months. In times of snow, when the roads were blocked, that saw you through. In those days there was more snow, more snow than we get now, it was more regular, now it's rain and wind the winter brings and people don't keep a winter store. The last time we had a lot of snow, people weren't ready for it. They had to send helicopters in. Operation Snowdrift is what they called it. The vans couldn't get through, so people ran out of food. With all their cars and televisions, the modern folk, they were in a more perilous state than ever we were. They had to bring a battleship into Loch Eribol to bake bread. When every house had a meal-gun, we had no need for battleships! Our table was frugal but our table was crowded. Now there's just one or two sitting down. Once it was the men who would go away to sea and to the herring fishing: now it's the girls and the youngsters who go and, of them, not five in a hundred return here to live. I was 22 years at sea, in the Merchant Marine, but I came home after the Second World War. I had my wife, Mary, and the children to think of. It was at sea that I composed many of my poems and I wrote a lot about Mary. After she died I wrote one last poem. It's called '*Sweet Memories*':

I sat down beside her for a moment in time
While she clasped my hand so tight —
'Twas the last goodbye in a lifetime for me
As we parted forever that night.
It was still very hard for me to believe
That this was the end of the road
And never again on the face of this earth
Would we meet in the flesh and the blood.

I stood in the doorway with tears in my eyes
As I watched her passing away —
What thoughts and sweet memories were crossing my mind
As there on her deathbed she lay —
I knew it was the end of an era for me
And my feelings I never can tell,
For sorely within my very sad heart
I was bidding my Mary farewell.

I knew she was dying but only to live
In a world without sorrow or pain
Where a place is prepared for each and for all
With life everlasting to gain;
What's more than a marvel and mystery to me
Is the hereafter that often I dread
For in less than a moment when the spirit had gone
I gazed on the face of the dead. (HM)

I'm on my own now and hard enough up – so I can see why those who get an education, get money, get into state employment, stay away, make themselves comfortable in the south. But the less people here, the more bleak north Sutherland becomes for the rest of us. I've written a song about the worst of this place. It's called, 'Bloody Melvich':

This bloomin' place is dead and dull,
You'd think the lot was on the pill
For everything is standing still
In Port Skerra and in Melvich.

I see the hills but not the moles,
The homes I see but not the souls,
They never leave their bloomin' holes
In Port Skerra and in Melvich.

I take a walk along the shore,
To where I've often been before,
For everything's a bloomin' bore
In Port Skerra and in Melvich.

There's not a bloody road to reach
Or take you near the bloomin' beach
But there's no further sense to preach
About that in bloody Melvich.

There's even not a path, be God,
To keep you off the bloody road
And Safety Rules are no damned good
Down in bloody Melvich.

There's not a bloody light to see,
It's dark and dismal as can be
And you canna tell a he from a she
Down in bloody Melvich.

The County should be losing face
With the bloomin' place such a damned disgrace
And I never saw such a bloody mess
As down in bloody Melvich.

With wrecks of lorries, vans as well,
You'd think 'twas under shot and shell
And that the place was bombed to hell
Down in bloody Melvich.

What the County's int'rested in
Is dig a hole and throw you in —
The more that's dead the less work for them
Down in bloody Melvich.

Well, my life is well-nigh worn
And all I do is moan and groan
But oft I wish that I'd ne'er been born
Around the bounds of Melvich. (HM)

Of course, it's not all bad in Melvich. We have the Melvich Inn — I wrote a song about the day a cow got in the bar! And a ditty about my friends — the drouthy drouths therein:

When I go to the Melvich Bar
To have my tootle dram
I know the drouths are already there,
I ken them every one —
There's Don Dall and there's Dondie,
Toomy and mysel',
There's Peter and there's Dodo
And Hugh MacLeod as well —
There's Ronnie, Gool and Logan
And Colin Fraser too —
And when Sandy MacKay, the King comes in —
We have the gallant few. (HM)

I feel very strongly about the decline of fishing as a viable local industry in Port Skerra. It's a tragedy I have witnessed in my own lifetime. Of course, there are many reasons: lack of capital investment, lack of a good harbour and large boats, distance from the market, competition. But when one sees the money and materials Britain is pouring into other countries, it makes us wonder about how we are neglecting ourselves. I have seen with my own eyes how small places abroad have benefited greatly from our invading armies. Harbours have been built where it would not have been thought possible, yet here in Port Skerra we have a fine deep creek which would be the foundation of a fine harbour and nothing's been done in over a century. I have seen railways laid in a matter of days and civilisations spring up in the desert, so I ask, why not here?

There was no scarcity of fish when I was young, and in good weather tons of fish would be landed on the beach each day. The main fishing grounds were within the three-mile limit but there was plenty beyond that. Many of the boats were 30 or 40 feet, not like the 15-footers in use today. In bad weather these big boats would have to make a run for Scrabster. But we also used scows, medium-sized boats of 24 feet, and the launching, beaching, hauling of these boats created a hive of activity. Just talking brings the picture back to my mind.

The scows had eight of a crew and the tackle used was handlines and the great lines, and there were lobster boats and rowing boats. Those scows carried large amounts of stone ballast, so the strength, the labour, needed to shift boats in and out of the water was tremendous. I saw all this with my own eyes. Bustle was not the word and everywhere there'd be the children in bare feet, fish curers bidding at the beach and the fisherwomen carrying the fish in creels, on their hips and on their heads, to the various storehouses. And the girls would be with them. They were very strong; a hundredweight was common enough, and they'd help haul or launch the boats on the nod. It was the women that set the hooks and baited the lines. And you'd see them sitting at the braehead, each waiting the return of their own boat, knitting, and picking out their sail at a great distance. The gutting was mostly done by women, who were crack hands at the job, but the packing and closing of the barrels was done by the men.

The rocks round the beach would be covered with salt fish drying in the sun. The children would help keep the gulls away. First every fish had to be gutted and split open like a kipper, then salted and packed in large tubs and pickled for the necessary number of days. Then they were taken out and dried – in the sun or by the fireside, in the rafters, along walls, across ceilings, up chimneys, hanging down from the thatch, even inside the old-fashioned boxbeds. Then they would be sold in hundredweight bundles. People slept with salt fish round the bed like angels. They had to make do, they had to make the money. People were homely, with no pretensions: to take salt fish into their homes was normal – but today if anybody did that they'd be asking for trouble – the Social Work would be round.

Then there was the job of getting the fish to the markets. The carters of Port Skerra and, in the high season, the carters for miles around, would be on permanent hire to transport the full barrels the sixteen miles to the railway station at Forsinard. Then it would be Billingsgate, or Glasgow for distribution. The long trail of carts leaving the shore each evening was a great sight and a sign of the prosperity here in those years before the First War. The smell of fish guts and oil was always with us; we got used to it, we even half liked it, because it was the key to our lives. I would say the Port Skerra of my boyhood was busy and alive like no village of its size in the whole Highlands and Islands.

All this, of course, was late in the year, September, October. Through the summer, things might be very quiet. Many of the men would go away to the herring fishing in May, to Wick, Fraserburgh and Peterhead. They signed on for a summer, as hands on the drifters, and each man received so much of the gross at the end of the season. Most would come home with a fair sum and a few do very well, making enough money to see them right through the winter and more. But on their return to Port Skerra the line fishing would be in full swing and they'd buckle down once more to months of hard work. Looking back on such lives, you can see what made these men such good sailors, such good soldiers; life in a trench or a greasy gun-turret was not so strange. Courage, boldness, hardship were just part of their lives and death not to be feared but met.

Hard drinking was part of the fisherman's life. Money in hand took many to drink. Many's the night I watched them stagger in relays from the hotel bar in such extremes of intoxication as might cause excitement amongst strangers or holidaymakers. That was not the case with us locals. We were so used to drunken characters staggering along the byways that we were not surprised to see men crawling on their hands and knees and anywhere but to their homes! So much so that on a Friday or a Saturday, if a sober man passed by in normal style, the question would be asked, 'Who is that man?' And the answer was, 'That man must be the hen-pecked product of a domineering wife!' And in the ceilidh houses things would go on all through the night, or for days on end. Songs there'd be, and the spinning of yarns, grumbles and squabbles and sometimes a brawl. Many would drink until they fell asleep where they were, and we boys would be bribed to hurl them home in wheelbarrows.

This is not hearsay from elders, all this I saw. Many's the night I worked as a runner carrying beer and spirits from the public bar to where some happy drinkers lay or leaned against a wall. We boys delighted in the job and

Hugh MacIntosh with big brother Bob,
Thurso, c. 1950. (LO)

would soon enough be partially intoxicated ourselves, for we would sip the ale
en route and be rewarded with a glass and seat amongst them. And we were
pleased to hear the crack and be like them and they would pass their pipes
around and, between the fumes of Black Twist and the beer, we learned a little
about the perils of the sea, and of the barley bree. And many was the song I
learned amongst those men. But despite all this, they still had a great respect
for the Sabbath Day and its approach would call a halt to the fuelling of those
burned bodies. They would make sure they had clear heads for morning
worship, which was still the regular routine in all the houses.

It's different now. The few fishermen we have go out alone or, at
most, in twos, and it's all nets or lobster creels. The long lines have long gone.
Like crofting, fishing has become a lonely business. In the old days there was no

Portskerra and Melvich school photo, c. 1910. Hugh MacIntosh marked with cross in front row. (LO)

help from the government but the village was prosperous. It was the twenties when things began to dwindle away. It was the seine-netting finished it. That bit of sea out there, the waters to the west of the Pentland Firth, was a great breeding ground for cod and haddies and all kinds of fish. Now the seine-netters get little and the line-fishing's been dead these many years.

My father was a crofter and in shore fisherman. We had one acre of ground and one cow. My grandfather also lived with us, he was a carpenter to trade. But all that's finished, even the crofting's finished. You hardly see a croft being worked today, they're all under grass. In my day, if you were out of work, it was your own fault. And you found work. Now it's not your own fault. And you don't find work. There's only ever been three or four salaried jobs here, postman, policeman, minister, school teacher. So you had to fit in, make do, or go away. When I first left school I worked on a farm for six months for ten pounds. Ten hours a day, six days a week and I was pleased with the pay. That was during the First World War.

School was also tough, there were no school meals. There was a fire in the school but you weren't allowed near it – unless you were sopping wet. We didn't have books. You had to wait your turn to get a book; we got books one at a time. Bare feet were normal. In wintertime, I've seen myself

Hugh MacIntosh (front) enjoying a day on the beach with his brothers and sisters, c. 1927. (LO)

wait in the house till the last moment – and then run up to the school in my bare feet so I wouldn't have to stand waiting on the freezing ground. But if you mistimed your run and were late, you were for it! Children used to be bought one pair of boots once a year, in September or October, and you had to look after them or suffer the consequences. A pair of tackety boots in my time cost five shillings. That was a lot of money and money was scarce. In a big family like ours, there would not be boots for everybody. So in summer we were all always barefoot and in winter some of us were.

We weren't what you'd call happy at school. But our teacher did his job. He taught us more than they get taught today. He was a one-man band, he taught us everything, science, reading, writing, even gardening. He was a very interesting man. He'd been out to the Colonies. You could hear him shouting a long way off. He was a hard man, he would use the cane on your knuckles. In fact, I'd say he was a very hard man! He terrorised us. It was a system that put you off school, off learning. Nowadays children want to stay at school but in our day we were only too glad to leave. That's something that definitely has improved. In addition to our fearsome 'taskmaster' there was also, in those days, what was called a Whipper-in, a man who went round to check on the children not in school. I've seen the Whipper-in chasing boys across the hills, bringing them back like stray sheep.

Gaelic was my first language, but when I went to school we had to talk in English and we had to pronounce it properly. Gaelic was just the local language, so at school it was all English except for the Book. We had the Gaelic Bible at school, as we had at home and as we had in church, and the teacher read that to us in the Gaelic tongue. In those days everybody went to church on Sunday and in every house you had prayers in the morning and prayers in the evening. Every day in every house. As you walked down the road here it was nothing to hear them singing psalms, singing in the houses, as you passed. Sunday was the Sabbath and very strictly kept. There was no work. It was a sin. We had to get our water from a well but it was understood that we should collect water on Saturday, or only go to the well with a small pail. A small pail or a drink wasn't a sin, but a big pail or three small pails, that was a sin! In Port Skerra, if you went out to your stack of peats on a Sunday, you weren't respectable. You brought your peats to the door on a Saturday and used them from there. Ooh, they went too far – but now they've gone too far the other way! There are two sides to every coin. It was for money and experience of the wider world that I joined the Merchant Marine.

BOUND FOR MONTREAL

We sailed from Glasgow's Princes Dock,
The night was Hogmanay,
And every sailor now on board
Was drunk as drunk could be
After bringing in the New Year
At every pub on call –
We told the pilots on the bridge
We're bound for Montreal.

We sailed that morning outward bound,
All full of joy and glee,
Steaming down the River Clyde
And for the rolling sea.
We passed the grand Dumbarton Rock,
So beautiful and tall,
And set our course on West-Nor-West,
We're bound for Montreal.

Again the old ship's under way
And in the ocean swell,
Steaming gracefully along
And all aboard is well;
Our bearing is on Instrahill
The last landfall of all
As we bid farewell to Erin's Isle —
We're bound for Montreal.

The tramp steamer Concordia
Was outward bound again,
Ploughing on through wintry seas,
The wild Atlantic main
But soon we reach the Belle Isle Straits
And sail along her wall —
The cry goes up 'Full Steam Ahead!'
We're bound for Montreal.

We're in the region of Cape Race
Where icebergs loom ahead,
Reported there by Ice Patrol,
A danger seamen dread,
And as we near that great seaway —
St Lawrence it is called —
At its other end our goal,
The Port of Montreal. (HM)

I sailed on many ships and for various companies — including 'The Prohibition Line', which cruised the east coast of America! I remember us loading a thousand tons of coal in bunkers at Immingham. We wondered where we were going. We went over to Rotterdam and pulled alongside a barge to land 40,000 cases of whisky! Down the Channel the captain called us together and he told us where we were going. America. We had been shanghaied! He told us we were signed on for Halifax but we didn't see a speck of land for eight months. We anchored about twenty miles off Cape Cod and stayed there all winter discharging. We sold the cargo to anybody who came alongside. Passenger boats would circle round us and the passengers would take photos of the bootlegging boats; ten or twelve cases would be put in a net sling and dropped overboard with a heavy weight and a marker-buoy. There'd be hundreds of these 'drops', in out-of-the-way places. At night, lorries would come along the coast, men would haul in the nets and stack

Hugh MacIntosh with shipmates (far left middle row), c. 1939. (LO)

the whisky in hidden tanks inside the lorries. It was a great game of cat and mouse between the bootleggers and the Customs. We saw some of the bootleggers caught. I've seen the American Customs firing into motorboats, forcing them to stop. They even brought Destroyers in to help round them up. We were all right, we were safe in international waters, outside the US national limit.

I sometimes think that that would have been the kind of thing that would have appealed to Rob Donn, the Bard of the North. He was the best bard we've had in Sutherland, at least in recent times. He was a cattle drover, and a poacher, and a bard much feared for the ferocious way he would attack his enemies in song. He didn't like to be tied down by rules and regulations, whether that meant shooting wild deer claimed by some landowner or drinking illicit whisky. One of my Gaelic songs was written in honour of Rob Donn, he's a hero to us. It's not been translated up till now.

HOMAGE TO ROB DONN

O come ye up to the land of Rob Donn,
Where the high mountains stand –
To the lochs and the rivers that the poet knew well;
The sons of the heavy-coated deer that he hunted
Still browse where he made a hard living
With musket and hound, with black powder and lead.

There were landlords here in this land of the mountains
Who paid great respect to his fame and renown;
Many a time they stood surety for him
And often enough they stood by his side.
And even when stooped in the grip of old age
They remembered him as he was in his prime;
A memory as precious to them as his musket to him
And his tireless hound so tall at the shoulder.

'Ah, did you hear that shot echo the glen?
Look, see the deer coming down from the ben,
Silhouette on the ridge in the light of the sun,
There on the hill with the great hound behind them
Bringing them down within range of my gun –
Hold still a moment – four hooves hit the ground!

'My thanks and a blessing go out to hard iron –
This musket so slender like the days of my youth:
Although often I cursed those slow-witted sheriffs,
With the years I admit – they tried to be just!
Small credence they gave to the truth that I told them
– the times were hard but my right was timeless!'

My listeners, I ask you – remember this man;
Imagine his thoughts as he made for the mountain
To bury the musket that had served all his days –
A friend always faithful in the moment of need:
Imagine the pain – turning his back on the sheiling
Where rocks and hard times had broken his heart;
And he climbing slowly to bury his musket –
High in the mountains out of sight and at peace.

Many was the shot you rammed down that barrel
And many's the aim you took at hoof and at paw,
Quick was your eye and steady your hand
And matchless your skill after hours in the chase;
In youth not a shepherd or keeper could match you
In fleetness of foot or knowledge of the wild
Where from a hook above flames your pot simmered
The kills you brought down for the poor.

That musket saw you safe from starvation and ruin
And gave you the plenty that all creatures need –
Now she lies buried in the lard of a cattle beast;
And although many's the foot's come down on her since
You put the tallow-fat through her, not a soul
Has glimpsed her since your hand laid her down.

'In the years since that day, old age has cut deeper,
Shortened my step and chopped down my pride;
My mind is oppressed, my freedom gone,
The whole world become like a burden to me,
The wild moorland is barred, my life in deep shadow,
What life can I lead without musket and hound?'

So his life in the mountains was brought to an end
And the Redeemer it was took him home to himself;
Now like his gun Rob Donn lies 'neath the turf.
So let this be a warning to all mortal men –
What came to Rob Donn will come to us all
And everyone know the graveyard of the dead.

O, the streams have dried up and the mountain is dark;
Evening itself now submits to deep sorrow
And Beinn Spionnaidh is silent to the song of the birds;
But walking the mountains are the shepherds and cowherds
And there by the sheiling in silence is waiting
The song that will waken Rob Donn from the dead. (TN/Mac)

Balnakeil graveyard, Durness,
with the Rob Donn Memorial,
inscribed in four languages,
on the right. (TN)

AIR CUIMHNEACHAN ROB DHUINN

O thugainn suas do dhùthaich Rob Dhuinn
Far 'm bheil na beanntan àrd,
Na lochan 's na h-aibhnichean
Air 'n robh èolas aig a' bhard;
Tha sliochd nam fiadh fionnach ann
Far 'n tug e bheòshlaint chruaidh
Le mhusgaid chaol 's cobhair nan cù,
'S le fùdar dubh is luaidh.

Bha uachdarain an tìr nam beann
Aig 'n robh meas mór air a chliù:
'S iomadh uair chaidh iad an ràthan air,
'S gur tric ghabh iad a thaobh;
'S ged chrom e bhàn le neart na h-aois,
Chum 'n eòlas suas na chuimhn'
A' mhusgaid phrìseil bheannaichte
'S am beathach spògach tuigseach grinn.

An cuala sibh an urchair ud
A' labhairt tro na glinn,
'S nach fhaca sibh na féidh
'S iad a' faotainn fuadach beinn
Sa mhullach àrd ri leus na gréin,
'S anns an reis bha 'n cù,
'S le sin 's ceart 's cinnteach sinn
Na thilg e ladhar dhiùbh.

Mo bheannachd aig mo mhusgaid chaol
Chum suas mo làithean òg,
'S ged mhullaich mi na siorraimh mhaol,
Bha iad uairean laghail leòr;
'S ged 's ainneamh thug iad creideas dhomh
'S don fhìrinn dh'inns mi dhoibh,
Gun robh ceartas 'na mo chaithe-beatha
'S bu duilich dhomh bhith beò.

Nach gabh sibh thugaibh na smuaintean aig'
'S e gabhail n-àrd a' bheinn
Dol dh'fholach mhusgaid phrìseil
Bha dìleas dha ri linn,
'S gur duilich bha nuair thionnd' e chùl
Air 'n àirigh bhris a chrìdh',
'S e fàgail 'chuid an tìr nam beann
A sealladh sùil 's aig sìth.

Nach iomadh urchair a loisg thu leath'
Air spòg 's ladhair sgoilt' –
'S e sùil do chinn bha glan 's geur,
Ged bhiodh tu fad' gun fhois;
'Nuair bha thu òg 's subailte,
Air na cìobairean fhuair thu buaidh –
'S tric a chroch thu pait ri bolla
Re aman goirt 's cruaidh.

Nach iomadh cruas as 'n tug i thu,
'S tric chuir i pailteas ort,
'S dh'fhàg thu 'n siud i beartach leòr
'S i làn de ghiorr nam mart;
'S ged iomadh ceum rinn cromadh orra
Bhon chuir thu 'n geir iad troimh',
Chan fhaca iad sealladh riamh dhith
Bhon dh'fhalbh i as do laimh.

Bhon fhuair na bliadhnan buaidh orm
'S bhon ghearr an aois mo cheum,
Tha cudthrom inntinn air mo cheann
'S tha mi gun móran feum;.
'S bho chaill mi saors' nam monaidhean,
Mo mhusgaid is mo chù,
Tha saoghal ann an neoni dhomh,
Gun cuideachd air mo thaobh.

Ach thug 'm Fear-Saoraidh dhachaigh e —
Thuig' fhéin a tha sinn 'n dùil —
'S chuir e cul ris 'n t-saoghal seo
'S tha e nis na laigh' fon ùir;
'S bitheadh siud na fhradhaidh dhuibh
Gur e sin a' chrioch thig oirbh
'S gum bi sibh uile mar tha e 'n-diugh,
'Na laigh' an cladh nam mairbh.

On tha na h-uillt air tiormachadh
'S na sléibhtean dorch fo bhròn,
Beinn Spionnaidh 's i toirt umhlachd,
'S cha chluinn thu guth nan eòin,
Ach bidh na beinn nam buachaille
Air 'n àirigh os a chinn,
Ach 'n duisg e 'n àird à cadal bàis
Aig crìoch 's deireadh tìm. (HM)

Four Gaelic stalwarts of the north Sutherland coast: left to right, Christie Campbell, tradition-bearer, Durness; Joseph MacKay, singer, Melness; Hugh MacDonald, genealogist, Melness; and Hugh's youngest brother Donnie MacIntosh of Port Skerra. (TN)

Rob Donn was a great man, like Robin Hood. He didn't want his gun to fall into the wrong hands; he greased it and wrapped it in deer skin and buried it, he said, 'in sight of the three kyles'. He left a mystery behind him. I believe the site is somewhere on Carn an Righ on Ben Spionnaidh, because from there you look north to the Kyle of Durness, south to Lochinver, which is a kyle, and east to the Kyle of Tongue. But I've heard others say he buried the gun where you can see five kyles. Certainly, no one's found the gun as yet, though you'd think, with a metal detector, it wouldn't be too difficult. He knew the hills so well; he must have discovered a spot where he knew he could align those kyles. It's very beautiful up at Carn an Righ but, if it was five kyles he saw then I would think the burial place must be somewhere on Foinaven which is just across Strath Dionard. But then the question of definition arises – what is a kyle and what is not? Rob Donn was a poet and a man of style and in his dying, I think, he wanted to raise these questions – about language, about geography and about the places that he loved. He created a myth, as the bards always have. People call me 'the bard' just because they've heard I write poems and songs. In fact, I sing songs and I sing all my poems. It's not difficult to get labelled a bard up here. If you just write one

poem in Melvich, they call you a bard. But Rob Dunn, he was a real bard.

I can't really remember when I started to write poems but, as a young man, travelling round Sutherland, ideas and images would start coming into my mind, a tune and the words of a song. I would get excited and want to turn these fragments into a proper song. I wouldn't be able to sleep at night. I would be up all night, putting new lines in as soon as they came to me, in case I'd lose any parts of the song as it was coming along. It was a bit of a nuisance to me sometimes. Sometimes I'd wish this voice would leave me. It was almost as if a wicked master was getting me up out of bed and forcing me, unwillingly, to work, but I had to go. Then for months the inspiration would leave me. That was sometimes a great relief. I would feel free. But if a long time passed with no compulsion to write, I would miss it and look forward to it coming back.

I've written hundreds of songs. For years I kept them mostly in my head. My first songs all came in Gaelic and I couldn't write Gaelic – so it wasn't till I met 'Dr Smiley' that they got written down at all. He wasn't a real doctor, he was a roadman like myself. His name was Charles MacKenzie. He was a man of scholarship and a happy disposition and he could write Gaelic. So I sang him all the songs I could remember and he wrote them down. He came from Dulrine. Most of my English songs got put down on bits of paper here and there, but I've always carried them in my head as well. I could always sing any of my songs at the drop of a hat. The songs I wrote to Mary, my wife, are my favourites: one is called 'The Fairy Glen':

> One evening as I strolled along
> The road that led me home,
> I met a bonnie lassie,
> A stranger all alone.
> Her face had blushed a rosy red,
> For she was shy of men
> And who she was I failed to know
> – Around the fairy glen.
>
> I asked her as I took her hand
> If she was far from home
> And why she wandered in this way
> And why the urge to roam?
> She answered, 'I was jilted once
> And never will again
> I trust a stranger's empty love
> – Outside the fairy glen.'

I told her I'd forgive her
If she'd do the same for me,
Although I knew my love for her
Was like the deep blue sea.
And when I clasped her in my arms
And kissed her o'er again,
I knew she was the bride for me
—Way down the fairy glen.

My bonnie lass, 'Will you be mine?'
She answered, 'Aye for aye',
The sweetest words of love that came
From her sweet lips that day.
And how we hugged and kissed and hugged
And hugged and kissed again
As we strolled together arm in arm
—Waydown the fairy glen. (HM)

Another song to Mary is called 'The Star O' My Dreams' and it tells its own story.

In a small coasting vessel that hails from the Tyne
I'm drifting along on the surf of the brine
With a fresh blowing breeze and a clear sky above,
I'm bound for Auld Reekie and the girl that I love.
As I pass by those headlands, those lightships and buoys,
Each mile takes me nearer the pride o' my joys,
Although it ain't long, it is ages, it seems,
Since last I saw Mary, the star o' my dreams.

When I see the May Island just right on the bow,
My heart beats with joy, for it won't be long now
And the lights of Auld Reekie so bright and so clear
Shine out to tell me that my loved one is near,
And while we are steaming full speed up the Firth
Our vessel will soon be made fast to her berth,
For here come the pilot and the mails that he brings
With love from my Mary, the star o' my dreams.

When at the pier head with our engines going slow,
Two blasts on the horn the pilot did blow.
As the telegraph rings we go slower and slower
Until we are berthed and all fast to the shore.
As soon as we're finished we fall in for pay
And all hands knock off for the rest of the day.
The married men go to their wives and their weans
While I'm off to Mary, the star o' my dreams.

She's the pride o' my joy and my heart's whole desire,
The only wee girl I will ever admire,
And wherever I wander, wherever I rove,
My thoughts always go to the girl that I love.
When I'm out on the ocean and far, far away,
I think of my darling by night and by day,
For there's no other belle, in the pride of her teens,
Yet sweeter than Mary, the star o' my dreams.

Her teeth are like pearls and her cheeks like the rose —
The bloom to her beauty, sure everyone knows,
With her lovely blue eyes and her raven black hair,
I can with my Mary no other compare.
When I see her come strolling along the main street
With her features and form so lovely and neat,
She's my pick and my choice from a thousand Colleens,
My winsome wee Mary, the star o' my dreams.

Come all ye princesses with your riches untold —
You can offer your love and your millions in gold,
Your lovely white castles, your houses and land —
They're no comfort or pleasure when my love's at hand.
Though all I can give her is love o' my ain
And all that I ask for is likewise the same,
For should I be master and king of all kings,
I'll always love Mary, the star o' my dreams. (HM)

It was after the Second World War that I gave up the sea and came home to
become part of what remained of the old life. For six years in the Royal Navy I
came back with six weeks' wages. That was a start, but it was still hard times. I
built our own house with stone I quarried myself. I got odd jobs, on the roads,

with the Water Works, with the Sewerage; I got a job with Wimpey, I worked on the croft. Then Dounreay came in on the wind. Some people are against it these days and they like to say there was a big controversy about them bringing a Nuclear Research Station here but there was very little controversy at the time and we were very glad to get it. It was the biggest thing that ever happened here. They supply work as far away as 60 miles. It's done a lot of good.

But in the forties, when I came home, things in Sutherland had changed very little. Families still shared the work and neighbours were used to barter and co-operative labour. The women did a great deal of physical work. It was them that went to the shore and cut seaweed and carried it in creels to the fields. Often they would be up to their waists in pools. In rain, they'd work soaked to the skin. Their clothes were heavy and took a long time to dry. The men did the digging, working the old hand plough, the *cas-chrom*. We didn't have tractors. Delving we called it. We liked to work in a team. A few days would see us cover three or four acres. The oats would be sown by hand and the harrows dragged by both men and women, working like horses. Many

Mary and Hugh MacIntosh (second left) at the peats with brother Rob (far left), 1940's. (LO)

The bard's father, Donald MacIntosh, his mother Georgina, his wife, Mary King MacIntosh and their daughter Georgina (in the arms of her granny). (LO)

would be well-nigh exhausted by nightfall. I've seen, myself, a woman fall in the furrow and not rise until helped up by her man.

The corn was cut with a hook, not the big scythe. Four or five men would move forward together, bending and reaping, it could be back-breaking work. The corn was gathered and sheaved and then stooked to dry in the wind and the sun. Much of that was done by the women and children. There were precious few horses and everything would be carried from the field on the backs of the crofters. It was then stacked in a rick or placed in a barn. There were no threshing machines up here. All threshing was done by the flail as in biblical times, the sheaves being laid end to end on a wooden platform and the flail wielded with all the strength in the man's power. It was first roughly fanned by hand, then riddled with a hand riddle and bagged, for use on the croft, or sent to the mill.

There were two mills in Port Skerra, one for oats and one for barley and they were kept pretty busy all winter. Because of the damp, some drying would be necessary and the crofters had to bring their own peats to fuel the kiln fire. Under the eye of the miller, they would then look after the grain, turning it occasionally with a large wooden spade. Sometimes the mill would run through the night. This would draw the old folk from miles around. And

there they would sit round the kiln fire smoking and spinn
with the world.

Our daily bread was oatcakes and girdle scones, and
they were. It would be most unusual for there to be a shortage of n
crowdie, or eggs. Peat was the fuel that serviced all houses in Port Skerra.
peats were cut with a tuskar and they still are; it's a spade-like tool with a blade
twelve inches long. At best one man works the tuskar, one man takes the peats,
and a third lays them out to dry. Like that three men can cut sufficient peat in
two days to keep a house fire going for more than a year. Such work was not
unpleasant. You could choose your day and go out onto the moor, listen to the
skylarks, take your time. Crofting was not a race like the fishing. We would take
our time, not like some folk but like others.

In the old thatched cottages the fire would be kept alive day and
night all through the year. Like religion, a peat fire was part of the fabric of life.
In my young days, Port Skerra was inhabited by a very religious race of people.
Chanted psalms and prayers began and drew to a close each day. And on the
Sabbath, the church, though it was three miles away, was full in every weather.
Over the years it fell empty, now it's been opened up as a museum. But the
people then, 80 years ago, served their Master with good heart, with body,
mind and soul. It was understood, as a natural instinct, that we were all one
family, irrespective of which roof sheltered us, and religion was a thing of
discipline and order.

The Sabbath was the day of rest. No work, no reading but the Bible
or religious books, no play. For the children this was very hard. Both at home and
at church, the groans that broke the silence of extended worship still stand like
scars inside my mind, and my stomach. For us children, the word 'Amen' was the
only sign that God's Covenant with Man was something more than torture.
Amens would come round far too slow and Sundays far too fast for us! How loud
I've heard Amens break from the throats of desperate boys. Sunday was a day not
of rest but imprisonment for us youngsters. If we went outside and quietly
started to play, it would not be long before friends or neighbours would round
us up and send us packing, back into the house for a dressing down.

Going to church, men and women would carry their great Bibles
under their arms with something close to pride. For those with bad eyesight or
a poor education, the big print would help them follow the service but they
also liked the weight of the book, it was a penance and a compensation. It was
the philosopher's stone they carried! The fear and love of God was deeply
rooted in the old people here.

There was no organ in any of the churches then. We had a
precentor and the sermons could be very long. The elders had their appointed

places round the table and they would keep a watchful eye on us but they had no compunction about falling asleep and snoring, if they felt a sermon was going on too long! It was the elders, rather than the minister, who had a grip on what happened both in the church and in the village. It was them that we feared more than God. But amongst them there was also great goodness. And the most notable of these good men were the two MacDonald brothers, James and John. They were disciples of Christ in truth and name; and I believe it true to say that no fault, in deed or word, could be levelled against them in all their journey from cradle to the grave.

Although I state that as a truth, James was a married man and towards middle age he fell into confusion and a great weakness of mind. Whether this was due to his fear of God and the insecurity of his soul, to schizophrenia, or to some psychosis, it is not for me to say. But what is interesting is this: he was not sent off to a Mental Institution. No, he was closely guarded and looked after by his sons and by his family and by his neighbours and his fellow elders. All offered their services in a weary watch that went on for years. For many years. But the watch was not in vain. James MacDonald returned to his old self, to his old gentle ways. His faith was stronger than ever and his life and his family were seen as an example to the whole community. And he was. In the absence of the minister, it was always he that would be asked to take his place. He would lead the service and preach and the congregation was always inspired by his presence and his word. He lived to a ripe old age, a matchless light to his people.

In our own family it was grandfather who led prayers. He wouldn't begin till the whole family was present and woe betide late-comers. The Bible lay on the corner of the mantelpiece and it's still there to this day. He would sit in his chair with the Book on his knees and before he began to read, he would give a few short coughs to ensure that nothing would disturb him in his reading of the Holy Word, which was always of a long duration. Then there would be the singing of a psalm. Sometimes I would listen carefully and sing with vigour but often not, and always I would be watching for him to raise his hand to begin removing his spectacles, the first sign that things were coming to an end. Then, on our knees, we'd say the Lord's Prayer and at last be free to enjoy the fields, the shore, the bothies and shebeens: a life that millions in the towns would envy. But his was a very stern hand. He really believed in the power of God and the importance of prayers and worship. He was always the last to bed and before he retired he would go into the closet, to converse once more with God before sleeping. For him it was love and a lifelong commitment. Times have changed. Although I am a believer, my life has led me in other directions and I'm glad that the old religion has gone. It could break your heart. It could force a man to write bardachd!

Mary and Hugh MacIntosh picnicking at the peats with a dram, c. 1950. (LO)

But there was one minister who was different. He was here for many years, the Reverend MacAuley. In him was a religious root uncommon amongst his reverend brethren. He did not chastise like the old ministers and the elders. He looked upon his congregation with equality and a great kindness of heart. If he saw three smiling faces in the pews you could feel his deep contentment. He did not order or command, he liked to see the children in glee and high spirits. Often enough the elders put him in his place and he would bend like a willow in a bitter wind but not give up the ground he held most dear. It was the Old and New Testaments. When the Second World War began, he had a vision and he prophesied that every young man called up for service from his parish would come home. And so it was. How many villages in all Scotland can claim that? He's buried now in Strathy Churchyard, alongside so many of those, who after years of active service returned safe, as he had prophesied, to their loved native place. And when in time I join him in the earth I have no greater wish than this – that he should greet me as a brother bard and be the man to welcome Mary to my side.

The Bards MacAskill

STRATHDEARN, INVERNESS-SHIRE

MURDO MACASKILL

Remembered by Margaret Begg of Inverness

My brother, Murdo MacAskill, was captured by the Japanese at Singapore. It was more than two years before we knew whether he was alive or dead. I remember him walking up to the door, coming back after all those years and us thinking him dead. That was in the autumn of 1945. We didn't know which train he would be on. And he walked all the way from Moy station, alone, in his army uniform. After all those years on the Burma Railway, he had to walk home by himself and he stood in the door with the light behind him. And he said he was lucky to be alive, and that his best friend had died in his arms just two weeks before the end. And we broke into tears to see him safe.

After that he spent all his life in Strathdearn, as a roadman. He became registrar for the Tomatin district, he wrote songs and poems, but he never called himself a bard. You see, his father, Donald MacAskill, spoke Gaelic and was bard to the Mackintosh of Mackintosh, whereas Murdo didn't write Gaelic, and he said he didn't write enough, or well enough, to call himself a bard. But he was a bard, and my favourite poem is about Tomnahully, which is a hill at the back of Tuach, where the Little Chef Filling Station stands today — just left off the A9, driving north.

> *Of Tomnahully old folks say —*
> *There the New Year's earliest ray*
> *Of sunlight strikes a certain stone*
> *Which has since olden times lain on*
> *A golden treasure — wrapped within*
> *The cover of a young foal's skin.* (MM)

Opposite:
The bard Murdo MacAskill,
Tomatin, 1940. (VR)

Our MacAskills came originally from Harris and they were related to the giant MacAskill who went out to Canada. It was the time of the big exodus and my grandfather came across to Strathdearn to work in the quarry at Kyllachie. For the last eight generations the eldest sons of the MacAskills have carried the name Donald and Murdo, alternatively. There were many bards amongst the MacAskills but, for the last four generations, the men of our line earned their living working stone. Murdo died in 1983. When he retired he wrote this little rhyme: it's entitled 'The Pleistocene':

> Retiring roadman, what have you done
> These thirty years in the rain and sun?
> 'Ach I've shifted some earth, I've moved some stones.'
>
> Yon great engineer with the famous name
> And the mining moles might also claim...
> 'Aye, and the River Findhorn the very same!
> They shifted some earth, they moved some stones.' (MM)

My father, Donald, he was known as the Strathdearn bard, died in 1943, before we had news of whether Murd was alive or dead. Father was a very good singer and fiddler, and he was precentor in Moy church, and he asked that if Murd did come back, that his fiddle should go to him. And so it did. Murd was a man of great talent, he knew history, music, poetry, painting. If he was young today he would have gone on to art school or university but he spent his life on manual work. He wrote a poem called 'The Dry Stane Dyker'; it tells you in rhyme how to build a wall. And, speaking it, he sounded like a druid.

> Bring me boulders from yon brae
> Weathered field stone, lichen grey,
> Binders from the boulder clay,
> Burn washed with colours gay.
>
> We will spare no time or toil
> To clear away all shifty soil,
> Our foundation we will lay
> On rock or gravel, pan or clay.
>
> Foundation stones are the elect!
> The best we have we shall select,
> The best side of the stone turn down
> However rough the face may frown.

Hammer dress to clear the line,
A dry stane dyke is masculine
And shows the world a rugged face
Where pretty smoothness has no place.

Levellings — must not be high —
The course above must bind and tie
Directly on the stones below,
These are things all men must know.

Wedge the horizontal spaces,
Build with care the upright places:
Gravity is not our friend
So use a wedge's thicker end.

Never let a chance go by
To dress your work to please your eye:
For every gap there is a pin,
As you find them, tap them in.

When the cope stones are in place
The rural scene our work shall grace:
Enduring as its weathered stones
When we are nought but crumbling bones. (MM)

Murdo MacAskill, c. 1930.

Snowy mountains, loch and
reflections. (TN)

I remember Murd very well. That's what we called him. He was handsome, he was the eldest and he was like a man to us younger sisters. He enjoyed horsing about with his younger brother, Hamish. They used to stand on their heads, do the high jump, run races, keep fit, ride out on their bikes together. There was no pub in Moy; the Mackintoshes wouldn't allow it. We were all brought up in the out of doors – on porridge, potatoes and plenty work. When Murdo went to school in Inverness, he stayed in lodgings and every Monday morning he'd walk the twelve miles there and every Friday he'd walk the twelve miles back. He used to come into the house and say 'J'famme, J'famme!', pretending he was one of Napoleon's Imperial Guard just back from Moscow. Later, he used to say that his stomach took to the rice and starvation in Burma, because it was a stomach well trained: that both he and ancestors had had plenty of practice surviving hardship. Like his father, he could quote reams of Burns:

> There's naething here but Highland pride
> > And Highland scab and hunger;
> If Providence has sent me here
> > 'Twas surely in an anger.

He was a good scholar and a very good artist. His pictures hung on the walls of Inverness Academy for years after he left. All the children, except me, got Mackintosh bursaries, to go to schools in Inverness. I left at fourteen to work at home and it was only later I trained to be a nurse. I think Murd stayed at the Academy until he was fifteen – but that was it – he came home to work on the roads. And, you know, it wasn't the Mackintoshes at Moy Hall created the Mackintosh bursaries – it was some old sea-captain from Inverness did that! There was a certain bitterness could arise in Murd, not against the Japanese, he accepted the fortunes of war, but against the class system here at home, the system that kept him out in the cold whilst lesser men lived protected, prosperous lives. He mended roads and dug drains to help his parents raise eight children, then raise his own. Our family would go out for one outing a year, with the Sunday School, taking our picnics. Murd was a big Labour supporter and he always read *The New Statesman* and *Nation*.

As soon as his younger brother, Hamish, reached the age of fifteen, the two of them went off to Canada, on the *SS Andania*. That was in 1929. We have a diary, telling of how the two of them got work on different farms in different places. He worked for a Mrs Miller, whose husband was in a lunatic asylum. He describes arriving by train at a place called Nepean, in Ontario:

> It was a beautiful warm spring morning, I was just a week off
> my 20th birthday and I was feeling on top of the world. I had

on a double-breasted blue serge suit. Over my left arm I carried
a gaberdine raincoat, a thing I cannot remember seeing anybody
in Canada wearing. The suitcase carried in my right hand was
still decorated with the shipping company's brightly coloured
labels.

'See that brick building standing there, beside the track?
That's the Condensery. The man who handles the milk from
your area's called Walter Hugebone. Go down the track and ask
for Walter Hugebone and you'll be OK.'

I saw a man facing me over a conveyor, stacking milk cans.
When I was still about 30 yards distant, he suddenly called out
loudly, 'How long you take coming over, fella?' Without a
second's hesitation I shouted back at him, 'Seven days, seven
hours and forty-nine minutes.' He kept looking at me very
intently until I got up beside him and enquired about Walter
Hugebone. He was big but he was not Hugebone! He was very
helpful, and he told me I had plenty of time to go downtown to
see the place and do any shopping...

I went into a shop and bought a pair of working boots,
about half the weight of our Scottish tacketies, which I had
always worn till then. In another shop I asked the girl attendant
for a bonnet. I settled for a cap, when she explained that only
grandmothers wore bonnets in Canada. Coming out of the shop
I almost bumped into a tallish, very erect, good-looking,
middle-aged, woman who kept staring at me as I came out past
her. Back at the Condensery, I found Walter Hugebone to be a
cheerful, talkative man who told me that my future boss, Mrs
Miller, had travelled into Nepean with him that morning and
driving through the town we picked up the woman I had met in
the shop doorway. Long afterwards she told me that as soon as
she saw me she was certain that I was the man who was going
to work for her.

The Miller family was descended from a Protestant pastor
who had, some time in the 17th century, led a group of
refugees from religious persecution in one of the German
Palatinates, to England. They then moved to Ireland, to New
York State and finally into Eastern Ontario. But Mrs Miller, Mrs
Florence Miller, had a grandfather from Ayrshire and she was
pleased to get a man from the Highlands. After training college
she had gone to teach at the school at Switzerville and lodged

with the Miller family. She married one of the boys of the house, Charlie Miller, and they had one son, Peter, who was one year younger than me. Well, the old man died and Charlie was left with the farm and very well-off compared to most of his neighbours, but ten years later he had nothing but a run-down farm and a much-reduced stock. He neither drank, gambled, nor smoked; he just kept on buying expensive machines he had no need of or use for! Selling them at a fraction of their cost when he tired of them. Finally, about to go into debt to buy a new threshing machine, his wife stopped the sale. After chasing her through a field of Indian corn with an axe, he was taken away and locked up in a mental home. That was in the fall of 1928 and it was the following spring I arrived. I stayed there on the farm with Mrs Miller for five summers and four winters.

Murdo was given a Canadian passport but when our father took ill he decided to come back to Scotland. He got work down in Strathspey as an insurance agent and he got married to Barbara, a local girl whom we all called Barby. He went off to the war on 19th December 1940. They then had three children, aged four, three and three weeks. After the war they had two more.

He didn't speak to us much about his years in the Japanese prison camps but after he retired he wrote up a diary. This was typed and passed around in Strathdearn. He always had a certain sympathy for 'the Nips', that's what he called them. They were ordinary soldiers, he said, just like himself, victims of history, victims of time and place. It was the Korean guards, he said, who were the most brutal. All the prisoners, officers and men, suffered terribly, I think about half of them died, but he found a comradeship there that was a beacon that burned for the rest of his life. He was one of those who made the best of things as they were. He made musical instruments and in the early months he was part of a small orchestra there in the camp. He was never asked to join an orchestra here! His father was a hewer, one of the stonemasons, who built the great viaduct at Tomatin, and he was one of the slaves who built 'The Bridge on the River Kwai'! These are extracts from his remembrances:

A strange sight we witnessed was the departure of our generals. All ranks from Brigadier upwards were at the gunpark one morning waiting for conveyance to Singapore where they were to embark for Japan. A single lorry drove up, similar to those which took working parties to the city. The very smartly uniformed Generals in their red braided hats clambered aboard.

There were over 20 of them, so it was standing room only, each holding onto the man in front. Although we sympathised with these unfortunate men in their humiliation, most of them middle-aged, we could not help laughing at such an incongruous sight. But the following episode gives a truer picture of the relationship between the officers and other ranks. A high-ranking Nip General was to inspect us one day. A couple of hours before the appointed time we were marched to a large, open, level area. After a lot of manoeuvring we finally stood ten deep round three sides of a square and were told to sit down. Our five ranks of signals were positioned behind five ranks of engineers. Our senior officer, Colonel Holmes of the Australians, stood right in front of us about 20 yards away. A very smart, red-moustached officer, Major Ferguson, was engaged in a final check of all units; this completed, he approached Colonel Holmes from our right. With truly guardsman-like precision he halted before the Colonel and put up a faultless salute. This so impressed some of the engineers sitting in front of us that they clapped their hands in applause. His report completed, the major took one step backwards and saluted again. Then, instead of making a right or an about turn, he made a left turn to face his audience, to whom he bowed deeply, then, straightening up, turned left again and marched away smartly. This manoeuvre, of course, was loudly applauded by all who observed it.

Every tenth day was a rest day, when one of the first things we did after breakfast, was to detach our bamboo bed slats, carry them out into the sunlight, and dunt them on the ground; hitting them with sticks to dislodge the bugs from crevices. In a short time the ground would be moving with thousands of these loathsome insects until they were overcome and killed by the strong direct sunlight. We were also very lousy and boiled our clothes whenever we got the opportunity. A dark coloured blanket hung out in the sun was soon dotted by plentiful white specks like a hirsel of sheep on a heather-clad hillside.

The most popular entertainment at the Tarsao Camp took place each evening at the beginning of dusk. Soon after the sun went down, at least half of us made our way outside. The conversation would die away and those still possessing watches would consult them and all eyes would stare upwards and

westwards to a high fork in a big tree that stood on the other
side of the road beside the Nip Headquarters. Then a loud
murmur: 'Here she comes!', as our flying squirrel appeared
from her nest in the tree fork. Silence again as she paused
before leaping nimbly upwards to a higher fork, to pause again.
Then came three horizontal bounds out on a limb, a final pause;
then the launch and a hushed murmur of 'There she goes!', as
she leapt out into the first glide of the night, down into the
forest. Every night this happened and every night she was
applauded by a near cheer from us. I have never been to a POW
reunion, but if I do ever go I will readily recognise the Tarsao
man by his answer to the question. 'Do you remember the
flying squirrel?'

The railway was designed to traverse the rockface, along a
five metre ledge, about 120 feet above the river. Our job
entailed the removal of a huge triangular slab of rock five
metres thick and sixty feet high at the apex. Drilling went on
day and night. A generator supplied current for the long line of
lights, while three large air compressors powered the drills.
Blasting took place every forenoon and evening. The main task
was the moving of the blasted rock to the edge of the bench
from whence it fell into the river. The biggest blocks were
tumbled over with the aid of crowbars, while the smaller pieces
were rolled or carried to the edge. Some of the less robust or
sickly-looking amongst us were given shallow little saucer-
shaped baskets for the small rubble. As the job was a very
'speedo' one, some of the Nips in charge were not slow in using
their bamboos on any slackers.

Two young friends of mine were there, Gerry Hall, a
student architect, whom I regarded as a considerable
intellectual, and Arthur Bacon, who was a bit older and who
had worked in his family's bookselling business in Hull, and
who was one of the most likeable fellows I had ever met. I still
smile to myself when I think of the two of them on one
particular day. They were both slightly built and starved-
looking. Each was dressed only in hat, jock-strap and home-
made wood-soled sandals. Gerry had a long tapering beard
halfway down his chest, while Arthur's was a straggly feature,
similar to the one I had tried growing in our early Tarsao days.
The two of them were squatted down facing each other on their

hunkers, with a single basket between, into which they occasionally and very languidly, dropped a small fragment of rock. They looked like a pair of Indian gurus. As I walked back and forth carrying lumps of rock to the edge, I caught snatches of their conversation. They were totally engrossed in an earnest discussion of the work of some (to me) obscure European writer and his influence on the work of later (equally obscure) writers. They may have escaped the bamboo because the Nip in charge that day thought it better to concentrate his attention on a fitter man like myself — who still *could* do a day's work.

I think it true to say that many comparatively physically frail people like Gerry and Arthur survived because of the interests they had in things outside their immediate environment; while others, although stronger but lacking such subjects, fretted themselves into a condition of pessimistic apathy and, when they fell ill, died of the want of sufficient will to live.

One morning on the check parade we were addressed by our British CO, Captain Cox. He told us that cholera had broken out at the Sawmill Camp, and that henceforth we must boil all our washing water and stop bathing in the river. Each morning after that he would give out in his clipped no-nonsense way the latest number of deaths from this terrible disease. Some time in the second week after that, I remember him announcing, 'The total number of deaths from cholera at the Sawmill Camp is now given as 120 British and Australian and an unspecified number of hundreds of Malays, Indians…' At the feeding point there was always an officer watching the sterilising of mess tins. When the water showed any sign of going off the boil, he immediately held back the queue with a bamboo pole, and only when the water was boiling furiously again would he allow it to proceed.

One day I met somebody who had an illustrated travel book about the Highlands. We made a swap. I began turning the pages over from one picture to the next until I came to one described, 'Strathspey, a sombre panorama'. And on my bamboo bed-space, in that outlandish camp, in tropical jungle, on the other side of the world, I gazed and gazed down the long slope behind Muckerach farmhouse, across the Dulnain to the dark mass of the Curr Wood and beyond to the murky mass of the Cairngorms. The photograph, taken on a dull day, was rather

The bard kept this photograph safe through all his years on the Burma Railway, as a Japanese prisoner-of-war. It shows his wife, Barby, and the three children he left behind. (VR)

indistinct, and some straggling trees hid the house which had been the home of Barby, our little daughter Florence, and myself for a year, and in which our son Donald had been born. I showed the picture to all my friends and must have been for some days quite obsessed by it. Then one night I dreamed that I was walking south down the Achnahannet road at a point a quarter of a mile west and not far downhill from the place from which the photograph had been taken. Realising where I was, I joyfully set out for home! And woke up! I can think of no other disappointment in my life as great as that one.

Sick parade. There were four or five of us. On my right, at the end of the line, was a tall man, of my own build, from Galloway. After a wait of ten minutes or so, a big Nip came out of the HQ hut, 30 yards away. It was the Tiger. His eyes travelled back and forth along the line then settled on the Galloway man for whom he then headed quickening his pace. The last five or six feet were covered in an athletic leap and the left cheek of his prey received a hard, open handed skelp, causing the man to stagger away to the right. The Tiger gave a growl and turned back towards us and gave each of us a hard, searching stare. Then he muttered something to the orderly at the end of the line, and headed towards his lair.

Dysentery. When I recovered I found myself in a new well-built hut, beside two Lowland countrymen. One of them used to sing 'The Auld Scots Sangs' in a thirties, crooning, tongue-in-cheek manner which I did not like. When I told him so, he told me I was a right old hill-billy, but I'd always liked the old songs sung with true feeling, and out there it seemed like sacrilege to hear those great songs sung without feeling.

My next bout of malaria struck me as suddenly as my previous one at Rintin. I was carried on a stretcher into hut number 13 on 13th of November 1943. As well as the fever, I had painful waterworks. Every half-hour I was compelled to stagger out to the urinal. At the end of each such excursion I would pass blood and then had to endure half a minute's intense pain. The only prescription the Aussie doctor could give me was a line to the cookhouse, enabling me to get my water-bottle filled with weak tea at any time of the day.

On a stretcher beside me was a tall young Dutchman. He had been an air-force pilot in Java. He told me of a very special kind of coffee which he said was peculiar to Indonesia. An animal akin to the American raccoon was very fond of the fruit of the coffee plant. The husks or shells were digested by the animal's stomach but the hard coffee beans were excreted. These were sought after and collected by the Javanese and, when well washed, were sold at high prices to connoisseurs of this unique coffee. I have never since met anybody who has even heard of this coffee; so he may have been pulling my leg, but I did not think so at the time. The name of the animal and the coffee was Luac.

On the other side of the hut was Arthur Bacon and beside him a small Australian, the only small Australian I can remember. Though short of stature, he had probably been heavy and well built, but was now just about the nearest thing possible to a walking skeleton. One day he disappeared for some hours but eventually walked in with a folded blanket over his arm. He had been down to the river to wash it. It must have taken a super-human effort for a man in his state to get back up that steep, rough, sixty-foot-high bank. Next morning, as breakfast time approached, he got out his mess tin and asked Arthur to collect his ration. Arthur took the two mess tins to the feeding point and I joined him in the queue. We would not have been out of the hut more than ten minutes but when we returned there were only bare slats to be seen at the small Australian's bed-space. Whilst he knew we would be chatting, he had just let himself die, and the medical orderlies had removed his body, his clean blanket, and all his few belongings to the mortuary at the end of the hut. He must have sought to make his dying easy for the rest of us. It took the kindly, soft-hearted Arthur several days to get over the shock.

For a time I was on light duties in the camp. I can only remember one. It was a morning burial party, a daily occurrence at that time. There were five bodies. The one I helped to carry was as light as a child. A much-used horribly stained groundsheet covered it and the body lay on another groundsheet laid on the stretcher. By means of the lower sheet the body was lowered into the grave. Then both groundsheets were removed for similar use the following morning. The little shrivelled body was curled up into its pre-natal position. It was bright pink all over, being completely covered with scabies.

A Thai funeral passed along the road by the camp one day. A
small band of brass instruments played a slow march, which
sounded familiar to me. The tune was short and repeated over
and over again. I still remember the main part, which sounded
exactly like the first two bars of the second measure of the pipe
tune, 'Dovecot Park'.

Fourteen old bullock-cart beasts were killed each ten day
period in Tamuan. As soon as a bullock was led up by the
Australian herdsman, Big Bill went into action, felling the beast
with one expert blow with the back of his axe. A hefty young
Dutchman quickly cut the animal's throat, while I thrust my
basin under its neck to catch the blood. Steadying the basin
with my left hand, I stirred the hot blood with my right, a most
unpleasant task, but very necessary if the blood was to be used.
A kind of glove of stringy material formed around my fingers
that was sometimes difficult to get off. Big Bill was expert at
splitting the skulls and extracting the brains, like large soft
walnuts. He also collected the tiny pituitary glands for an
elderly Nip who used them, hopefully, for rejuvenation
purposes.

There was much pessimistic speculation about our ultimate
fate, and it became harder to disregard gloomy rumours of
impending massacres. One day, as I lay quiet beside Vic's empty
bed space [Vic Hipple, his best, oldest friend in the camps, had
died following a beating just a week before], out of the blue
came a bugle call, not the Nip call to which we had been
accustomed for years, but the British 'Fall-in'. 'Fall-in A, Fall-in
B – Fall-in every Company!' We slid off our beds and
stampeded for the door. The rain had ceased and the ground
was drying under a strong sun. We assembled into our 'check'
positions in record time. There wasn't a Nip to be seen. Our
senior NCO, a stout man in his forties, wearing a Red Cross
felt hat, climbed up the steps onto 'Laughing Dog's' platform.
We were called to attention and stood silent for some seconds.
Then the man on the platform was only able to shout one short
sentence, 'This is the happiest day of my life.' The parade
instantly erupted with a loud roaring and broke ranks. As I
turned towards the gate, I saw a flash of yellow to my right, two
men were hoisting a large Lion Rampant, the flag of Scotland,
on a bamboo pole. Ecstatic, I slowly made my way among

dozens of tearful men, dancing, shaking hands and hugging one another.

Back on my bed-space, I lay down. I remember saying, 'Good God,' to myself, aloud, 'I really will see Barby and the bairns again. Yes. I will sit by the bright fire of dry Curr Wood fir, whilst Barby bends over our home-made fireguard attending to her cooking. Dear Barby…'

Three men parachuted into the camp. One was an operator of the Royal Signals, like myself. From him, we learned the grim story of the atom bomb, but to which, of course, we owed the sudden change in our fortunes. We also heard the good news of the new Labour Government with its landslide majority. Lady Mountbatten paid us a visit and we paraded in Indian Army Surplus uniforms, which hung on our greyhound frames like scarecrows. I have a clear picture of her addressing us, though no memory of her words. I am sure she was never more heartily or sincerely cheered than by us, and I still am an admirer of hers.

Soon we were getting into a Dakota at Bangkok, en route for Rangoon. It was my first flight on a plane. Two or three Jeeps, driven by Sikhs, came tearing up to us like unleashed dogs, and then shot off with us, eight per Jeep, to a small building at the edge of the airport. Here we went up a few steps and entered a room containing armchairs and tables bearing newspapers and magazines. We had hardly begun to look at these when a door opened and an ATS girl called us into another room for tea. The tea was richly yellow with tinned milk, and sweet. The food was simply plain bread and butter, but in all my life I never tasted anything more tasty or more satisfying than the bread and butter we ate that day after three and a half years of boiled rice.

There were several bare-legged ATS girls moving amongst us, acting as waitresses, and the only time we could take our eyes off them was when we took hurried gulps of tea. To this day, the taste of plain bread and butter brings back to me the memory of those bare-legged lassies.

Postscript. Back at home after a joyful reunion, Barby and I passed through a period of adjustment and readjustment. I was then 36 and Barby almost 29 and no longer my carefree girl-wife. She had a broad band of premature grey hair on her dark

head. She too had suffered much. Shortly after I had gone
abroad, she and her young family had been practically hounded
out of our little home to make way for a farm worker.
Subsequently all our household goods were lost in a fire in
another old farm cottage, and since I was the holder of our fire
insurance policy the claim was not paid until I returned home.
Such treatment of the young family of a soldier serving abroad
in wartime, though common enough in the Highlands of the
19th century, must surely have been rare, if not unique, in the
mid-20th. But events in Scotland, at their blackest, were mild
compared to those in those camps of hunger, dirt, disease and
death; those camps of hope, humour, and the comradeship of
cheerful companions; that camp of 'the flying squirrel', at
Tarsao on the River Kwai.

You can see that Murd was a very vivid writer. So why did he write so little
poetry? Perhaps, after all his struggles, Murd thought poetry inadequate.
Perhaps he didn't have the time or energy to write poetry, working long days
on the road, but I think it's more likely that it was just that he was never asked
or expected to write. He was given little respect being a roadman. I heard once
how he went to put a new fireplace into a house on the Mackintosh estate, he
having good masonry skills, though not being a mason to trade like his father.
Well, the lady of the house said she wanted something very nice, very smart for
the times when the Mackintosh of Mackintosh visited. And Murd got suddenly
angry and he said, 'And it doesn't matter about me and the others who come!

*'Alt Dhuagh', the house Murdo
MacAskill dreamed of building for
his family whilst a prisoner and which
he completed, with help from his
brother Hamish, in 1947. (VR)*

We can stand before a dead fireplace. We can sit looking at an ugly mantelpiece but the Mackintosh of Mackintosh must have the best of the best! Not just at home – but in every house he thinks fit to receive him!' And Murd picked up his tools and walked out of that house never to return. He was a passionate believer in equality.

He was very upset when he saw his parents' house burned to the ground. It was still a good, habitable house, Rose Cottage, and it was burned to the ground. It was the BBC that did it. They paid money and they burned it down for one of their serials about life in the Highlands. It was burned to the ground and never replaced and there's nothing where Rose Cottage once was. The BBC has played its part in the Clearances.

Murd worked on the roads because, when he came back from Burma, he wanted never to leave Strathdearn alive. There was no other work for him. He wanted an outdoor life. He loved the people and the history of this place. He knew the genealogy of all the old families here and most of his bardachd is about local events, things that happened round about. Most of them were humorous. He used to sing 'The Ballad of Allan's First Tractor' to the tune 'Cawdor's Fine Braes'. It describes an incident in the life of Allan Tulloch, one of the old-time characters in Strathdearn:

O, Allan's first tractor, a famous machine
Was made by himself from an old limousine,
A very good worker until it got riled
And then it was apt to be wilful and wild.

Said Allan one morning, 'I must break ye in,
So I'll steer up the stubble before we begin.
It's "Hi here" to go west, and it's "Wheesh" to go east –
For all yer ill looks you're a mettlesome beast!'

The end-rig was nearby when Allan cried 'Whoa!'
The throttle was thrawn, the machine widna slaw!
The clutch widna clear, and while Allan did yank
The tractor arrived at the high river bank.

O, steep was that bank with the water beneath,
That bolted machine had the bit in its teeth!
But Allan, undaunted, did not turn a hair,
Right gallant he rode his mechanical mare.

Down into the river the tractor did plunge
The stotter behind wi a stot and a lunge,
'Get up there,' cried Allan, 'Just have your own way,
You'll be glad o' a rest by the end o' the day.'

The salmon fled seawards, the seagulls did scream,
As Allan's wild tractor tore through the mid stream,
Out onto the far bank, then on a west tack,
Two miles to the bridge and two miles to come back.

Its fuel all finished, the tractor did cough,
And come to a halt at the watering trough.
Allan sat smiling and said — 'Aye, ah think
Yersel and masel, we could do wi a drink!' (MM)

Another poem comes straight out of his work on the road. Its called 'Cutting the Peat':

Deep centuries the peat knife stabs,
The wet black moss falls back in slabs
Books of brown-stained sodden pages
Dull records of far distant ages,
And here is one broke clean in two
With something pale exposed to view —
An axe-hewn chip of ancient pine
Cut by a blade as keen as mine.
My fascinated fingers feel
A tiny ridge left by the ancient steel;
Its edge was dented thus to mark
Each chip with this fine curving arc,
A segment of the axeman's swing.

How close he is, brought by this thing,
I feel his grip upon the haft,
I know his strength, his skill, his craft,
His axe strokes strike upon my ear,
The moss is gone, the wood is here.
The rain-filled centuries I span;
Before me is this brother man.

But ah! The rumbling of that train
Brings me to myself again,
Thinking how I might contrive
That some small chip of mine survive
In someone's thought, somewhere, somehow
A thousand years ahead of now. (MM)

He had the poet's wish to be remembered, to be immortal, but felt himself rejected. He'd built himself the little house he dreamed of building when he was a prisoner, yet felt himself a failure as a man and as a husband. There was never any money for anything like luxury. Barbara was always a stylish woman, she liked to dress well. He wrote her a poem and signed it 'The Has Been'.

I wish you a Happy Birthday
With many more to come.
I drink your health in lemonade
Although I'd rather rum.
I'd like to give you two fur coats
And several diamond rings,
A pair of scarlet wellingtons
And other lovely things,
A poncho and an ermine cape,
A sheenyol and a shawl,
A velvet tartan mini-skirt,
And still that isn't all.
I'd feed you steak and curried eggs
Marsh-mallowed-flavoured honey,
And all that's left in me of love
And all I have of money. (MM)

Murdo and his wife Barby in Inverness for a wedding, mid 1950's. (VR)

It's a nice poem but it's a sad poem. He also wrote a poem to celebrate their 43rd wedding anniversary and it was read out at Barbara's funeral in 1997. It's called 'The Forty Third Milestone':

Baba bright-eyes in the snow,
since that springtime long ago,
in check coat and yellow tam,
you've made me who and what I am.

Brave sweet Barby, half of me,
With our children at your knee,
That height of happiness attained
No other way I've ever gained.

Lady Barbara of my heart,
only death will make me part
from you the anchor of my life,
my dear delightful dreadful wife.

Duchess Baba all tartan clad,
laughing loud or raging mad!
I am proud and very glad
you still accept me as your lad. (MM)

Another of his poems is just a scrap jotted down on the back of a raffle ticket for the Christmas Draw of Rothes Football Club. The ticket number is 7138 A. It cost two and half pence and the draw was made on 5th December 1975. It's called 'The Triple Trinity', and it makes me proud that Murdo MacAskill was my brother.

Opposite:
Murdo MacAskill at home by the
fireplace he built with his own hands,
1980. (photo, Ian MacKenzie)

On a cold summer evening
I walked out the hill,
The north wind in my face,
Thoughts afar, until
Peering over an esker ridge
Below me, close and clear,
I spied the triple trinity,
A family of red deer,
Three hinds, three yearlings and three fawns.
It was a magic sight:
I'd hope in vain to live again
That moment of delight. (MM)

THE STRATHDEARN BARD
DONALD MACASKILL

Remembered by Margaret Begg of Inverness

Donald MacAskill, my father, was a very different poet to Murdo. In 1928 a book of his poems was published by Alex MacLaren and Sons in Glasgow. It was titled The Mixture, A Collection of Verse by Donald MacAskill, The Strathdearn Bard. It was dedicated to The Mackintosh of Mackintosh, 'In acknowledgement of his generous patronage and shrewd counsel.' It cost one shilling.

Donald MacAskill was another ordinary working man but he, unlike Murdo, was somewhat honoured and recognised as a bard in his own lifetime. You see, he was still part of the old order; his father had come over from the Isle of Harris and he met and married my grandmother, Margaret MacPherson, in Strathspey. Both his parents were native Gaelic speakers, they mixed the dialects of the Western Isles and the Grampian mountains. Strathdearn was still half Gaelic in those days. In Harris, old Murdo had grown up with the sea all round him but in Strathdearn his horizon was always the mountains and many was the time I heard my grandmother speak of how much he would long for a glimpse of the sea. He died at quite a young age, in 1877, but he fathered four children, of whom the bard was the youngest. My grandmother had a great struggle bringing up four young children alone. First she had a small croft at Woodend, Tomatin, on the Coignafearn road. Then they moved to Rose Cottage on the Kyllachie Estate.

The Strathdearn Bard,
Donald MacAskill
1872/1943. (VR)

My father left school at the age of thirteen. He became an apprentice mason. The big thing then was the railway, they were building the Tomatin viaduct and he worked on it for years. It's a beautiful example of the stonemason's craft and stands in perfect condition 100 years later. After that, in search of work, he travelled the country and he married my mother, down at Shotts, in central Scotland. They had eight children. During the First World War, he was batman to the Mackintosh of Mackintosh and bard to the chief. My father was a handsome man, especially in his uniform. Fairish hair. He had four years with the Camerons. And after that he became a general worker to the Mackintoshes on the Moy estate, looking after the walls and the stonework.

His earliest bardachd was all in Gaelic but later he wrote only in English, with touches of Scots. I don't know any of his Gaelic songs, I think they're lost, but his most famous English poem is 'Coignafearn'. It's still sung here: Angie Dunbar of Invereen would sing it to the tune of Mairi Mhor's 'Eilean a' Cheò':

COIGNAFEARN

We boast of Scotland's beauties, and our boasting is not vain,
Hers is the wooded slope, the loch, the rich expansive plain;
But her greatest beauties lie among her mountains wild and stern
And they rise in rugged majesty surrounding Coignafearn.

Ben Nevis' crest may pierce the clouds, and bear the changeless snow,
And next to it Macdhui first may catch the morning glow;
After such giddy altitudes my spirit does not yearn,
But it loves the massive solitude surrounding Coignafearn.

The nearer slopes are tender green, with tops of brownish hue,
Then further off the purple, and further still the blue,
Till the furthest ridges of the sky the eye can scarce discern,
The artist revels in the shades of lovely Coignafearn.

Here, free upon his own domain, is seen the stately stag,
Browsing upon a grassy slope beneath some beetling crag,
Or nobly silhouetted on some purple crested cairn,
The most majestic picture of the charms of Coignafearn.

And here the monarch of the air soars o'er the mighty ben,
Now on his rigid pinions poised, now sweeping down the glen;
Here truly nature's student of her grandest page may learn,
Amid the pregnant silences of lonely Coignafearn.

I've wandered over Scotland, and I've seen her choicest sights,
And in her lowland beauties I have found some keen delights,
But I ever turn with fondness back to beautiful Strathdearn,
Where the lovely Findhorn leads me to the hills of Coignafearn. (DM)

Coignafearn captures the imagination and there are many stories and rhymes about it. Donald knew it from his boyhood but he was brought up at Moy where the Mackintoshes lived. It was all very feudal. My aunties have told me how they were warned to keep away from the house. There were two paths to get to the dairy, the shortcut was the private path of the Mackintoshes and the long path was the way we had to go. And even then, going to get the milk, we'd hurry by, fearful of getting our father the sack. The chauffeur, the carpenter, the forester were always on the watch. Or we thought they were. Even the

Bard to the MacIntosh of MacIntosh
of Moy, Donald MacAskill (in hat),
with family and friends,
c. 1935. (MB)

dairymaid ruled with a rod of iron – if we were late she'd give us 'a reprimand'. Reprimand was her favourite word and many was the reprimand we got. And the keepers would keep a very sharp eye. No one shot so much as a rabbit around Moy. We didn't even have a gun. That was best, my father said. We lived in isolation and as children we had no idea that we might be described as 'deprived'. We had plenty of space to play and there were no dangers in those days. A child could walk for miles through the forest without fear. The only thing that might hold us back would be heavy snow.

My father was a great admirer of Robert Burns. He sang Burns songs and he spoke at Burns Suppers. In 1908 he wrote a tribute: 'To the Shade of Robert Burns':

> *Dear shade, in some Elysian sphere,*
> *That knoweth neither sigh nor fear,*
> *Where with congenial spirits dear*
> > *You tune your lay,*
> *We hail with warming hearts and cheer*
> > *Your natal day.*

More than a century has fled
Since you laid down your weary head,
And ceased the struggle for your bread
(But seldom buttered),
Since then what wealth's been used to spread
Each word you uttered.

Tonight your memory fills each thought,
The kindly lessons you have taught,
How pomp and pride have come to naught
Through your straight preaching,
And how to see things as we ought.
Has been your teaching.

On honest hearts, both high and low,
How eager were you to bestow
Praise that sets true men aglow
With warm assent,
And aye the hypocrite's o'erthrow
Was your intent.

Each helpless thing your love would shield;
The turned-up daisy in the field,
The mousie driven from its bield
Your pity moved,
And so our hearts to kindness yield,
Because you loved.

Each Scot who loves his motherland,
Each man who for the truth will stand,
Each generous heart on every hand,
From pole to pole,
Pays homage to your genius grand
And noble soul. (DM)

My father was an excellent fiddler. In the evenings he would play and the children would gather on wee footstools round the fire. Every week the Moy church choir would come to our house for singing practice. They would sing the psalms, hymns, and every other kind of song, but he never sang his own songs, or spoke his own poems in the house, as far as I remember. We children

Father and son, the Strathdearn
bards at home at Moybeg,
c. 1929. (MB)

joined in with the choir and so did my mother. And she always gave out tea and hot scones. They were very enjoyable evenings. My clearest memory of my father is of him standing in church and striking the tuning fork and holding it still in his hand and his beautiful loud voice leading the choir into the first hymn.

The Great War had a tremendous influence on the whole way of life in the Highlands. Many of my father's poems make reference to the war. There's one, a bit like Thomas Hardy, called 'Three Years Ago':

> *Three years ago he laboured on a farm,*
> *And forked the fragrant clover to and fro,*
> *Nor gave a random thought to war's alarm,*
> > *Three years ago.*

> *He watched the waves of gently rustling corn*
> *(The breezes whisp'ring in the forming ears),*
> *Nor ever dreamed of human waves shell torn,*
> > *This time three years.*

I met him after thirty months of fight;
The rustic gravity had left his face,
And though he'd witnessed many a ghastly sight,
                Mirth took its place.

My grave concern but made his laugh more gay
The day he left again to face the foe;
Was this the youth I saw among the hay
                Three years ago?

Yes, 'twas the same, a simple British Youth,
Who felt the patriotic glow,
Strong in the 'cause' that rallied round the truth
                Three years ago. (DM)

Most of the Strathdearn men, and all the Mackintoshes, fought with the Camerons. As bard to the Mackintosh, my father wrote a song for the regiment. It's called, 'The Camerons':

When Allan of Eireacht, great Chieftain of yore,
Arose to the help of his country at war,
His kinsmen and neighbours were swift to the fore,
                For fighters of old were the Cam'rons.
Right fiercely they fought with a martial fire,
And gathered the laurels that heroes inspire,
Till all the brave lads in our great Highland shire
                Were eager to fight with the Cam'rons.

CHORUS — Cameron men from the foot of the ben,
From village and clachan in many a glen,
From castle and sheiling the flow'r of our men
Came into the ranks of the Cam'rons.

And when the great conflict for woe and for weal
Took toll of our armies with shell and with steel,
Old Scotland sent forth, at the call of Locheil,
                The best of her sons with the Cam'rons.
Their prowess and daring have finally sealed
The truth that 'A Cameron never can yield,'
And the glory of many a death-stricken field
                Is 'graved on the shield of the Cam'rons.

CHORUS — Cameron men from the foot of the ben,
From village and valley, from city and fen!
Forever shall live with the sons of the glen,
The deathless renown of the Cam'rons. (DM)

He would be asked to write poems for special occasions. After the war he
wrote various remembrance poems; the one I like best was for the unveiling of
the 'Strathdearn War Memorial':

Before this monument of granite grey
            We stand with sorrowing yet thankful hearts;
Our grief for those who lie afar this day,
            Our thanks that they so bravely played their parts.

The crash of Freedom's struggle for the right
            Awoke the echoes of our peaceful Strath;
And, as of yore, with fiery cross alight,
            Men left their hearts and homes for glory's path.

We proudly hailed them as they marched away,
            Their going made us hold our heads erect;
Worthy their sires who never shunned the fray,
            Nor failed their sacred homeland to protect.

The path of duty took them far afield
            And some no more the Findhorn shall behold,
For Freedom's victory with their blood was sealed,
            And with the heroes are their names enrolled.

Then let us reverence our noble band,
            Like them, put duty first whate'er befall,
For duty's higher than a King's command,
            And sacrifice the noblest thing of all. (DM)

When I was a teenager my father was diagnosed as having TB. The doctor took
just one look at him, put a hankie to his nose, his own nose, and said, 'It's TB.'
That was a death sentence in those days. He had to be locked away in a room
of his own, like an isolation ward. My mother would take him things. Of
course, his work with the choir had to stop. We got some help from an
insurance company in Inverness and later Murd came back from Canada. But

something strange happened, the years passed and my father didn't die. The doctors decided to have another look at him and he was rediagnosed. It was silicosis, not TB. Granite had ruined his bronchial tubes. His last years were not easy, but at least he knew what he had and he got his family back round him. One of his poems describes the kind of work he did as a young man. It's called 'The Rumper' and it describes the competitive striving of one workman against another, which the bosses encouraged in those days. It's dedicated 'To the best of "butties", Bobby MacBeth, Barmuckity, Elgin'.

THE RUMPER

'Twas in the hewing shed,
To earn our daily bread
        We worked the whole day long;
We scorned to take our ease
And with plenty elbow grease
        We struck it fast and strong.
We all got bankered on the same,
Then each man tried the striving game,
Nor stopped to light his cutty;
Along the shed the signal ran
'Walker' expects that every man
This day will rump his Butty.

'Twas Newton, hard and tough,
But we cut it fast and rough
        Through moulding, splay and check;
Our rumper Sandy Grey,
He avowed aloud each day
The record he would break;
Like shot and shell the chips did fly,
Each mash and mallet swung on high
        Like horseman's flashing sabre;
And swiftly flew each point and drove
As doggedly each mason strove
        To rump his friend and neighbour.

Lal MacDonald, a gaelic-speaking friend of both the Strathdearn bards, walks beneath the viaduct Donald MacAskill helped build over a hundred years ago. (TN, 1997)

At last the joyful day
On which we got our pay,
> *The joyful day came round;*
We hailed the welcome sack,
And with kits slung o'er our back
> *We started townward bound.*
The dollars made a pleasant clink,
We all went for a parting drink
> *And filled a brimming bumper;*
And every man in that gay crowd
'Ere drinking, cried this toast aloud:
> *'Confusion to the Rumper!'* (DM)

I don't carry any of my father's poems in my head but I remember very well the beautiful letters he wrote me when I was a nurse down in Salford, in Lancashire. That was during the first years of the war. He never once told me about goings-on at Moy, not once did he lower himself to write gossip. It was always about the hills that he wrote, about the high hopes that he had, about the

Margaret Begg with Murdo MacAskill's two daughters, Lorna Payne and Vivien Roden, Inverness, 1998. (TN)

beauties of nature. Unfortunately I have none of these letters. On Christmas Eve, 1940, the Salford hospital was bombed and not one of those letters survived. But one of the poems in his book gives you an idea of the letters he wrote to me. It's called 'A Sigh to the Hills' and it shows you the kind of man my father was.

Bright summer sun on the plain,
  Brooks smiling back to the sun;
Freshness of green after rain,
  Meadows with flowers overrun;
Here it might surely be pleasant to dwell,
But Oh! for the scent of the sweet heather bell.

Gaily the blackbird at morn
Startles the glade with its notes,
High o'er the thick shooting corn
  Skylark in melody floats;
Joyous the music each day they renew,
But Oh! for the cry of the plaintive curlew.

Up on some Grampian height,
  Ptarmigan white flashes by,
Grouse crowing loudly alight,
  Startling the deer where they lie;
That is the picture at which my heart thrills,
There's where I'd be, on my own native hills. (DM)

Part Three

The Many-Coloured Coat

Charlotte Munro

PITLOCHRY AND KINGSKETTLE, FIFE

I was born at Moulin, Pitlochry, in Perthshire. My father was Charles Riley and my mother was Jean Power. They had a family of frocks, eight girls and no boys. I was born on 24th January 1940, the third oldest in the family. I've made poems, sung my songs, and acted out my plays since I can remember. I'm a loner. I left school at fourteen, I've worked, I've had a family, I've been ill many times. I've lived my life in tortuous waves. I really feel for the homeless, the sick, the afflicted. I've written poems about Aids. I've a song about an alcoholic. It's to my own tune and it's called 'Back on the Sauce':

> *Back on the sauce again*
> *Singing his song to the stars,*
> *He's off on a pleasure cruise*
> *Clowning around the bars:*
> *And it's no use complaining,*
> *You brave fellow you,*
> *The dastardly's done,*
> *The borrowed, the blue,*
> *The perfume, the magic*
> *Have all fallen through*
> *And he's back on the sauce — again.*

Opposite:
The bard Charlotte Munro,
Kingskettle, Fife, 1998. (TN)

Dropped by his snow princess,
This foolish man's alone.
He left her in dire distress
Now the battle colours are down:
And it's no use complaining,
You brave fellow you,
The dastardly's done
The borrowed, the blue,
The perfume, the magic
Have all fallen through
And he's back on the sauce – again.

O, captain, the moon's
Just deserted the sky,
The weather's for changing
And the rain is close by.
There's a pain in his heart
And a chill in his bones.
O captain he's falling
And the waters so cold.
His aspirations – his dreams –
Are lost in a stormy sea –
Sunk in an endless wave.
At last this poor man is free
And it's no use complaining,
You brave fellow you,
The dastardly's done,
The borrowed, the blue,
The perfume, the magic
Have all fallen through
And he's back on the sauce – again. (CM)

My grandmother, on my Dad's side, was a Burns from Ayrshire. Margaret Burns was her name and it was always said she was related to Robert Burns. My grandfather Riley was a wool merchant with a smallholding at Moulin; that's where they found the skulls of the Oroc, the ancient wild cattle, the only two in Scotland. When my father came home from the war, he bought a bus that then became our home for many summers. We travelled all over Scotland spray-painting farm sheds and industrial buildings.

I hardly saw my father till I was five. He was a tank sergeant in

The bard's parents William and Jean Riley, 1941. Charlotte is the seated toddler. (CM)

William Riley (front right) with 'Shirley' (for Charlotte) emblazoned on his vehicle, Germany 1945. (CM)

the Black Watch and he was away at the war. Our family came in two halves, two sets of four girls seven years apart. And it's a strange thing but my father was a different man to the two sets of children. The younger ones remember him as an intelligent man, a gentle man who told jokes, they loved him, but to us older ones he was Frankenstein, Dracula, and Wolfman all rolled into one. He had been a corporal, he was shell-shocked, and we older girls got treated like squaddies. 'Stand Up Straight! Attention! Straight! Polish Your Shoes! Hi You! This you, that you!' He didn't hit us, just a backhander every now and then but we feared him, we were afeared to be in the same room as he was. If you cooked a tomato and it wasn't just right, underdone or overcooked, he'd throw it straight out the door. If you broke an egg yolk in the pan....

My mother used to say it was the war and that we had to be patient, that he'd been affected by all he'd seen and done, that we had to be nice to him. He had shrapnel in his head. I've seen him squeezing slivers of metal from wounds that came and went behind his ear. Mother was a quiet and understanding woman. She used to say her Powers were cousins to Tyrone Power, the actor. Her father had come over from Ireland and married a Margaret MacArthur from Argyll and she was born down there on Loch Fyne. My mother was used to hard times. Her father had a reputation for violence and her own brother was killed by the Germans in North Africa. We older girls used to give father a wide berth but gradually, over the years, he changed, and by the time the younger girls were growing up he was talking to them in a way he never talked to us. It was a great disappointment for him to never have a boy. Each time my mother was delivered of another baby, friends would be calling 'Hullo there, Charlie – is it a boy?' and every time he'd bellow back, 'No such luck, another split-arse!'

My father used to sing us songs but the funny thing was, he sang them all to the same tune, or near enough the same tune, in fact it was hardly a tune, more of a chant. I used to think his songs weren't very good but then no one thought my songs were any good at all! I liked pop music.

I made up every kind of song. I'd feel one coming on and lock myself away till it was finished. Words and tune. My grandfather Riley made up his own songs and I remember that he was very fond of riddles. 'Sit you down,' he would say and then he would start. He was full of sayings.

> *A wee, wee thing made of leather*
> *Running up and down the heather,*
> *Through a rock, through a reel,*
> *Through my granny's spinning wheel,*
> *Through a miller's happer,*
> *Through a bag o' paper,*
> *Through sheep shank marrowbone.*
> *What is it?*

And the answer was a maggot. And if he got started on a story he'd soon enough be carried away. He had inspiration and I've got inspiration. At four o'clock in the morning I'll wake with my head full of nonsense and I'll jump out of bed and put everything I've been thinking down in a flow. When I look at what I've written next day, I might leave it, or I might change it, improve it. I know when I've done something good. I'm always thinking about words, about phrases, images. Words keep flooding into my head and sometimes they form themselves into a poem just as though they had a mind of their own. 'Shaded leaf', 'bonnie black and blue', 'Dante's Inferno', 'stout hunting grounds', they may be clichés but I turn clichés into poetry and song. 'When earth's adorned in winter frock/When sunshine all but falls asleep/When life is cold and drab and lost/I, the spiteful wind will reap.'

My father's family was always collecting bits and pieces, scrap, art, antiques. I remember going up to visit my uncle, Eddie Riley, up above Pitlochry, and he riding out to meet us on a horse in full armour, all polished and shining; over the brow of the hill he came and circled round us. I remember my Auntie Doris and I, walking home in the dark after going to the pictures and suddenly this hand would come through the grass and grab you by the ankle. That was my Uncle Eddie. A person needs to have a bit of character, before you remember them. I remember my Uncle Eddie very well. He was dedicated to frightening us. I've written a story about wizards, with poems and songs:

> *When darkness offers cover*
> *Of spells he castes none.*
> *Desire to court a lover*
> *Of spells he castes none.*
> *If wealth be part of lifeblood need*
> *Of spells he castes none.*
> *When gluttony grows like a seed*
> *Of spells he castes none.*
>
> *If memory be truly jaded*
> *Of spells he castes one.*
> *If tempers tarry unabated*
> *Of spells he castes one.*
> *If truth be hid in forest or face*
> *Of spells he castes one.*
> *If a silver lining merits grace*
> *Of spells he castes one.* (CM)

I've always loved to sing. I can sing for hours. I've still got a good voice – I'm a wee dynamo, a ball of dynamite! But illness has kept me down and, when I say that, I'm not making it up, I've got diabetes, I've got a rogue thyroid, the nerves to my hands and feet have more or less gone, I can only walk with a stick. In fact, everything about me is buggered, everything but my lungs and my head. I've got all these ideas, and nowhere to go.

> *With severed thoughts my brain does play*
> *as I struggle with resentment.*
> *This dire dilemma illness brings*
> *has pickled my contentment.*

I send my poems down to England to be published. I'm a member of ISOP, the International Society of Poets. Seventeen of my poems have been published in

Breadalbane Academy, first year class photo, 1953. Charlotte Riley is in the second row, far left. (CM)

England but not a single one in Scotland. It might sound conceited but I really feel I have something to give the world. My poems and songs cover a huge range of subjects from the stage to the grave.

When I was young we used to go to the berries, take the bus and spend three weeks picking the raspberries up at Blairgowrie. Many's the summer we were up there, and my uncle used to come down from Aberdeen, Willie Murison. He was married to my father's sister, Jessie. In the evenings all the children would get into this big bath for a scrub-down and afterwards we'd all be sat on a bench outside Uncle Willie's caravan for a story, 'a Jake story'. He died of a heart attack, years ago, in his forties. But in those days, up at the berries, every night we got a story, the never-ending story of Jake. And, looking back, I can see that Willie was one fly man. He didn't really tell us a story at all, all he did was get us going and keep us going. I used to get so excited, so involved in the story. They'd all be an adventure and Uncle Willie would get Jake to the point where he would be hanging on a cliff, clinging on for dear life and his fingernails would just be breaking when he'd say, 'Now, you weans, off to bed! Away you go and tomorrow I'll tell you what happened to Jake.'

I couldn't bear it. All night I'd be thinking about Jake and worrying about him and the next day at the berries we'd all be discussing it. 'How do you think Jake's going to escape this time?' 'He can't escape, he's going to die this time!' Well, when the evening came and we were sat down, Uncle Willie would start again and just say, 'Well, Jake was walking down the road when…' And we'd all shout, 'But, Uncle Willie, he was hanging from the cliff – tell us how Jake got down from the cliff!' And he'd laugh and he'd say, 'How the bloody hell do I know how Jake got down from the cliff, I've been pickin' rasps all bloody day!' And we'd all moan and cry out and he'd say, 'You'll have to work it out for yourselves!' And we'd all start arguing about what really did happen to Jake, till he'd shout, 'Shut up! Now I'm going to go on with the story…' and we'd all be very quiet and he'd begin, 'Now, as I said, Jake was walking down this road when he came to a crossroads, and sitting in the middle of the road was a very old woman and her name was Winnie the Glutton and it was said round about that she was a witch. And when Jake saw Winnie the Glutton his heart turned to stone…' And he'd pause, and he wouldn't go on , and the questions would start.

'What's a glutton, Uncle Willie?' 'Was she a real witch, Uncle Willie?' 'Can a witch really turn your heart to stone?' And Willie would say, 'I'll tell you this, she was nae a witch but she was a glutton and she'd eat the f…ing legs aff ye! She'd eat your arms right off yer body and she'd eat your toes with the nails on and she kept a row o' noses in her big black purse…' And everybody would start squirming and talking and wondering, till Willie would shout, 'Right, on we go! Quiet! Now, Jake took a short-cut round the crossroads and he came to this wee village and as he turned the corner there, lying on the ground, was a man, with a very dark skin…' And the questions would start once more. 'Is he dead?' 'It's a golliwog!' 'Is he a black man? Is he an African?' 'He's a Red Indian been shot with an arrow! Waaawaaa!' 'I know, I know, he's the man wi' the turban that sells the ladies' underwear!' And so on. And all the children would be shouting and clamouring when out of the blue, Willie would say, 'Aye, that's the man! That's who he is! Now, Shirley, you tell us how he came to be lying there in the road.' And so it would go on till he'd get Jake stuck up a tree or bound tight with rope and suddenly he'd stop. 'Right!' he'd say, 'That's enough for tonight, off you go to your beds and we'll go on with the story tomorrow.' And so the Jake stories went on and on and they never got anywhere! Looking back, I can see that he was a teacher, he was giving us a learning lesson each night. He was getting us to think and tell our own stories. He was like the Mad Hatter! But we had good times in the berry fields, with the campfires and songs. I've written a poem called 'The Berries':

> We a' went tae the berry picking
> Aye! When we were young,
> Wi' our luggies, hooks, strings and pails
> Boy, did we have fun.

We went in the summer, when the berries were ripe
        And the sun was high in the sky,
Wi' our sloppy joes, jeans and boppers sae white
        A bottle o' juice and a pie.

We met lots o' new friends, we shook lots of hands
        And we greeted the auld weel kent set.
Sticky juice o' the berries was stuck roon oor mooths
        It's a sight I'll never forget.

We sookit the big anes, then made oorselves sick
        And mother was fair black affronted.
We turned a shade green, were in bed for a week,
        A doctor was a' that we wanted.

We grafted and blethered, we rested and sang
        While filling our pails. It was fun!
We a' went tae the berry picking —
        Aye, when we were young. (CM)

I have my grumbles but in many ways it was an excellent life, touring Scotland each summer in the bus. We never went without. We travelled all the islands, Arran, Mull and Skye. We went down to Manchester. I remember being out on the Isle of Arran. It was September. I was there with my cousin Shirley, we were starting to grow up, and I was beginning to think spray-painting wasn't the thing for a young woman to be doing. All we two Shirleys really cared about was Bill Haley and the Comets! Although I'd been christened Charlotte everyone called me Shirley and they still do. My father painted the name 'Shirley' on the front of his tank. So out there on Arran, we were the two Shirleys! Two adolescents, and we'd be wondering who was watching us behind each window we came to as we spray-painted a house or a big shed. After a hard day's painting, we older girls would go down to the bay to swim and wash the spray away out of our hair. The weather was perfect, an Indian summer. One evening, about half past eight, a great harvest moon was rising, the tide was right in and we swam out into deep water. I was floating on my back when suddenly, Shirley whispered quietly: 'Shirley! Whatever you do, don't look down, just turn and follow me, swim very slowly to the rock...'

Well, I couldn't help but look down. And there, right by my face was a monster! A shark! A huge basking shark! A whole school of sharks! Just a yard below us, swimming by, I could see their eyes, their mouths open like great pale suns in the water. Now, I'd never seen sharks and I panicked. I started thrashing out for the shore, like a fool! I lost all my strength and I couldn't swim a stroke. My legs started to sink and I could feel the wash from their tails coming up beside me. Then the fins started coming out, cutting through the water. I gave a great scream. It was Shirley who helped me back in. They were harmless but that was the end of swimming on Arran!

We grow and vanish
*   down dark lovers' lanes*
Where the shackles of innocence
*   go up in flames.*

Here passion's forthcoming
*   as desire runs strong*
And everyone's caught
*   in the eye of life's storm.*

With a pressing of flesh
*   we devour and discover*
In the name of true love —
*   that immaculate cover.*

It's simply amazing,
*   all cradle days gone —*
We transform forever
*   into adults by dawn.*

When all passion has climaxed
*   and the dastardly's done —*
Enter blind panic
*   along with the sun;*

For all shrouded in darkness
*   a third party sits —*
Unused in a packet
*   purchased cheap at the Ritz.* (CM)

I'm a big believer in Safe Sex. That's a poem I wrote years ago, called 'Scatter-brained Chances'.

My father was what you'd call a shrewd businessman. One year he bought a big house in Canal Street, Aberdeen, and we lived up there.

The bard's sister, Jessie Smith, poses by a bus of the kind in which the Riley family travelled when young.
(CM)

Another time he bought an ironmonger's shop and a garage in Bank Street, Aberfeldy, where he made shooting-brakes for special customers. He was very, very practical, very good with his hands. He began to get quite proud of us girls. Walking down the street, people would say, 'Here's Cherlie Riley, and his beautiful daughters!' And, though he wouldn't admit it, he was proud of us. We were fast runners. We went to Breadalbane Academy, up by 'The Birks o' Aberfeldy', about which the bard wrote. We could run most of the other kids right off their feet, boys as well as girls. One sport's day, the Riley girls won every race for girls there was! We cleaned up. We won the High Jump, Long Jump, Fancy Races, Long Races, Short Races, the lot. It was in the newspaper. 'The Life of Riley', that was the headline.

Although we spent the summers travelling, we were not like the people they call Travellers nowadays. We girls used to be told to keep well away from the tinks, what we called 'the wood minks'. Some of them used to live in the old bow-tents, hide away in the woods, too shy to come out and black with the stove smoke. Father kept a strict eye but one summer, up at Oban, we three oldest daughters entered a beauty contest at the dancing. And we won the first, second and third prizes. Lena, the second oldest, won, Margaret was second and I was third. I was too young, only sixteen.

The winter after, we were in Crieff, when my father took ill with a bad chest. I'd started work and month after month it was my wage that kept the whole family going. Lena and Margaret had gone away, so every penny in my pay packet went to my mother to keep the five young ones at school. I was working on a big farm, cleaning tractors and machinery. Six days a week. I was a young woman. I should have been out enjoying myself and there I was working every hour of the day. One year of that and I'd had enough. At seventeen, I went away to live with my Auntie Maggie in Kirkcaldy, and I became a weaver. Then I moved across to work in Nairn's linoleum factory and I was there for four years.

I got married to Hugh MacKenzie and we took a place in MacKenzie Street. His people worked the chip shop at Gallatown and his granny owned a lot of the buildings in the Gallatown. We had two children but after eight years that marriage ended. Later on I met my husband, David. His father was a colonel in the Polish army. We've been together for seventeen years and married for fourteen. He worked for the Council in Glenrothes: he was a heating engineer till he took early retirement. Now he does part-time work on the chicken farm. He's a fine man, a wonderful husband, and I wrote this poem for him. It's called 'The Bees Knees':

> *You do not have the sight*
> *to follow the stars into the heavens.*
> *You do not have the hearing*
> *that can tell when mountains sway.*
> *You do not have the reach*
> *to touch the birds as they are leaving*
> *But to me*
> *you are the bee's knees anyway.*
>
> *You do not seek a quest*
> *to pull that sword from out that stone.*
> *You do not have a plan*
> *to save the day.*
> *You do not have the means*
> *to tackle poverty alone.*
> *But to me*
> *you are the bee's knees anyway.*

You cannot solve the secrets
beneath the desert sands.
You cannot sail the seven seas
by two o'clock on Sunday.
You can't control the high winds
or the waves that wash the beaches.
But to me
you are the bee's knees anyway.

You can become a legend,
especially in my time.
You will release the magic
that I hope for when I pray.
You must be sure you love me
just as much as I love you.
For to me
you are the bee's knees anyway. (CM)

For fifteen years Dave and I had a caravan up in Glen Devon. I wrote a lot of my poems up there. One night we were with a big group of campers, drinking in the Dungeon Hotel, when we got talking about poetry. They didn't believe I could write poems, so I came back the next night with a different poem about each one of them, about them all rolling back to their caravans drunk! They were amazed, they got them all specially written out by a calligrapher, on great scrolls, and put them up on their walls. I like to be asked to write poems. I write poems for weddings and anniversaries. I wrote a lovely poem for my daughter, Christine. She was unfortunate, she married a man who didn't want her but he didn't want anybody else to have her either. So she had a hard time. She's with another man now. She's a most beautiful daughter. This is the poem I wrote for her when she was still a girl. It's called 'Christine':

You're as pretty as a picture
In your bonnie party dress.
You're all the things a lass should be:
You're young, you're pure, you're fresh.

You turn the heads of all the lads
As you walk down the street —
For a smile like yours never grows on trees
So gie them all a treat.

Your sparkling eyes would shame the skies
On a cold clear winter's night,
And you'd turn the head o' any man
Be he red or black or white.

Now the thing that bothers me the most
Is the sadness in your eyes,
You should not think about the past
Forget the who's and whys.

Enjoy yourself, you're only young –
Leave memories alane:
Put on your bonnie party dress
Take my hand – we'll both gang hame. (CM)

Opposite:
Charlotte Munro, Kingskettle,
1998. (TN)

My poem, 'The Dream', came to me in minutes. I was in the kitchen talking to my husband about the garden, when this poem started coming and I wrote the whole thing down whilst I was still talking. I said to David, 'Listen to what I've just been writing.' And he said, 'You just did that? Whilst talking to me?' I test all my things out on him. He tells me whether he likes them – but I know when I've got a thing right. With songs, it's always the tune that leads me to compose and afterwards it's always the tune that brings the words back to my mind. I never forget a song I make. But with my poetry, it's pure inspiration and the spur of the moment, so sometimes I might forget a poem, and I usually write them down. 'The Dream' is one of my best poems:

We are the messengers of life,
          The passing strangers in the night.
In flights of fancy we may seem
          A yellow road of sheer delight.

We set the rhythm and the tone,
          The mind to stretch in many ways.
We touch the soul, the heart, the bone,
          We are the master and the slaves.

We are the guts o' life's machine,
          The passion of forgotten times.
We are the blankets or the ice,
          We are names on a parchment signed.

We are the aches, the hurt, the blight,
> *We are the angel or the freaks:*
We can delay the planned awake —
> *Then take great care before we speak.*

We are the keepers of each thought.
> *To each his own in deepest sleep.*
This strong desire to dream alone
> *Does help the Lord one's soul to keep.* (CM)

I lived in the New Town of Glenrothes for many years and I worked in Eastwood's chicken factory. I helped work out all the bonus schemes for collecting the eggs. The trouble was that some people would collect thousands and thousands of eggs and others would collect next to none. I enjoyed the work. We used to push the trolleys along with our stomachs, stacking the eggs in those square, dimpled trays, 36 by 36. I used to sing and make up songs as I went down the battery and it was the cure if the hens got over-excited! I used to say, 'Now, listen to this, you birds,' and I'd start to sing, maybe one of my folksongs:

I climbed a mountain
And I wandered to the top:
I fished a river
But I did not catch a lot.

I saw my true love
And he passed by:
And I wish, I wish,
How I wish I could die.

I walked a long road,
A road that had no end.
I searched the byways
Looking for a friend.

I saw a fountain
And dark turned into dawn:
I asked three wishes,
Then in I threw my coin.

I saw my true love
As he passed by:
And I wish, I wish,
How I wish that I could die. (CM)

I'd sing that and the hens would all go quiet. They'd start clucking away, and purring, purring away, and laying more and more eggs!

My son, Hugh, went to university. He's now general manager of one of the big electronic firms in Glenrothes. He's done very well in business and, like me, he writes songs. He plays bass guitar and he sings. I used to write funky rock songs for the band and I didn't find it difficult. After they broke up I started writing a musical for the stage. It's called 'Fine Men Are We'. It tells the story of a soldier away at the war, who comes back to marry his bride. The father owns a tweed mill and his two sons are fighting over the same girl. It's the old story of the good brother and the bad brother. Whilst one is 'lost in action', the other steals his poems to make up to the girl. I have my own tunes for every song. One is called 'Brotherly Love':

CHORUS:
We were born to love and care,
Fine men are we,
But we chose to fight and swear.
Fine men are we.
What gift this be — fine men are we.

Tae gad aboot wae shrugg-ed shoulders,
Tae perish fae the thochts that goad to us,
Tae wish that things could be the t'other.
What gift this be — tae love one's brother.

Tae speak oor minds, tae be forthcoming
Tae shout and scream, then end up running,
Nae seasoned thoughts, just tongues o' thunder.
What gift this be — tae love one's brother.

CHORUS:

Tae cherish a' the best o' living,
Tae be benevolent and giving,
But it is sair to split asunder.
What gift this be — tae love one's brother.

Tae whisper words that hae nae meaning,
Tae suffer frae the guilt we're feeling,
Better be gone, than beset each other.
What gift this be – tae love one's brother. (CM)

At the end of the musical, the lost brother comes home and everything turns out well. As the bride gets ready for her wedding, she sings this song, 'Tomorrow':

Tomorrow is Friday, tomorrow is my day,
The best day of the week.
Tomorrow's a good day, tomorrow I should say,
The best day of all time.
Everything's just fine,
I'm going to make you mine.

I've waited so long for this day to arrive
I feel like I'm walking on air.
I'm so glad that I'm living I feel so alive.
I hope that the weather stays fair.
My doubts have all vanished,
My thoughts are all clean,
And I'm just the prettiest girl you've ever seen,
Tomorrow is my day, you know what I mean,
It's Friday, tomorrow is Friday, tomorrow is my day,
The best day of the week.
Tomorrow's a good day, tomorrow I should say,
The best day of all time.
Everything's just fine,
I'm going to make you mine.

My mother and father are in such a state;
Why, they can't relax for a second.
My sister and brother well they think it's great,
To this wedding they've both been invited.
But sad I do feel for myself in a way,
For I will be single for just one more day;
But I cannot wait to hear my lover say,
Its Friday, tomorrow's a Friday, tomorrow is my day,

The best day of the week.
Tomorrow's a big day, tomorrow I should say,
The best day of all time.
Everything's just fine,
I'm going to make you mine... (CM)

There's a full orchestra playing, the whole stage is filled with spotlit dancers, the confetti is being thrown and wild rice. The audience is joining in the chorus... I can see it all in my mind's eye. I'm just waiting for it to happen.

John MacAskill

BLACKPOINT, GRIMSAY, NORTH UIST

Robert Burns chose Gaelic tunes for more than a third of all the songs he wrote but Burns was not popular in the Islands. Myself, I've always admired Burns. He speaks for the common man. If he had failings, they were failings inside each one of us. I wrote a poem which honours his genius and ponders the reasons why so many have raised stones against him. I call it 'Robert Burns – Poet of Scotland':

Opposite:
The bard John MacAskill,
North Uist, 1997. (TN)

ROBERT BURNS, POET OF SCOTLAND

I stand in the house of the poet of Scotland,
Silent thoughts rising at the thought of his birth.
There can be no better place for composing a poem
To honour the bard than here, where he first opened
His eyes and took his first step:
It's his inspiration and spirit I seek strongly now –
Warm was his heart and deep were his depths.

I write not to put a stain on the character of Burns
(As though I was never a prey to temptation!)
But to conjure the man who was a man among men,
On whom destiny shone and from whom poetry flowed.
Where is the man who lives just as he ought,
I ask, where is the man who never sought girls?
We are all, but more feebly, like the great Rabbie Burns.

From whom beauty of soul welled forth like a spring.
The man's mind was enquiring, with hardly a flaw,
And matchless he put his passion in words –
The loveliest words that live in our language.
Though his legacy were to be no more than those verses
Sung the world over to start the New Year –
He would never be forgotten.

Those simple words are immortal,
Wrought in fire of love:
They bring to our memory all who have gone,
Drawing tears and remembrance to all who live on.

Poet you were of what it is to be human,
Poet you were of the unobscured truth;
You understood nature like no man neath the sun.
Would you had known how high we regard you –
Your words and your music precious beyond flesh:
To the world you gave genius of heart, mind and soul:
We hold what you gave us before death and the grave. (TN / Mac)

RAIBEART BURNS, BÀRD NA H-ALBANN

An taigh san do rugadh bàrd na h-Albann,
smuaineach balbh a' dol air ghleus –
chan fhiosrach mi air àit' a b'fheàrr leam
airson dàn dhuibh chur ra chèil',
far an do dh'fhosgail e a shùilean,
far an do dh'ionnsaich e chiad cheum –
a spiorad bhios mi sireadh làidir
nuas o mhullach blàth gu stèidh.

Chan ann chur smal air mar a ghluais e,
mar nach deach mo bhuaireadh riamh,
is fios agam nach eil mi ionraic
ann an smaointean no an gnìomh;
chaidh òrdachadh a bhith na bhàrd e
's fhuair e tàlantan da rèir,
ach mar dhuin', air leth o thiodhlac,
ana-miannach mar sinn fèin.

Cò am fear tha mar bu chòir dha,
's duilleach òig' air tighinn fo bhlàth,
nach robh 'g iarraidh measg nan nìonag
cheart cho cinnteach ris a' bhàrd?
Ailleachd anam' mach a' brùchdadh,
inntinn sgrùdach, 's i gun mheang,
'n àm bhith cur a ghaoil am briathran,
an dòigh as brèagha tha sa chainnt.

Ged nach fàgadh e de dhìleab
ach na rainn a thèid a sheinn
aig deireadh cuirm is toiseach bliadhna,
cha bhiodh dìochuimhn' air a chaoidh:
faclan sìmplidh 's iad neo-bhàsmhor,
teine gràidh gan ceangal suas,
toirt nar cuimhne na th' air triall bhuainn,
tarrainn dheur gu iomadh gruaidh.

The bard's house at Blackpoint,
Grimsay, North Uist. (TN)

Cliar na cneasdachd b'e da-rìribh,
nach do chuir air fìrinn sgòd,
meud a thuigse 's maise nàdair
dèanamh chàich nas slàine beò;
fhathast labhairt bhriathran prìseil
ged nach eil e leinn san fheòil,
sìor phàirteachadh a chridh' is inntinn
nuair a shìneas e fon fhòid. (JM)

I was brought up a native Gaelic speaker and, since I was a boy, I've composed poems, always in my head. I'm not a singer, I don't even sing in church, and I never write a poem down until I've finished it. Many I've never written down and some I've forgotten. I might be anywhere. I worked on the alginate for 25 years and sometimes when I was at work on the seaweed, a poem would start coming, and maybe for weeks I'd chip away at it, letting it run fore and back in my mind. Sometimes I'd wake at three in the morning with lines going round in my head. And, although I know people who lose their dreams before morning, I don't think I've ever lost a poem like that. I was inspired to write one of my best poems whilst walking on Ben Lee, the mountain that lies to the south of Lochmaddy. It's a poem about nature, about the visible and the invisible, about the world being made out of things man cannot see. It's about geological time and the idea of there being a beginning even before the rocks were laid down. We have rocks here on Uist more than three thousand million years old. Rocks that were once huge pockets of gas – rocks hard as granite, which once were smoke. The poem is called 'Ben Lee':

BEN LEE

Truly it is a wonderful thing to stand on Ben Lee
In the warm sun. Worries, I cast them in prison!
Unbound on a mountain with untroubled mind
I breathe the sweet air coming up from the ocean,
Wave-salted, the heather sways lovely around me,
Solitary, tranquil, at peace in the glen.

Thirsty – I know, I'll find a drink to drink here,
A soft wind will gather water from clouds
And the mountain channel a clear stream before me:
Here thirst and death will be ushered away,
Neither I nor my kinsmen will fear drowning or flood
And round us in plenty the food will be free.

Listen — I hear, the birds sing their chorus,
For they too are happy and faultless their music
Cascades from each wing. No judge
Among the thousands who've listened intensely
Has ever found fault with the song that the skylark
Sings out in the morning to welcome the sun.

Mystery — inexplicable in the hard grey rocks:
the age of the universe is in them, say the wise
But imperfect the guess of all who have tried!
They feel the need for a beginning to age
And The Beginning is lost to them. They seek
Appearances alone — these men of the Lowland mind.

The Earth — and all that is in it is as the dew,
The dew that is there in every form that is:
The same dew that dissolves in the light or grows hard
As ice to the hand. Throughout eternity things have
Disappeared but nothing has gone back to nothing:
The eye sees not the substance of the thing itself.

What we see is what is temporal. What we cannot see
Is permanent — for it is not things that are seen
That make up the things that are seen — atom and galaxy —
And the real proof of the thing that cannot be seen
Is the essence of the great hope for Hope: for hope
That can be seen by man — is no longer Hope at all. (TN/Mac)

SAORSA AGUS DIAMHAIREACHD BEINN LI

Gur cinnteach is nì prìseil e
Bhith 'n Lì an seo sa ghrèin;
Uallaich, chuir mi 'm prìosan iad,
Inntinn fallainn, rèidh;
Slàinte thar a' chuain a' tighinn
Air bàrr gach stuaigh tha leum,
Maise 'n fhraoich mun cuairt orm
'S an gleannan uaigneach sèimh.

Gheibh mi deoch an seo ri òl,
Treòraichidh gach gaoth
Uisge shùghadh do na neòil
Dhan lòn a tha ri m'thaobh;
Cha toir tart dhomh ann am bàs
'S cha bhàthar mi le tuil;
An asgaidh, faisg, am biadh as fheàrr
Son sàsachadh a' chuirp.

Cluinnidh mi na h-eòin a' seinn,
Tha aoibhneas orra fhèin,
Ceòl as foirfe ruigeas cluas
Tighinn thugam nuas thar sgèith;
Cha tàinig britheamh fhuair dad ceàrr,
Am britheamh b'fheàrr a dh'èisd,
An òran uiseig a' cur fàilt'
Air gathan blàth' na grèin.

Tha diamhaireachd nach d'fhuaradh
Sna creagan cruaidhe glas,
Aois a' chruinne-chè annta
Don duine 's léir toirt às;
Ged tha cuid bheir tuairmse dhuinn
Le beagan tuaileas Ghall,
Tha feum air toiseach dèanamh aois,
'S tha toiseach orr' air chall.

Talamh 's na bheil ann mar dhriùchd
A thèid 's gach caochladh cruth,
'S urrainn dhol à sealladh sùl
No làimhseachail a deigh;
Na chaidh à sealladh, cha deach sìon
Gu neoni riamh air n-ais,
'S gun ann an fhaid a chì an t-sùil
Ach susbaint rud nach faic.

'S e na chì sinn a tha aimsireil,
Tha an nì nach faic sinn buan,
'S chan e nithean tha rim faicinn
Nì nithean chithear suas;
Dearbh chinnt' an nì nach faicear
Brìgh an dòchais mhòir,
Oir dòchas leinn a chithear,
Cha dòchas e nas mò. (JM)

All my serious poems are in Gaelic but I write some light verse in English. My doctor in Lochmaddy is very interested in poetry. He likes to go sailing and one day when I was up there getting my heart tablets, he asked if I would write a poem about the blowing up of the rock at the mouth of Balmullagh Bay. He said he thought I should – so I wrote a few lines and I carried them about in my pocket for almost a year: then one day I remembered to give them to him, at the surgery. He liked the poem and he passed it round. It gets the facts down in a humorous way. It's called 'Major Crow of the Rock':

At the entrance to Balmullagh Bay
Stood a navigation hazard –
Which no mortal man since time began
Till recently had tackled.

The year was nineteen ninety-two,
The month it was October,
The twenty-seventh was the date –
The man a British soldier.

Some mighty atoms were let loose,
The rock became a chasm –
Now mariners who take this route
Have got an extra fathom.

So into Balmullagh – whenever you go
Raise up your hand and bless Major Crowe! (JM)

There are two kinds of poetry, two forms, you might say: those which are inspired and personal, like 'Ben Lee', and those which are written to order. The latter do not usually have the depth and the feeling that the former have, or should have. I write them down and give them away; it's like lending books –

you're lucky to get them back or hear of them again! I've another which falls somewhere between those two stools. South-east of Lochmaddy harbour, two large rocks called Am Madadh Mor and Am Madadh Gruamach stick up out of the sea. Everybody in Uist knows them and I wrote a poem to them called 'The Madadhs':

> *O, Madadhs, I have often wondered*
> *How you got your Gaelic name:*
> *Many eyes have since beheld you –*
> *But your name remains the same.*
>
> *Were you always standing lonely?*
> *Were you once a part of Lee?*
> *Are your bodies grinding slowly,*
> *Pounded by the raging sea?*
>
> *Awe-inspiring in the winter,*
> *When the seas are raging high;*
> *Beautiful in peaceful slumber,*
> *When the summer days draw nigh.*
>
> *Every time I sail beside you,*
> *I start thinking of the past*
> *But for now here's to the future –*
> *May your name and beauty last.* (TN/Mac)

By tradition our MacAskills were oarsmen on the longships of the MacLeod chiefs. There have been many strong men in our family. The giant MacAskill came from Bernera but how closely I am related to him I don't know. My great-grandfather was Alasdair MacPherson. He was said to be the strongest man in Uist in his time. One day a herring boat came into Lochmaddy from Harris with a man of enormous strength aboard and he started lifting the herring barrels into the waiting carts by himself. Now those barrels weigh over 400 pounds – and they're very difficult to get a hold of. The skipper shouted out, 'There's not a man in Uist can lift barrels like that!' and he ordered his man to leave a barrel on the quayside.

   Well, from the crowd that had gathered, the word went out for MacPherson. He was having a dram up in the bar. At first he wouldn't go, but he was persuaded to go. He had another dram and he walked down to the pier with the barman, his mates and the children behind. When he got to the quay,

The young Johnny MacAskill at play,
1930's. His mother is pouring
the tea. (JM)

The bard's wife, Morag MacAskill, 1998. (TN)

MacPherson shouted across to the skipper from Harris, 'If anything happens to the barrel, who pays?' And the skipper said, 'I'll pay! Now get on with it!' And Alasdair MacPherson, Alasdair Mòr, bent down, picked up the barrel and flung it right over the cart! It exploded – shooting out herring like rats from a cage. Alasdair MacPherson's daughter was my mother's mother, so there's strength on both sides of the family. I heard that story straight from the mouth of a woman who lived to be one hundred and three, Sheila Nicolson. She knew my great-grandfather very well and she had many other tales of that man's strength.

I was born in 1925. We learned a lot of poetry at school: Sir Walter Scott, 'The Lady of the Lake', that sort of thing. I left at fourteen in 1939 but my father, he left school at ten. I don't write many poems but I've always made poems and I often think, 'How easy this is – everybody must be able to do this!' But then I think, 'Those who sing think it's easy to sing – and I can't sing a note. I love to hear the psalms – but if the whole congregation here was like me, there'd be silence!' My voice is a one-off – like Dolly the sheep's!

I did four years in the army from 1944 to the end of 1947. I was in India and Singapore but I had an easy war, not like many round here. The Bomb had been dropped and that saved us another two years of fighting. Then I worked on the Hydro schemes. Then at the alginate. I retired after my second heart attack and I've recovered. I walk every day, and I've done a fair bit of travelling. My son, Iain, used to work for British Airways and got free tickets. I was in Moscow, in Germany, Italy, France, Holland, Iceland and Ireland. He lived a very gay life, though it's better I should say 'a very happy life' – parties and all that. Then he became dissatisfied and he came home to become a minister. He married a Catholic girl from South Uist. She joined the Free Church and now he's a minister in South Uist. I'm an adherent of the Free Church but I'm not a member.

We have no croft, just the house. I have a small boat to take me out in the summer. It's very quiet here now, but Grimsay, when I was young, was bustling. We had boatbuilders, tailors, cobblers, weavers, shops – but about real quiet you should ask my wife, Morag, Morag MacKinnon. She was born on the island of Rona, which lies just a few hundred yards off the east side of Grimsay, her father was shepherd over there. They were the last family to come off the island. She used to skin otters with her father, she used to come to school by rowing boat. She has more stories of the old ways than I have – but all the old people here have stories.

People used to go out to the island of Haisgeir for the great seal hunts. Seal flesh was once commonly eaten on Uist. I remember hearing how, one harvest time, some young visitors from the mainland sat down to eat and a crofter's wife brought a huge piece of meat on a large ashet and one of the young

North Uist. (TN)

men said, 'By Jove, they're fine big wedders you breed here'. And her uncle replied in Gaelic, 'They should be big considering the miles of fine pasture we've got between here and St Kilda!' and all the visitors tucked into seal they thought was best lamb! But seal meat can be good. The tinkers used to eat any number of seals. They were free. And everybody used to eat sheep heads. When the old people were ill, that's one of the things they liked to eat. A sheep's head, when boiled up, is so beautiful and white and, when they were brought to the table, the women would always have them decorated. There was no worry about scrapie or BSE then. It was mutton just as much as lamb we ate.

Most people kept cows and I always liked cows. It was a lovely thing to hear the women calling in the cows. They would go out at much the same time and you would hear all the different voices with all their different calls, calling cattle for milking. And if you stood you'd see them coming in. They'd be down on the shore or out on a promontory and, when they heard the call they knew, you'd see them raise their heads and start coming in. And some would trot, so pleased they'd be to be milked or get a little treat from the pail.

Over on the west side, on the machair, they had a herd, a man with a great handlebar moustache like General Kitchener. He was an old soldier come home from the wars and each morning he'd take the cows out with the dawn. At about ten the women would go down to the *cuidhe* and the whole township would gather at the pen. The *cuidhe* was like a large sheep fank, but the wall was only about three feet high and there was a wide entrance. You still see plenty of sheep fanks but all the *cuidheachan* seem to have gone. In the old days, that was *the* place for meeting and talking. And, going down, many of the women would be taking the calves to their mothers. At first they'd be frisking or pulling back but when they saw their mothers they'd take off! With the women and the children fleeing behind them! Straw halters we had and at a distance you'd think the women were men with great hounds straining at the leash! Thinking of it reminds me of John Keats's 'heifer lowing at the skies and all her silken flanks with garlands dressed'.

Inside the *cuidhe* the calves would have their fill and then the cattle would be milked and afterwards the women would take the milk home for setting, for crowdie, for butter and cream. The children would play and the women would talk and wander home. Cross-Highlands they were mostly, with lovely natures and they gave plenty of milk. At about twelve o'clock they would be let back out of the *cuidhe* and meander slowly out onto the machair to graze, sometimes with the old man and sometimes with the boys, if they were home from school.

Except for the herd and the children, it was women who looked after the cattle, it would have been shame on a man doing the milking. Out at Claddach Kirkibost, the herd was Ruairidh Nicolson and each day he would have his breakfast in a different house because he didn't get a wage. Everybody took it in turns to feed him. He was the son of Sheila Nicolson. She was blind but she remembered back to the time of Napoleon and she lived to be 103. I remember those days - the flowers in May and June, the smoke coming up through the thatch, the children playing, the old men talking into the evening, the women singing.

I remember an old woman telling me about an old *bodach*, an old man called Gillespie. She said he was the ugliest man in Uist but when she was a girl she loved him. When she was about three she used to toddle after him everywhere he went. Huge big ears he had, full of dark pitted holes, and very, very hairy. She used to think him the kindest man in the world. She used to go down to see him at breakfast time. He'd be there, sat at his chair with another chair in front of him and on it there'd be a boiled egg and a scone. He always wore braces over his shoulders and a striped shirt with no collar. And he had a song he'd sing for her, each day after breakfast.

And there was a *cailleach*, that's an old woman, down at Claddach Kyles, in the days when there was no Poorhouse. She couldn't walk, so she was carried round on a stretcher. She couldn't look after herself so it was agreed in the village that the last crofter in with his harvest had to take the *cailleach* through the winter, harvest to harvest. Well, after that all the crofters worked night and day so as not to be last and have to take this poor soul on. But he that was last had to take her! And do you know this, there was one old man who was always last with his harvest! He was either very slow or very unfortunate or he liked to take her. He lived alone. And he looked after the old *cailleach* year after year; so she, who might have been a burden to some, must have been company for him. And she stayed with him till she died.

There's a story about the mother of the herd, the old woman who lived to be 103. She lived with her daughter and she spent the last 20 years of her life in a box bed. The two of them slept in the same bed and the daughter nursed her. And that daughter kept her mother so clean – for 20 years she lay in that box bed and not a single sore did she take. The bedcover was red, a woven red blanket. And there was something special about that old *cailleach* because, although she was bedridden and blind, she always knew the state of the tide. For 80 years she'd followed the tides – the men would be fishing, the sheep would be grazing by the shore, she herself would be after the spout fish at the low tides – and all this must have locked in her brain; so until the day of her death, that woman always knew the state of the tide.

Some people call the new moon the new light and Sheila Nicolson knew all the phases of the moon; she'd tell the children to look out for it as she lay in her bed enjoying their visits. And so she lay for 20 years until, one day, her daughter woke to find her mother cold beside her and she ran across the grass to the next house. It was a beautiful morning in June. There were no locked doors to houses in those days, so she went straight in calling out, 'Mother is cold and she will not wake up!' Now the name of this daughter was Kate and, it's a strange thing, although she was an old woman herself, she must have been 80 and people looked very old in those days, she seemed not to know what death was. She had never married; mother and daughter were like the dearest of sisters to each other. They had lived so quietly, so happily and so long together that the idea of death seemed beyond her. So death came as a surprise at the age of 103!

It was normal and necessary for every family to provide its own 'social work' in those days. It was just part of what everybody's life was, but many people here would not see a doctor through the whole of their lives. I heard about an operation carried out one Saturday night by old Dr MacKenzie. It was an appendectomy and the man's name was Donald. The operation was carried out in his house, on a table, with just the instruments the doctor carried in his bag. There were no proper roads in those days, the doctor came in by horse and he went back by horse – to Scolpaig. And when he left he asked a neighbour to keep watch on the patient and to be sure to ride over and report to him as soon as the man passed wind. That would be the sign things were getting back to normal and no further visit necessary.

All night the man sat by his friend waiting, and at last with the morning came the wind. Now it was the Sabbath but, of course, in an emergency journeys must be undertaken, so this man saddled his horse and rode at full speed to Scolpaig, just as everybody else was setting off for church.

And each party that saw him flying towards them knew something was wrong. So, one by one, they waved him down and asked, 'Can we help?', 'What's the matter?' Well, he couldn't tell a lie! So bending low in the saddle, still riding at speed, he would shout, 'Donald has farted! I ride at full speed to Scolpaig to tell Dr MacKenzie that Donald has farted!' All his life he declared, 'That was the most embarrassing thing that ever happened to me.' But we used to say, 'We know you enjoyed it!' We have a saying here, 'After a storm the wind comes from the south,' meaning that after a wounding comes healing and balm. Well, that's how it was for Donald and he was soon right as rain! That's the kind of medicine that was practised here till well after the war.

The crofters with good land on the machair didn't go away to the fishing like those on the poor ground on the east of Uist. They could spend the whole year at home. They would work hard but it was always in their own time at their own pace. They'd be bringing in seaweed, harvesting, building, dyking, thatching, out with the animals. There was time for everything. Some would go for lobsters out to Heisker; fish would be eaten, lobsters put aside to be sold. Each season had its different work. All the corn was cut by hand but each house had many hands in those days. It was sickle and scythe and everybody cut their own harvest. No stacking was done until everybody had their whole crop cut and bound and stooked ready for drying. So the first would be there to give a hand to the last. Most families would have ten or twelve stacks. It was a healthy life and, although the thirties were hard times, I look back with nothing but pleasure on the days of my boyhood.

The bard Johnny MacAskill, North Uist, 1997. (TN)

All the threshing was done by hand and the wind. There was a big barn where they winnowed the seed and the chaff would be blown out the door. They would choose their day. Some would strike corn against their harrows, they stood clear of the ground on spikes and made a convenient thresher. Oats and barley and rye were for the people but also for the cattle and horses. Most of the crofts had two horses. They did all the ploughing in my day, they carried the peats and the seaweed. It was corn, not hay, that fed the animals through the winter.

The Uist people were very proud of their horses. Up until the First World War there were races on the sand and on the machair. Up until the Second War the big horse markets continued every year. There was wrestling on horseback. That was a favourite exercise of the Lovat Scouts. The men, bare-torsoed, would grapple, circling round and round, till one fell. Many men went away with the Lovat Scots in both world wars. One of them came back to South Uist last year after more than 50 years away. His name was Angus MacPhee and he was from Iochdar. It's a beautiful story. We saw a man talking about him on the television.

Two sculptured weavings by Angus
MacPhee draped in the undergrowth of
Craig Dunain Hospital, Inverness,
1996. (TN)

From Iochdar, you look west to St Kilda and east across Uist to the Cuillin mountains on Skye. It's good crofting land with green machair, white sand and good fishing; better than here. Angus MacPhee was a Catholic. He grew up a big, handsome young man; he swam, he played the bagpipes and we hear he had a lovely singing voice. When he was seven his mother died. He left school at thirteen to work on the croft with his father. He loved horses. Like most of the boys, he joined the Territorial Army and on 3rd September 1939, he rode out on his father's horse, to join the Lovat Scouts at Beauly Castle. The horse was bought by Lord Lovat for £70 and, coming in as a horseman, he got five shillings a day extra pay.

After training in Scotland, he was sent across to Canada and then on to the Faroe Islands. But in 1941, Angus became mentally ill. He was brought back to Scotland, first to Larbert Asylum and then home to Iochdar. He was very confused and extremely difficult. He didn't look after himself. His animals were dying of neglect. His people couldn't look after him, couldn't handle him, so in 1946 he was put in a straitjacket and taken to Craig Dunain at Inverness. And there he remained for 50 years, till he recovered and he was brought back by aeroplane, all those years after he set out on his horse. He came back to Uist House, the Old People's Home at Daliburgh, and he died there: aged 82. Now that might seem a sad story but the wonderful thing is this: in Inverness he became an artist and his last year was a time of contentment for him.

Angus MacPhee was an unusual artist. What happened was this, at Craig Dunain, Angus was set to work on the asylum farm but he was always wandering off up into the woods, and he was allowed to do this. And there in the wood he made ropes and clothes and boots and shoes and harness and reins for horses, out of grass! He made them out of hay, wool, twigs and leaves, anything he could find. And this kept him quiet. He was so strong he could be dangerous. He was a schizophrenic but, working at his ropes, he became meek as a lamb and the staff let him get on with it. He used to hang what he made up on trees and in hedges and stack them under the rhododendron bushes. Over the months and the years they rotted away into compost.

He had this compulsion to be useful, to earn his keep. He had a dedicated sense of service. He must have remembered how his father had made ropes of grass and heather, how he'd helped his sisters carding wool, how they'd made horse-bridals and collars out of marram – so, in his madness, he made length after length of string and rope. Then he would weave these ropes into hats and cloaks and leggings, knapsacks, holdalls, and strange things that look like giant horns. He made needles out of wire and knitted vests from the wool he collected from the thorn hedges. He made trousers out of beech leaves and tobacco pouches out of birch and great sea-boots out of hay. He lived in a world of his own but it was also a world like the past, like the old days Màiri Mhòr wrote about in her song:

> When Martinmas came
> And the livestock and crops were all put away,
> The men would be making their ropes of heather
> And the rush-bags stacked in a heap
> By the clamp built high for potatoes,
> And the barrel would be full of salt-meat:
> That's how things were for us,
> Growing up on the Island of the Mist.

And Angus never stopped making these things. At last his illness burned itself out and he came home to be looked after amongst his own people. He was blind when he came back but how pleased he was, you can imagine. Care in the Community proved good to Angus MacPhee.

Angus MacPhee of Iochdar,
South Uist, after his return from
Craig Dunain Hospital in 1996.
(TN)

It was a woman called Joyce Laing, an art therapist, who discovered him. On the television he was called 'A Hero of our Time'. They said he was like that Iceman they found up in the Alps, carrying everything he needed with him when a sudden snowstorm took him by surprise and he froze to death. Angus loved horses and there in the wood he set out bridles, collars, halters, reins, harnesses, nose-bags and hunting horns. They were like offerings. He would put feathers round his bonnet and stride through the trees broadcasting seed to the right and to the left. And in time he was healed and he came back to Uist and he had Gaelic all round him again. And till the day he died, he would walk very straight, like a soldier. After 50 years of silence, they say, he even began to talk again. He regained his pride, then he died.

When I heard the story of Angus MacPhee, it's a very strange thing, but a lullaby came into my mind. Its called 'Blue Donald's Lullaby" and it used to be sung by Mrs Archie MacDonald, up in South Uist. She's dead these many years. It's a lovely song and it's very old.

The sun rising
And it without a spot on it,
Nor on the stars.
When the son of my King
Comes fully armed,
The strength of the universe with you,
The strength of the sun
And the strength of the bull
That leaps highest.

That woman asked
Another woman,
What ship is that
Close to the shoreline?
It's Donald's ship,
Three masts of willow on it,
A rudder of gold on it,
A well of wine in it,
A well of pure water in it. (Trad. trans. HH)

Two Bards from Skye

CALUM RUADH AND THE SKIPPER

The names of three poets stand out across the last three centuries of Gaelic history, Duncan Ban Macintyre from Argyll, Màiri Mhòr nan Oran from Skye and Sorley MacLean from Raasay. Each represents the genius and historical character of their times. Of these three only Màiri Mhòr nan Oran might be described as a 'village bard' of the kind presented in this book, but Duncan Ban Macintyre is part of the same tradition and one defining characteristic of the great modernist MacLean was his adherence to the Gaelic continuum of which he was part. MacLean has become one of the recognised 'art poets' of 20th-century Europe but he also remained a deeply 'local' poet, fascinated by the landscape, the history, the folklore, the language into which he was born. These things are keys to the originality of his world view and the strange beauty of his verse. In future years MacLean will be seen to stand as a fulcrum to the long history of Gaelic literature, and appropriately so because the Isles of Skye and Raasay lie geographically and culturally at the heart of the Scottish Gaidhealtachd.

> *... great beautiful bird of Scotland,*
> *your supremely beautiful wings bent*
> *about many-brooked Bracadale,*
> *your beautiful wings prostrate on the sea*
> *from the Wild Stallion to the Aird of Sleat,*
> *your joyous wings spread*
> *about Loch Snizort and the world ...*

Opposite:
The poet Sorley MacLean looking towards Skye from his birthplace at Ostaig, Isle of Raasay. (TN, 1982)

Great Island, Island of my desire,
Island of my heart and wound,
it is not likely that the strife
and suffering of Braes will be seen requited
and it is not certain that the debts
of the Glendale Martyr will be seen made good;
there is no hope of your townships
rising high with gladness and laughter,
and your men are not expected
when America and France take them.

Pity the eye that sees on the ocean
the great dead bird of Scotland.

… eòin mhóir sgiamhaich na h-Albann,
do sgiathan àlainn air an lùbadh
mu Loch Bhràcadail ioma-chùilteach,
do sgiathan bòidheach ri muir sleuchdte
bho'n Eist Fhiadhaich gu Aird Shléite,
do sgiathan aoibhneach air an sgaoileadh
mu Loch Shnigheasort 's mu'n t-saoghal …

Eilein Mhóir, Eilein mo dheòin,
Eilein mo chridhe is mo leòin,
chan eil dùil gum faicear pàighte
strì is allaban a' Bhràighe,
is chan eil cinnt gum faicear fiachan
Martarach Ghleann-Dail 's iad dìolte;
chan eil dòchas ri do bhailtean
éirigh àrd le gàire 's aiteas,
's chan eil fiughair ri do dhaoine
's Ameireaga 's an Fhraing 'gam faotainn.

Mairg an t-sùil a chì air fairge
ian mór marbh na h-Albann.

from 'An t-Eilean' ('The Island') (with the permission of Carcanet Press)

Bards have always played a consciously integrated role in the culture of Gaelic society. They have been servants of chiefs, guardians of the name, the honour, and values of the clan, chroniclers and remembrancers. But they have also been idiosyncratic servants of 'the voice of truth'. They have had an oracular function and this has sometimes forced them into the role of 'outsider'. Some have suffered the kind of opprobrium flung at Court Fools and certain bards have taken pleasure in their reputations as 'black sheep', as rebels, as those who, in MacLean's words, seek 'to say the unsayable'. This has been true in the home, at school, within the community and away on military service. Bards have never been strangers to exile and it is noticeable how many bards remained privates, able-bodied seamen, ground aircrew: they tend not to join the establishment, they rarely become officers. 'Calum Ruadh', 'Red-haired Calum', Calum Nicolson of Braes, was just such a bard.

A distant relation of Sorley MacLean, Calum Nicolson was a natural rebel. Calum Ruadh did war service in the RAF, but when he returned to run his small croft at Camustianavaig, the nature of his bardachd ensured him a private rather than a public life. He revelled in satire, he had a quick sense of humour, he liked company, he enjoyed an audience, but too rarely found one. He liked to over-emphasise his under-achievement at school. On the croft he laboured as he felt necessary, not to show his neighbours what a hard worker he was. He had a keen sense of social justice. His bardachd was conservative in style but almost always contemporary in subject matter. One of his brothers was killed in the First World War, another was the first British soldier killed in Malaya during the Communist Emergency. By aptitude, choice and experience Calum seems to have been a 'throwback' to earlier times when life, poetry, relationships and tragedies were heroic or elementally simple. At the end of the Second World War he wrote a powerful song about 'The Nuremberg Trials':

THE NUREMBERG TRIALS

A Sword of Justice was brought into Nuremberg Hall
To cut out bad flesh that had caused murder and war
To spread its curse like a gangrene across
Every door sheltering a family in Europe.
A trial is no more than the best form of justice
But I shall be shocked if the men accused live —
They know what they did — just think of the children:
Justice and peace must be theirs for a lifetime.

Words cannot describe the crimes committed,
The lustful desire to conquer all Europe,
Treacherous deception and great nations invaded,
Death Camps established and the land laid waste.
Only the ocean saved the Kingdom of Britain,
Only the Channel kept those curs from our shores —
Till sun-wise good fortune turned in our favour
And leathered and routed the brute brought to his knees.

When these savages heard the charges against them
They vauntingly smiled and, to their shame, boasted
Of their pride and their duty! Odious beasts,
They were found guilty and hanged by the neck.
And if you doubt for a moment the fate that they suffered,
Think of our gallants brought down in their blood,
Think of the merchant ships sunk when full-laden
And those seamen now deep in water so still. (TN/Mac)

The bard Calum Ruadh Nicolson,
Braes, Isle of Skye, 1962. (SSS)

ORAN NUREMBERG

Thàinig claidheamh ceartais
Chun na h-aitreibh san Roinn-Eòrp'
A th' ann am Baile Nuremberg,
A ghearradh às droch fheòil
A rinn am murt 's am mallachadh
'S a thug an doineann mhòr
Air na h-uile thìr is àite
'S air gach fàrdach san robh beò.

'S ann ormsa bhiodh an t-iongnadh
Nam faodadh iad bhith beò —
Bhiodh sin air clann nan daoine
San t-saoghal sa gu leòr;
An t-sìth a th' air a gealltainn dhuinn
A bha 's bhios ann ri ar beò —
Ged a dh'iathadh là mu làimh,
Gheibh an t-aingidh mar as còir.

Chan urrainn dòmhsa cainnt chur air,
Air naimhdean bha cho mòr
'S a rinn a h-uile call oirnn
'S a mheall air ioma dòigh:
Na rìoghachdan bha teann orra
Le foill a' tighinn nan còir
'S a' dèanamh àit dha champaidhean
'S e 'n geall air an Roinn-Eòrp'.

'S e shàbhail Rìoghachd Bhreatainn
Bhith na h-eilean anns a' chuan,
Is gur e Caolas Shasainn
Chum na madaidhean ud bhuainn;
'S an uair a fhuaradh deiseil,
Chaidh am bleadraigeadh 's an ruaig,
Is chuireadh air an glùinean iad
'S thug sin na brùidean suas.

Buchenwald Concentration camp,
1945. (IM)

Nuair thainig cùirt na breith aca,
Nach b' eagalach air sgròl
Mar bha na daoine ladarn' ud
A' dèanamh uaill à feòil;
Fhuaradh ciontach, gràineil iad
Mar bha iad an tìr nam beò;
Is ann mar sin a bha —
Chaidh 'n cur gu bàs le ròp.

O, saoilibh nach do choisinn iad
An crochadh mar a bha —
Nach ioma fiùran eireachdail
Chaidh leagadh sìos gu làr;
Nach lìonmhor bàta marsanta
Chaidh bhualadh às 's i làn,
Toirt leotha sìos nam maraichean
Gu calaidhean nach tràigh.

Rugadh agus thogadh sinn
Air machraichean 's air fonn,
Thus' à bail' no ionad
Agus mis' à Innis Ghall -
An ann gu feum no cinneachadh
A bha sinn idir ann,
No 'n ann gu sileadh faladh
Ann am machraichean na Fraing? (CN)

Right up till his death in 1978, Calum Ruadh Nicolson practised an archaic, oral style of bardic composition and his style of rendition was a controlled and dramatic chanting, his rhythmic melodies acting as a kind of foreplay that brought the words not so much into his mind as out of his mouth. His very pulsing, rythmic singing seems to have been crucial to his remembrance of the words. Is there a better way of retrieving many thousands of lines of poetry from one's memory bank? It seems unlikely, and the Danish scholar, Thorkild Knudsen, has suggested that Calum Ruadh is a key figure in the continuance of an ancient practice found amongst oral poets from Romania to Iceland.

Calum Ruadh wrote numerous songs which honoured local people and describe local events. Calum Ruadh's people, like Sorley MacLean's forbears, were directly involved in the famous resistance of the Braes crofters to eviction in the 1880's and 'The Battle of the Braes' is frequently referred to in his bardachd. His 'praise poems' are excellent modern examples of the ancient panegyric tradition. One of the best is his 'Song to Sir John William Nicolson':

SONG TO SIR JOHN WILLIAM NICOLSON

This year a great honour was bestowed
On the Isle of Skye of the Gaelic:
A crofter's son from Gead an t-Sailleir
Was made a Knight of Her Majesty the Queen.
John William Nicolson is the name of our hero,
As a boy he went to school here in Braes,
Now he has brought fame and bright history
Home to the land of high mountains.

Sir — you are a man of the pure blood
Of Clan Nicolson and it was from Sgoirebreac
You rose to become our noble champion.
You have known dread and the horror of war,
You were an officer in arms for King George
In the Great War against the Kaiser —
Though young in years, great was the reputation
You gained in the face of the enemy.

And also I sing of Clan MacLeod of Drumuie —
Proud kinsmen of your mother's people.
Were she alive, her pride would be great
In you — her noble, youngest son.
A great doctor you became in the city of London;
The Queen did her duty in honouring you —
And proudly we say, here in the mountains,
We know Johnny William — he's just one of us.

These Highlands are home to very brave men
And a strong arm was needed in a place such as this —
A spirit of resistance was necessary here
Or you'd be flung off the land like a stone!
Little your father would have thought for a moment
When he stood his ground and his right
At the Battle of Braes that his son
Would in time be honoured so greatly.

Now I must draw my song to a close —
May you enjoy good health and live long:
We know you love well the land of the mountains —
Know well that your kinsmen will welcome you home
To Ollach, your very own place here in Braes.
Things here will be once again as they were —
Before you went South — and your speech
Crystal-clear like the speech of your mother. (TN/Mac)

ORAN AN RIDIRE IAIN UILLEAM MHICNEACAIL

Chuireadh urram mhòr am bliadhn'
Air Eilean Sgiathanach na Gàidhlig:
Mac croiteir à Bràigh Ghead an t-Sailleir
Fear de Ridirean na bàn-righinn;
Iain Uilleam MacNeacail —
Siud an gaisgeach is an t-àrmann
Bha dol a Sgoil a' Bhràigh' na bhalach
'S thug an eachdraidh thìr nan àrd-bheann.

Tha thu dhen fhìor fhuil Chlann 'acNeacail —
'S ann à Sgoirebreac a bha sibh —
'S dhearbh thu sin, a churaidh uasail,
Anns na h-uabhasan a bha thu
Nad oifigeach 'n arm Rìgh Seòras,
Am a' Chogaidh Mhòir sna blàran,
'S fhuair thu cliù ann ged a b' òg thu
Ann an còmhrag ris an nàmhaid.

Gur e clann 'acLeòid Dhruim Aoidh,
B' iadsan muinntireas do mhàthar —
I bhith 'n làthair, 's i bhiodh pròiseil,
Mac a b' òige chaidh cho àrd riut;
Lighiche ann am baile Lunnainn
'S fhuair an t-urram on a' bhàn-righinn,
'S b' eòlach sinn air Seonaidh Uilleim —
Rugadh air an Talamh Ard e.

Talamh Ard nan daoine tapaidh —
Siud na balaich a bha làidir,
'S dh'fheumadh iad a dhol a shabaid
Air neò air an cur às an àite;
Aig am bualadh nam buillean,
Bha Somhairle Uilleim air an àireamh —
Bu bheag a dhùil am Blàr a' Chumhaing
Gum biodh an t-urram seo san àite.

Crìochnaichidh mi dhut m' òran —
Guma fada beò is slàn thu,
'S thu bhith tighinn air chuairt dhan Olach,
D' àite-còmhnaidh anns a' Bhràighe;
Chionn gur toigh leat tìr nam beanntan
'S gu bheil mòran ann dhe d' chàirdean,
Chan aithnicht' gu robh thu riamh air Galltachd —
Chan eil blas air cainnt do mhàthar. (CN)

Calum Ruadh also made humorous song-poems. One pokes fun at two of his lady neighbours. It is highly personal but never degenerates into superior 'contempt'; and the bard seems to recognise the 'teuchter' in himself, and us all, as he describes a Mrs Bean-like chapter of accidents. The song delights in the Chaplinesque confusion where two languages, long distances and modern machines collide. Well sung in Gaelic it can still reduce a Highland audience to tears of laughter. It's called 'The Song of the Donkey':

THE SONG OF THE DONKEY

I was born in Gead an t-Sailleir,
A little township here in Braes,
Beneath a handsome mountain,
Where youngsters learn brave ways.
But I'm sorry to say
There's few here today
Can match the men
Fought the Battles of Braes.

But as it happens,
It wasn't this battle
That wakened my thought to write verse,
But a story much worse and entirely true
Of how MacFarlane of Greenock
Sent a donkey by train
All the way up to Braes
And left everybody wondering why!

It all started with a couple of ladies
Or that's what we thought at the time!
One was called Annie
And one was called Mairi
And they wanted potatoes to grow,
It was Kerr's Pinks they ordered
But forgot to write 'pink'
And they posted their letter away.

When in Greenock the letter was opened
MacFarlane's two eyes gave a blink!
'It must be a chair they're wanting in Braes,
Let there not be a minute's delay!'
So the very same day
One was put on a train
To arrive like a throne in Portree
And the news sent to Braes right away.

So next morning these lassies,
For that's what they were,
Jumped out of their beds looking lively!
Of powerful physique, they trotted over the moor
To ask at the store for the spuds
They presumed would have come — not a chair!
'What a knave! What a dog!'
The two cried going spare!

A telegram was sent straight away to MacFarlane:
'Send as required. . .A.S.P.'
That's what they meant!
But what they actually sent
Was a telegram saying
'Send as required — an ASS . . .
We expect it to come by train straight away!
Action this day, not a minute's delay!'

And back by return
Came the thing they had ordered,
As big as a camel and wild as a lion
Hee-hawing and braying like a beast out of Hell!
Not with ropes but with hawsers
They tied the brute down —
And put sand in his ears
To waken the two ladies of Braes!

A second message was sent
And they came again for potatoes
But what they found in the store
Was nothing less than a monster!
'Glory be,' shouted Annie,
'It's the great Bunny of Satan!'
'Hold your tongue, silly billy!' said Mairi with glee,
'It's a pony will give us a carry!

'It's one of the breed Old Joseph had
When banished with all his relations
And we must take him home!'
So trotting they praised
Their prize to the skies —
'If he's not a cow, he's a stallion!
He'll carry the seaweed up from Portmore
And the peats from the Aird to be sure!'

And that's how the donkeys got started in Braes. (TN/Mac)

ORAN AN AISEIL

Rugadh mise ann an Gead an t-Sailleir,
Baile beag a tha sa Bhràighe
Is e fo shàilean na beinn bhòidhich —
'S ann a fhuaradh na h-àrmainn;
Ach 's e dh'fhàg an sgeula duilich
Nach eil duine 'n-diugh dhiubh 'n làthair
Dhe na seòid a thug na buillean
Anns a' chomhrag aig a' bhlàr ann.

Cha b' e siud a dhùisg mo rann-sa
Aig an àm seo mar a tha e
Ach ciamar a thàinig na h-aisel
Gu bhith fantainn anns a' Bhràighe:
Innsidh mise 'm beagan bhriathran
Mar as fìor is mar a bha e —
Monsgaid rinn MacPhàrlain Ghrianaig
Dh'fhàg na biastan ud san àite.

Bha dithis mhaighdeann sa bhaile,
Tè air an robh Anna agus Màiri —
Chuir iad fios air falbh a Ghrianaig
Is iad ag iarraidh buntàta;
Kerr's Pinks a bha iad ag iarraidh —
'S e bu lìonmhoire gu fàs dhaibh —
Is dh'fhàg iad Pink às anns an dìochuimhn'
As an litir chiallach chàirdeil.

Nuair a dh'fhosgladh an Grianaig an litir
'S a chunnacas am fios a bha innte,
"S e tha iad ag iarraidh ach chair
Anns a' Bhràighe,' ars MacPhàrlain;
'Cuiribh fear air falbh le rèile -
Na biodh mionaid fhèin a dhàil ann',
Is chuireadh gu cidhe Phort Rìgh e
Is chuir Port Rìgh fios chun a' Bhràighe.

Dh'fhalbh na gruagaichean air madainn
Foghainteach, sgairteil mar a bha iad,
Rachadh iad ri muir is monadh –
'S ann a' trotan a bha iad;
Nuair ràinig iad stòr a' bhaile
'S a chunnaic iad an rud a thàinig,
'Nach e an tràill e,' ars Anna;
'Madadh,' 's e thubhairt Màiri.

Chaidh teileagram air falbh an uair sin
Glè luath gu MacPhàrlain:
'Send as required,' 's e fhuair e;
Ass a sgrìobh Màiri.
Muinntir Ghrianaig rinn an lasgraich:
'Aiseal, 's e bh' ann,' thuirt àsan,
'Is cuiribh fear air falbh le rèile dhaibh –
Na biodh mionaid fhèin a dhàil ann.'

Tighinn a-mach ann am Port Rìgh dha,
Bha e pìobaireachd 's a' rànaich,
Is chuir iad a-staigh dhan an stòr e –
Cha b' e ròp a bh' air ach hawser!
E cho fiadhaich ri leòmhann
Is e cheart cho mòr ri càmhal,
Is bha iad a' cur gainmheach na chluasan
Gus an cluinntear shuas sa Bhràigh e.

Chaidh an darna fios a-rithist
Dh'ionnsaigh nìghneagan a' Bhràighe,
Is dh'fhalbh iad an dàrna h-uair
Dol a thoirt a-nuas a' bhuntàta;
Nuair a chaidh iad staigh don Stòr
Is sheallte 'm beathach mòr a thàinig,
Dh'èigh Anna, 'Thì na Glòire –
Coineanach mòr an t-Sàtain!'

'Cum do theanga, òinnsich -
'S e th' ann ach pònaidh,' arsa Màiri,
'Tè dhen bhriod a bh' aig Iòsaph
Nuair a dh'fhògradh e bho chàirdean;
Bheir sinn dhachaigh e, a bhrònag —
Mur e bò a th' ann, 's e àigeach —
Is bheir e 'm brùc far a' Phort Mhòir dhuinn
Is bheir e mhòine far an Aird dhuinn.' (CN)

Calum Ruadh died 20 years ago, but over on the west side of Skye, John Nicolson is still going strong at the age of 98. Known since boyhood as 'the Skipper', John is another man of independent character and lively humour. He lives at home with his wife Mary. His sons now run his farm. Like so many of the bards, he lives in splendid rural isolation, his house at Cuidreach stands alone above Loch Snizort looking south to the Cuillin mountains. He has recently achieved a certain fame and is now the subject of a major literary and biographical study by folklorist Dr Tom McKean. Iain MacNeacail is the archetypal Gaelic township bard.

'When did I start writing poems? When I was young. When I stopped school I started writing songs. I'm 97 now and I've forgot them all. Except the ones that others took. When I hear others sing them I remember them by ear again. Dr Tom McKean he came to see me and he's written a book about me. I sang my poems for him and they're all set out. The book is called *Hebridean Song-maker*. Everything's in there, or so they think! So you won't need much from me! But I'll give you 'Nach Bòidheach Uige – The Beauties of Uig':

THE BEAUTIES OF UIG

Uig is beautiful,
Fragrant and gay,
With its green woods so verdant
And its dewfall in May;
With its song birds so joyous —
They sing in a rapture,
Their music cascades
From high in the trees.

Glorious are the mountains
Encircled by sea —
They shelter each homestead
No matter where the wind blows
And sunshine brings warmth
In the bitterest weather,
Each plant here unfolds
To the kiss of the sun.

A beautiful green lights
Each bank and small hollow —
And lovely the daisies
Dance in the breeze.
Round the edge of each spring
Grow the green cresses
And tall stand the rushes
Where the clear water flows.

The shore-line is perfect
As the curve of a horse-shoe
And unceasing the ocean
Puts new beauties on it.
Many are the streams cut
Through the green hillocks
To meet in the valley
And run to the sea.

Proud rise the cliffs
Like a wall against water —
To fling back the challenge
Of the billowing waves.
With regards to wild nature
You'll not see its equal —
This place is the loveliest
Place in creation.

And the people who live here
Are kind and so tender —
And they show in their nature
Deep love for each other:
This song is no fable,
I tell you the truth —
The fame of this beauty lives
Long as the cattle graze here on the heath. (TN/Mac)

NACH BÒIDHEACH UIGE

Nach bòidheach Uige, gur e tha cùbhraidh,
le choille dhlùth-ghorm fo dhriùchd a' Chèitein,
le eòin cho sùrdail a' seinn gun tùchadh
's gach seòrsa ciùil ac' air bhàrr nan geugan.

Tha bheanntan àghmhor mun iadh an sàile
ri cumail sgàil' air gach àit' on séid gaoth;
tha fiamhan gràsail ri geamhradh geàrrt' ann,
gach lus a' fàs ann ri blàths na grèine.

Gu bileach, snuadhmhor gach glac is bruachag,
le neòinein ghuanach 's an tuar cho èibhinn;
ann an cois gach fuarain tha 'm biolair uaine
's tha badan luachrach ri bruach gach fèithe.

Tha dealbh a thràghad mar lorg a' chapaill,
tha 'n cuan gu sàmhach cur àilleachd fhèin air,
gach allt gu siùbhlach a' ruith an cùrsa
'n teis-meadhan ùrlair a' dol 'na chèile.

Tha chreagan uaibhreach mar bhalla suas ris,
ri freagairt nuallan nan tonnan beucach;
thaobh obair nàdair, chan fhaicear àicheadh
gur àit' as àille sa chruinne-chè e.

Tha 'n sluagh tha tàmh ann gu h-iochdmhor càirdeil,
ri nochdadh bàidh ann an gràdh da chèile;
cha sgeul air thuairmeas a ta mi luaidh air:
bidh eachdraidh buan fad bhios buar air slèibhtean. (IN)

'As far as I know, there were no bards in my family. The poems, they just came to me when I was young. And when they came, I'd order them inside my head and later on I'd sing them. Forty or fifty poems I had, or more. I'd make them up in the field when I was working, then sing them at a ceilidh. That was the custom here, in the old days. It's not so common now. You'd be called to your neighbour's house here and there and you'd have songs. I made songs about the people round about and they'd be new to them, so they were interested to hear them. There were many people making songs in those days but there's not so many now. Every township would have a bard. That was the only amusement you had. If a notion came to me, I'd start working on it and it wouldn't leave me alone. I'd have to keep at it till the poem was finished. I'm not so keen on all that now – thank God! There were nights I couldn't sleep. That's how it was. I've stopped it now, for good, I hope! All my songs used to come in Gaelic, except my last song about the Clearances; it's in English.'

A time will come, a time will go,
Preserved by God across the sea.
The Highland Clearances deprived
Our land of stalwart heroes.

They were men of great renown
For repartee and freedom,
But all they gained of freedom was
Exile without reason.

Their land was wrenched out of their grasp,
Their homes were burnt to cinders:
No evil could be worse than this,
Nor any type of landlord.

Prime Minister Gladstone was to blame,
An evil clique around him
Sent a thousand marines to Skye –
The people there to hound them.

The Skyemen gallantly did stand
As honest men before them;
And did not yield an inch to them
But routed all before them.

The Skipper with his wife Mary
Nicolson, 1997. (TN)

The final end to this dispute
Came by Carmichael – Lawman:
That the land be graced by gallant men
That own to fame and glory.

The wounds may heal, the scars remain
And so lie waste the Highlands:
The men that made our nation great
Gained nothing but remembrance. (IN)

'At a ceilidh I'd sing some of the old songs, like Màiri Mhòr, but mostly I'd sing
my own songs. It would be in the wintertime. In the long nights after work. I
never wrote them down. It was all memory, memory. For amusement. I liked
to make them laugh. I made the song to the rhyme, the rhyme of one line with
another, that was the way I put them together – with the rhyme. I used to play
the bagpipes, I wasn't great but I could hold a tune. We'd always have a piper at
a ceilidh. It was always Gaelic that was the most important thing. That was my
own language. It does you no harm to have as many languages as you can. You
get a better understanding of humanity.

'I've been in this house 40 years. I was very lucky. There were
two ladies who took the big house here, and they bought the land but they
didn't want the land. They got me to take the land and they gave me this house;
all free of charge. And they just lived in the big house themselves. It turned out
very well for us. I'd been away five years at the war, so I was pleased to come
back to the land and to get married. My wife is Mary Munro. Her house was

The Nicolson farm at Cuidreach on Loch Snizort. (FN)

the first house you see going off the road to Portree, at Kingsburgh. Two hundred and fifty acres we have here and it's very handy for the sea; for fishing. It was a good place for the children and it's nice when a bard has a roof over his head.

'I've spent all my life on the land, amongst sheep and cattle, lambing, ditching, horses. All the ploughing was with horses here. And all the cattle had to be driven to the local sales. Then the drovers would take them on, down to Kyleakin or to Armadale, then they'd go by boat to Kyle of Lochalsh or to Mallaig and be put on the trains and shipped out. That would be at the end of the year – but it's all lorries now, floats they call them, and it's tractors not horses. Up till the war my life was not so different to Rob Donn's.

'Why am I called the Skipper*? That's because I liked to be going about in boats. I used to put the small boats out on the loch and send the younger boys out fishing. I used to look after things. Somebody gave me the name "the Skipper" and it followed me on after that. It's like my songs, I'm tarred for life.'

* Further information about the Skipper, Calum Ruadh and Màiri Mhòr is set out in Dr John MacInnes's historical perspective, pp 321.

Duncan Williamson

ARGYLLSHIRE TRAVELLER

My mother was born in a cave at Muasdale, Kintyre, up behind the shop. And I was born in a tent in the wood at Furnace, looking out over the waters of Loch Fyne. I was thirteen of sixteen children, the seventh son of a seventh son. It's a strange thing, but my mother had boy, girl, boy, girl right down the line. I'll be 71 on the 11th April 1999. I'm the father of nine children. Seven by my first wife and two by my second wife, four boys and five girls, and fourteen times I'm a grandfather. I live here in Fife, in this little cottage on Straiton Farm, but I travel the world. I'm a storyteller, a singer and a bard. I'm one of the Travelling People.

I ran away when I was thirteen. It was the beginning of the war. We all lived in two big tents and things were crowded, so I decided it was time to leave, leave my parents, strike out on my own. I went north up into Argyll. It was summertime and after Inveraray, I took the shortcut over the mountains and there I came on an old man cutting peats. When I saw him, I went over and begged a cigarette off him and he stopped digging and took a packet of 20 Woodbines out of his jacket. 'Well', he said, 'I'll give you a smoke if you'll give me a lift with me house'.

His name was Patrick O'Donnell. He was an old Irishman and he lived in a hut that was built on a stretcher and two men could carry it anywhere. He opened the packet and we sat down on the heather and we each had a fag. Then he took up the front end of the stretcher and I took the back end and we carried his house over the moor. It was a nice wee hut with a chimney, a stove and a bed in the corner. When we put it down, he asked me inside and started to move the blankets up, so I asked him what he was doing.

'Well,' he said, 'Duncan, I know you're Jock Williamson's son, I've talked with your father in the pub and we've worked together, taking the coal off the Puffers on the shore. Well, I need a hand with the peats, I need somebody to rue the peats in fours to dry. I'll pay you five shillings a week. You can sleep in that corner and I'll sleep in this corner and you can eat all the food you can eat and you can smoke all the Woodbines you want.' Well, I thought that was a good deal, so I decided to stay up there in the hills. And for weeks and weeks I didn't see a living soul but old Patrick O'Donnell.

Each Saturday he'd go off for the messages, with an empty sack on his back. And watching this figure coming back over the moor with the darkness of the gloaming coming down, I used to think he was like a snail, with his pack on his back and a house that followed him wherever he went. And he'd hand over two packets of Woodbines and unpack enough food for the week, oats and potatoes, a few bones for soup, a loaf, a piece of cheese and two packets of tea. Well, I've travelled far and wide since those days, in many countries, and I've met many educated and intelligent people. I've been to Cambridge in England, I've been to one of the biggest universities in America, Cornell in Ithaca, but I've never met a more intelligent man than Patrick O'Donnell. He had a mountain of knowledge. He could tell you about the smallest insect that creeps in the bog and the largest fish in the world, the great Blue Whale. To me there seemed to be nothing he didn't know and he knew more songs and stories than any man I ever met. He was my master.

The men who went whaling always called a whale a fish and Patrick O'Donnell was an old sailor who'd travelled the world many times. And from each port and each country he brought news of who the people were, how they cooked and what they ate and how they spent their lives. Well, there we were, on the top of the moor in the summertime, digging peats; and we lived in that wee hut together. I slept in my clothes and he slept in his rug with a wee pillow for his head and under the pillow was his Bible and the Bible would rest his head through the night. He used to sleep in his long-johns, with his feet sticking out by my head. Now, Patrick O'Donnell couldn't read and he couldn't write, so, before going to bed, after telling his stories and singing his songs, he'd lean across and take out the Bible from under his pillow. And he'd sit by the stove and let it fall open, then he'd give it to me and ask me to read, and I'd read a page or chapter. I can see it like yesterday. The two of us sat by the wee square stove, with the chimney elbowed out through the wall, the peats singeing up in the draught and a candle down waxed to the floor. And a wee black drum, on the stove full of tea; and the same drum would be used for potatoes and soup.

Well, old Patrick O'Donnell taught me many things and many ballads, Irish ballads. I know more ballads than any Irishman alive today: 'Mr

McGraw', 'Glen Swillie', 'If I was the King of Ireland', all those beautiful ballads. I can go on forever and ever. First it was the ballads and then it was the Bible. Oh, I liked reading to the old man and when I finished, he'd say, 'God bless you Duncan, my son.' Then he'd whisper, 'Goodnight, Duncan,' and blow the candle out and I'd creep away to my bed. And the door would be open to the dark blue of the sky and the Milky Way arched over. And sometimes I'd wake with a little rain on my face, coming in through the door.

Old Patrick told me about his work as a cattleman, as a horseman, as a farmer; he'd driven a tramcar in London and cut timber in the snows of Canada. And when he sang a song, he'd get me to sing it back to him. 'Good man,' he'd say, 'Good man.' Now, it was not more than two months I stayed working the peats but I tell you this – those were the happiest days of my life and I'll not forget those days till I go to my grave. Many's the song I sing to this day that I learned from Patrick O'Donnell. One day I was in Gray Steel in Northern Ireland, in a little pub called The Rising Sun – the pub where the terrorists came in and slaughtered the people. 'Trick or treat!' they shouted and mowed the drinkers down. The publican was killed and so was his son and five of the people. Well, I was in that pub a year before it happened, and I sang 'Glen Swillie', just as old Patrick taught me. And they made me sing it three times! Because they'd never heard a Scotsman sing that song and they loved it, they loved hearing it sung the way I sang it: he was my master, Patrick O'Donnell.

> *...Brave-called men around me stood,*
> *Each comrade bright and true,*
> *And I shook each well-known hand*
> *To bid a last adieu –*
> *Says I, my fellow countrymen,*
> *I hope you'll soon be free*
> *And wave the green flag proudly over*
> *The hills of Glen Swillie.*
>
> *No more among the saggy moors*
> *Will I hear the blackbird sing,*
> *No more to me the blithe cuckoo*
> *Will welcome back the spring,*
> *No more will I see the fighting fields*
> *Of Colveen's clan McCree,*
> *For I'm fond to roam to America*
> *A stranger for to be....*

Old Style Travellers on the road, Perthshire, 1920's. (UK)

I sang that song in Dublin, the night Chris Collins came back from winning the World Middleweight Championship. Daniel O'Donnell was there, and he came over and he asked me to sing a song. And I said, 'Come on, it's you should sing, not me! You're the greatest singer in Ireland' And he said, 'I might be the greatest singer in Ireland, but I'm not the greatest singer in Scotland!' And he got me to sing that song. They like me over in Ireland.

Any singer or bard needs to have a good memory, but everybody needs to be taught. Now, in the old days, when a boy went away to the Clan Chief to be a bard, he was put to be taught by another bard. And nowadays a lot of people come here to me. They don't get sent by the Clan Chief, they just come, like David Campbell and Padraigh O'Neill, and others from all over. They use my tapes and stories in universities. I've had American students here and people paid by the Canadian Arts Council. It's the student gets paid – not me! I've got thousands of stories and thousands of songs and riddles. The world's full of stories but a bard needs to know how to tell them. I got the best of my stories from my granny, from my parents, from Travellers I've met on the road, from the old crofters, the fisher people, and Patrick O'Donnell.

So that's how my life on the road got started. I ran away and met a man cutting peats. Going away is the natural thing for the Travelling People. A wedding with us was running away! Two youngsters would go away up the glen and when they came back they were married. And usually the mother and father would welcome them back. They used to dig a wee hole in the ground and stick a tin can in it. Then they'd get the boy to pee in it, and the girl would pee in it, and the mother would stir it up with a stick and the girl would taste it and the boy would taste it – and they were bound for life. After that, only He who could separate that which the stick had stirred would separate those two people. That was it.

My eldest brother, Jock, he ran away to get married, to the Isle of Skye. He never went back there after his honeymoon, so he asked me to write a song about it. Skye is a beautiful island and it was full of memories for him. He's dead now, he died at Lochgilphead, but my song about Skye was his favourite and when he'd had a few drinks, that was the song he'd always ask for, 'The Skylines of Skye'.

What happened to Jock was this. He ran away with his cousin, Mary Townsley, and her father tried to stop them going. The two men had a fight and neither would give in till Jock broke his father-in-law's arm with a ploughshare. Then the two of them made a run for it. Later on, the police got to hear and they followed the two youngsters out to Skye and three months later Jock was arrested and brought back in irons and he got three months in Gateside Jail, down at Greenock. But he was not jailed because he made use of the ploughshare! It was because Mary's parents told the police she was only fifteen! Jock was done for sex with a minor, a girl under sixteen. Now, that was wrong, but it took them 50 years to find out. Because when Mary went for her old-age pension, at 65, they told her she was 67! She was two years older than she thought! Everybody told her she'd run away at fifteen but she was seventeen! And my brother should never have gone to prison! He did six months for nothing! Never had sex with a minor, Mary was a young woman of seventeen. It was Jock who was fifteen! He was two years younger than Mary and he never got a pension at all, he died. Well, after the happy months of his honeymoon, Old Jock never went back to that beautiful island, so he asked me to write a song and I call it 'The Skylines of Skye'!:

> *O, the road winds far*
> *To my dear distant homeland,*
> *Where those heather-clad mountains*
> *Reach into the sky.*
>
> *And I think of those footpaths*
> *Where I used to wander,*
> *For my heart it is heavy*
> *And often I sigh.*

And what would I give
For one glance of those mountains
And to walk in the heather
Once more at my ease.

As the cry of the wildfowl
Floats over the heather
And is carried so far
In the evening breeze.

O, to catch once again
A sight of the red deer
As he stands like a king
On the mountains so high.

As the scent of the pine trees
Blows over the heather
And in the distance I see
The Cuillins of Skye.

O, some day I'll come back
To my dear Scottish homeland
And on the sweet-smelling heather
It's there I will lie.

My heart will be gay
As I watch the sun setting
On those far distant mountains
Those Cuillins of Skye. (DW)

After a horse, heather was the most important thing for Travellers, it made their bed and gave them a roof, it made besoms, it made ropes, it made beer, it made honey, it made the distant mountains blue. I love heather. We sold it for luck and it kindled our fire.

Leaving the peats, I went to work on a croft at Auchindrain, which is now a museum, but in those days there were five crofts and I worked on them all. Men and cows went in through the same door. I'd sleep with the sound of the chewing of cud and the plopping of shit. The smell of cud is a beautiful smell. I worked with horses, did years of stane dyking, worked in the wood and out on the hill. I fished with the long-lines, went snaring for lobsters.

Traveller camp, Kintyre,
1975. (TN)

I played the tin-whistle, I played the Jew's harp, I played the chanter. I don't play the great Highland Warpipe, but Hamish Henderson once said, 'Duncan,' he said, 'you're the whole Scottish tradition rolled into one person!' I've done many things and I can't help remember. I remember swimming horses across to the small islands. I've swum the cattle from the island of Luing across to Kilberry. We haltered the bulls and swam them across. There were no piers on the small islands in those days.

It was John Lorne Campbell, the scholar, who built the pier on the Isle of Canna. He was a poet and a song collector and a very dear friend of mine. Once I had to call in at Canna, on the way back from Eigg where I'd been telling my stories – so I phoned to tell John Lorne Campbell that I'd have fifteen minutes at the pier. He said, he'd be down to meet me, and we had good crack. Just as the boat was about to leave he said, 'What the Hell, Duncan!' and he came up the gangplank and sailed all the way to Mallaig and took bed and breakfast before sailing home the next day. He liked a wee bit crack about the old days and ways. It was my father used to trim his uncle's corns – with a cut-throat razor. And we chatted away all the way to Mallaig and I sang the songs that his uncle liked and he, like the perfect gentleman, was buying the drinks. And he told me how very disappointed he was – with what the National Trust was doing to the island he'd given them.

He collected many Gaelic songs, and he asked me how I made up a new song. I told him, with me, the words always come first. Then, when I've got the words, I choose a tune – but then I thought, maybe the tune's already there in the back of my mind – giving me the lines. And I'm still not certain which comes first – the words or the tune – or if they come together. Certainly, when it comes to remembering words, it's the tune that brings them. One thing is clear – with a song – I have to know the story I'm going to tell. When I begin to compose a new tune, I like to start by thinking about the person for whom I'm writing. I think – what's this person's favourite car? If it's a Ford – that gives me an F. Then I think – what's his favourite colour? If it's green – that gives me a G. Once I get one or two notes in my head – I'm away – then the whole tune comes tumbling out. I like to ask a person which month they were born in – if it's September that's no good, but if it's April, that gives me an A and so on. I make up tunes all the time.

I wrote a pipe tune called 'Mount Tumbledown'. That was during the Falklands War and I gave it to the Cowdenbeath Pipe Band. I also wrote a pipe tune for Betsy Whyte, after she'd written her book, *The Yellow on the Broom*. I went to the launch of the book in Edinburgh, and when I saw her, and Brycie, her husband, coming up the steps this tune started coming into my head – I call it 'Betsy's Welcome to Edinburgh'; and I wrote a tune for Betsy's old Mum and Dad, Maggie Johnston and Sandy Whyte. They lived up at Blairgowrie through the winter but when they saw the yellow coming onto the broom, they'd get what the Travellers call 'Spring Fever' and they'd be wanting to be off - out on the road, so I wrote this song for Maggie and Sandy:

> *O, come sit beside me, Maggie, lass,*
> *I hate to see you gloom*
> *For I will take you from this place*
> *When the yellow's on the broom.*
>
> *When those Angus hills are free of snow*
> *And the swallow he's on the zoom,*
> *I will take you from this place*
> *When the yellow's on the broom.*
>
> *O, to Loch Leven's bonnie glen*
> *Or to the River Spey,*
> *Where I can fish for pearls, my love,*
> *And there the pipes I'll play.*

So it's put a smile upon your face,
I hate to see you gloom,
For I will take you far away
When the yellow's on the broom.

When those Angus hills are free of snow
And the swallow he's on the zoom,
O, I will take you from this place
When the yellow's on the broom. (DW)

I'll tell you the story behind another of my songs. One day there was heavy rain, and we were up at Crieff, shawing potatoes in the wintertime, and an old beggarman came into the camp and he came up to the fire and he asked if we would boil his drum, his little can, for his tea. He was dressed in rags and it was a Saturday morning. The women it was looked after him and they asked if he wanted sugar and did he want a piece, you know women. But the old man wouldn't take a thing, just the boiled water for his tea. And away he went up into the wood.

Well, next morning, Sunday morning, the police came in to the camp. I was up, I was just kindling the fire when they came in and they asked, 'Did any of your people not come home last night?' I said, 'We're all here, they're all sleeping, it's Sunday morning.' 'Well,' he said, 'I want youse to go in and check because the shepherd's just come down from the wood and he's found one of youse, and he's dead.' 'Oh,' I said, 'that'll be the old beggarman who came in to the fire yesterday. He wouldn't eat, and went away into the wood with his can of boiled water.' So they took me up to the mortuary in Crieff, and I identified the body and it was the old beggarman. No one knew who he was or where he came from, and no one even knew his name. I felt very sad about this; that that old man should die by himself in a bloody wood. And that night I wrote this beautiful song. 1964. It's the tune carries the rhythm of the words.

O, the night was dark and the night was cold
And the rain had been falling down
When an old beggarman lay down to die
Upon the cold, cold ground.

He had no one to comfort him,
No one who would understand,
For he was just a lonely,
A dying old beggarman.

Top to bottom:
Archaelogical reconstruction of
Palaeolithic shelters found in Siberia,
c. 20,000 BC. (HH)

Highland Travellers campsite,
Sutherland, 1957. (HH)

Lap camp, northern Scandinavia,
c. 1930. (HH)

Brian Stewart, Highland Traveller
erecting his bow-tent in North
Scotland, 1957. (HH)

And then he saw a beautiful light
All coming down from the sky,
Such a beautiful light, such a wonderful light
To the bush where he did lie.

'O, who are you?' the old beggar said,
'And why do you trouble me?
For I am just a dying old beggarman,
As you must surely see.'

'O, I have come,' the stranger said,
'From my Father's home far away
And this long dark cold wild winter's night
I will keep you company.'

'But I am a beggar,' the old man said,
'Just a dying old beggarman,
And why you come to comfort me
I do not understand.'

'In my Father's home,' the stranger said,
'In the place from where I came,
The tramp and the beggar and the poor and the rich,
They're everyone the same.

'And I have come to comfort you
And it's with you that I will stay
This long cold dark wild winter's night
I shall keep you company.'

Next morning that old tramp was found
In the bushes where he lay.
There was a happy smile upon his face,
For his soul had passed away, away
For his soul had passed away. (DW)

The Travellers care very much about death. I remember my mother telling us how they buried her uncle, old Geordie Townsley. He was wrapped in the tarpaulin taken down off his tent and laid in his grave with a tin cup, a piece of bread and a silver coin in his hand. That was my mother's father's brother, he

came from Campbeltown. The bread was to keep him going on his journey —
to Heaven or to Hell. The cup was for his tea or drink and the sixpence to pay
his passage over the sea. He was a piper, so the pipes went into the grave, his
head resting there on the bag and the drones all down his back.

All my life I've collected riddles. I don't make many up but I can
remember hundreds and hundreds and I like to test them out on children.
They're good for getting the brains working.

> *The man who made it*
> *Did not want it.*
> *The man who bought it did not need it.*
> *The man who used it never saw it.*
> *What was it?*

> *The answer, my friend, is A COFFIN.*

> *What is it?*
> *That's higher than the highest thing,*
> *Lower than the lowest thing*
> *Better than God,*
> *Worse than the devil.*
> *Dead people eat it*
> *But if we eat it — we die?*

> *The answer, my friend, is NOTHING.*

I told that riddle to a primary seven class in Glasgow and a little boy put up his
hand and answered, 'One of my daddy's Socks!' A good answer but not the
right answer! Now try these:

> *1. It's got a little round body*
> *And it's got six arms.*
> *It's got no legs.*
> *It can cover a mountain.*
> *It can fill a valley*
> *And some day it might become part of a man.*
> *What is it?*

2. In marble hall as white as milk
My lining is as soft as silk,
No doors or windows in my stronghold,
Yet thieves break in and steal my gold.
What am I?

3. This is an old Traveller riddle –
What always walks with its head down
And is no good with its head up?

4. You go in through one door,
You come out through three,
And when you're in you're ready for out
And when you're out you're already in.
What am I?

5. Always drinking
Never thirsty –
And always cold as death.
What am I?

That's an easy one – I am A FISH.

6. The ones you catch
You throw away.
The ones you miss
You keep.
What are they?

And the answers, my friend? They are:

1) A SNOWFLAKE. A snowflake comes down round – but under a microscope a snowflake will be seen to be a crystal with six arms leading out to its six points, snowflakes cover mountains and fill valleys – and sometimes a child will heap them together to make a snowman.

2) AN EGG, a white hen's egg.

3) A NAIL – the nail in a horse's shoe.

4) A JERSEY, A JUMPER.

6) The answer, my friend, is FLEAS.

Duncan Williamson singing his cousin, Big Willie MacPhee, to death, 1996. (TN)

The Travellers are always poking fun. You know Big Willie MacPhee, up at Perth, he's a great, great, great, grandfather. Well the last time I saw him, he told me he was on a diet! He said, 'The doctor's told me to lose three stones, Duncan.' So I told him, he'd have to lose a damn sight more than three stone if he wanted to get back in the ring! He's 90 years old. He used to be a boxer, like me. Then he asked me, 'Duncan, when's a man not a man?' 'When he's a boy,' I said. 'Wrong answer,' he said, 'A man's not a man when he turns into a field!' So then I told him if he really wanted to lose weight he should lose a bit of his head! 'It's a fat head, not a fat belly, that's your problem, Spottie!' That's his nick-name, Spottie MacPhee. All the Travellers have nick-names. I wrote a song about nick-names:

> *O, there's Gravits and there's Spotties*
> *And there's Piggys from the glens,*
> *There's Hardfish from Argyllshire*
> *And some they call the Hens,*
> *With me he riddee doo*
> *Me re riddee doo*
> *Me re riddee doo riddee di dye doo.*

There's Old Game Befukum
And Old Scabby Kate,
O, yin they call the Hedgehog
And yin they cry the Skate
With me he...

There's Breid and Milk frae Aberdeen
And Danny's from the south
And Big Daddy Danny
Who's famous for his mouth
With me...

O, on and on the nick-names go
From old men to the young
But before I give away too much
I'd better hold my tongue,
With me he riddee doo
Me re riddee doo
Me re riddee doo riddee di dye doo... (DW)

'The Hardfish', that's me! All of us Williamsons were known as the Hardfish from Argyll, because my grandfather used to hawk salt fish when he was a young man. Down in Kintyre, the crofters would salt small fish and hang them all round the eaves of the houses. Grandfather was a tinsmith, and he'd bargain a tin cup or a skimmet for a few of these salt fish. And one day some Travellers came from the east and they saw him with this basket of hard fish on his back, all sticking up straight round his head. So they called him Hardfish Williamson and it stuck with all his family. And it's the same with the MacPhees – they're all known as Spotties – since when I don't know.

I was a boy very keen on poetry at school. When I go to London, I like to visit the poets' houses. I've been to Keats' house and I've been to Tennyson's house, and in America, Longfellow's house. I always loved Wordsworth and the poetry of Thomas Campbell. 'The Burial of Sir John Moore', 'The Slave's Dream', 'Lord Ullin's Daughter', I love those poems. I learned them by heart and I can never forget them. I like to put them to music. I sing all those poems like ballads. 'The Wreck of the Hesperus', I put that to music and it makes a lovely ballad. The old poets must have had some kind of tune inside their heads but today, most modern poets don't like to sing. They don't even remember their own poems, let alone other people's poems. I'll tell you a story about that. One day I was sitting with Dr Tom Burton of the

University of South Carolina. He's a big big man on Tennyson, he did his doctorate on Tennyson, and he teaches Tennyson all over the world. We were in Margaret Bennett's house in Edinburgh, and he asked me if I knew any Tennyson – so I recited some and I sang some and I asked him to recite his favourite. And, do you know this, that man couldn't recite one poem out of his head, not one.

Tennyson's 'The Brook' is a great poem – who could describe a wee burn better than this:

> *I come from haunts of creeping heron,*
> *I make a sudden sally,*
> *I sparkle there among the fern,*
> *And make on down the valley...*

And I have another poem. It's called 'The Web-Spinner' – it's brilliant: spiders were very important to the Travelling People and when Bruce was in the cave on Rathan Island it was the spider made him think again.

> *Web-spinner he was a miser old*
> *And he came of low degree.*
> *His body was large and legs were thin*
> *And he kept bad company.*
>
> *His house was seven storeys high*
> *At the corner of a street*
> *And it always had a dirty look*
> *When other homes were neat.*
>
> *O, up in his garret-flat he lived*
> *And from his window high*
> *He looked out upon the dusty streets*
> *And to the passers-by.*
>
> *The day was hot, the air was poor*
> *And the night came on apace*
> *When a brawny baron of a bluebottle*
> *Came riding from the chase.*

Ah, says he, I'll ask for lodging
At the first house I come to
And at that the gate of web-spinner
Came suddenly in view.

O, loud was the knock the baron gave
And web-spinner came with glee.
Come in, come in, kind sir, he said,
And spend the night with me.

At that he ran and locked his door
And a loud loud laugh laughed he!
Then each upon the other sprang
And fought most furiously.

Now the baron he was a swordsman,
A swordsman of renown,
But the spider he had the strongest arm
And kept the baron down.

And out he took a little cord
From the pocket by his side
And with many a cruel and crafty knot
His hands and feet he tied.

And then he went about his house
Arranging dish and platter
And doing all that work with care
As if nothing was the matter.

Then he seized on poor bluebottle,
A strong and burly man,
And step by step and step by step
The hoisting up began.

And step by step and step by step
They went with weary tread
And when he reached his parlour door,
Poor bluebottle, he was dead.

Just then a lady came that way
With a long and cruel brush,
Which she raised above her carefully,
Web-spinner's house to crush.

Now that wicked churl through all his life
Had looked for such a day
He passed through a trapdoor in the wall
And took himself away.

As to where he went no one can tell
But it was underground –
Where he died a miserable death
And his body ne'er was found. (Anon)

I haven't found the right tune for that poem yet, so I just recite it, but it tells a wonderful story. That's what I like, stories – not this abstract modern stuff that only makes sense to a university professor! 'Not a drum was heard, not a funeral note...' That's the kind of thing I like – 'The Burial of Sir John Moore After Corunna'. I learned that poem at school and I've never forgotten it. That was what we used to do in the winter in the tent – learn poems. We had no television, no radio; times were hard, there was no money for drink so we learned poems and songs and made up songs, round the fire. And sometimes we added new bits to old songs.

Duncan Williamson, 1998. (TN)

You'll know Yeats's poem, 'The Sally Gardens'. It's only four verses long and the last verse seems to be missing. Yeats tells the story but he doesn't finish the story. People in many countries have searched for the missing verse but no one has ever found it, so I thought I'd complete the poem myself. And when I went over to Ireland, I sang 'The Sally Gardens' with my new verses added on – just to see how they'd go down. And afterwards a woman came up to me and she asked me, 'Duncan, where did you find the lost verses of "The Sally Gardens"? In my book, Yeats only wrote four verses.' So I told her that I wrote the new verses myself. 'Sally' is the Irish word for a willow and it's the Traveller word.

In a field down by the river
My love and I did meet
As she crossed the sally gardens
In her little snow-white feet.

> *She bid me take love easy*
> *As the leaves fell from the trees*
> *But I being young and foolish*
> *With her would not agree.*

> *In a field down by the river*
> *My love and I did stand*
> *And upon my leaning shoulder*
> *She placed her snow-white hand.*

> *She bid me take love easy*
> *As the grass grew on the weir*
> *But I was young and foolish*
> *And now I'm full of tears.* (WB/Trad.)

That's as far as Yeats ever got, but my verses finish the song.

> *Now the sallies they have turned to brown,*
> *The weir has ceased to flow*
> *And a voice it will always haunt me*
> *Wherever I do go.*

> *And though I shall never see her*
> *Through the rest of my weary years*
> *When I think of the sally gardens*
> *My eyes they fill with tears.*

> *For she bid me take love easy*
> *When the leaves fell from the tree*
> *But I being young and foolish*
> *With her would not agree.* (DW)

The sallies do turn brown in wintertime and the weir freezes over with ice. The woman wouldn't give the man what he wanted so they parted and he never saw her again. She was a fairy woman. Well, the woman in Ireland must have been pleased with my version of 'The Sally Gardens' because she wrote me a letter asking me to finish another song, 'She Walks Through the Fair'. It also ends all of a sudden so I wrote another verse to the song and I'm waiting to hear what she thinks.

I've put a tune to Sir Thomas Campbell's poem, 'Lord Ullin's Daughter'. The poem is about a MacQuarrie chief, who owned the island of

Ulva, and Ullin Campbell, who owned Millport across from Dunoon. There was a feud between them. MacQuarrie was the son of two second cousins, so when he wanted to get married, he went to the mainland to find a strange wife and there he met Lord Ullin's daughter. They fell in love and eloped to Dunoon, taking the shortcut over the top of Loch Goil. Many's the time I was over there myself. Lord Ullin ordered a great hunt for the runaways. They had horses and rode for their lives. Fearful of capture, they jumped into a boat whilst a storm was raging. The boat capsized in Loch Goil and both lovers were drowned. It's a story that makes a beautiful ballad, so I put a tune to the poem. There's a big stone in memory of the two lovers on Ulva yet, just across the Atlantic Ocean from Mull, by the bridge.

> *A chieftain to the Highlands bound*
> *Cries 'Boatman, do not tarry*
> *And I'll give you a silver pound*
> *To row me o'er the ferry.'*
>
> *'O who are you would cross Loch Goil*
> *This dark and stormy water?'*
> *'O I'm the chief of Ulva's Isle*
> *And this is Lord Ullin's daughter.*
>
> *'O fast before her father's men*
> *Three days we've fled together*
> *And should they find us in this glen*
> *My blood will stain the heather.*
>
> *'His horsemen hard behind us ride*
> *Should dare our steps discover*
> *And who will cheer my bonnie Meg*
> *When they have slain her lover?'*
>
> *Up spake the hardy Highland wyte,*
> *'I'll go my chief, I'm ready,*
> *It is not for your silver pound*
> *But for your winsome lady.'*
>
> *'O hurry please' the lady cried*
> *'The tempest round us gathers*
> *I'll meet the raging of the seas*
> *But not an angry father.'*

The boat has left the stormy land,
The stormy sea before her,
We know too strong for human hand
The tempest gathered o'er her.

'Come back, come back,' Lord Donald cried
Across the stormy water
'And I'll forgive your Highland chief,
My daughter, O my daughter.'

But in vain the loud waves lashed ashore
And in turn all aid preventing,
The waters overwhelmed his child
And he was left lamenting.

I can't sing that line, 'My daughter, O my daughter' without feeling the tears. For me, all poems should be sung. I've got my own variation to the tune to 'Thomas the Rhymer' and John Purser wrote about that in his book *Scotland's Music*: 'Of the many versions of the words, Duncan Williamson's is one of the finest, preserving the deep symbolism rooted in Celtic mythology. His tune also contains, within its own structure, a sense of the marvellous. It is largely confined to the interval of the minor third, but the middle section is sung up an octave, and the tessitura (or average pitch) is high, which gives an eerie effect so that the voice enters another world in each stanza... Duncan Williamson is one of the travelling folk, and their respect for their traditions is such that any modelling he has undertaken has probably been done in the same way it would have been in the thirteenth century when the material first drew breath.'

I've written some beautiful Homeland Songs, emigrant songs about the people going away to all different countries – one's called 'Home to Barra'. One day, way back in the sixties, I picked up the paper, the *Sunday Post*, and I read a story about a man from Barra, whose father had taken him away to America when he was two years old. His mother stayed behind in Barra and he lost contact with her but when he was about 50 years of age he heard that she was still alive and he set sail from America to visit her. Well, when I read that story, I immediately wanted to write a song – as though I myself was that man coming home:

O, Barra, my homeland,
O, Barra, my isle,
Soon I will see you

Again in a while.
As I gaze at this water,
My laughter, my love,
I'm coming home to Barra.

O, I'm watching the sun
Sink down in the west
With love in my heart
And joy in my breast.
I'm coming home to the island
That I love best,
Home to my island of Barra.

Those lovely white beaches
All covered with foam,
Where me as a laddie
Those beaches did roam.
Now there's joy in my heart
For I'm coming home,
Home to my island of Barra.

There's a dear little cot
Nestled close to the sea
Where a dear sweet mother
Will be waiting for me
And I'll gaze on the face
I'm longing to see
Home in my island of Barra. (DW)

That's it – a song straight out of the *Sunday Post*. I made that song more than 30 years ago, I haven't sung it for years, but I remember every word. Duncan Ban Macintyre, the bard, he could recite dozens of poems of 500 lines and so can I. He could recite the genealogy of his chief back ten generations and more. He couldn't read or write. His monument stands between Inveraray and Dalmally, up on the hill, not far from where I stayed to work with old Patrick O'Donnell, so I'm very fond of Duncan Ban Macintyre. He went away to Edinburgh but he used to write about the world he knew when he was young. And I do the same in many of my songs.

O the Summertime is come again,
It surely breaks my heart
When I think of the happy days I've spent
With my old horse and cart.

The roads they were not long for him
Nor yet too long for me
It's on the road I used to go,
My old horse and me.

From Aberdeen to Galloway
We tramped the country round,
From Edinburgh down to Stranraer
And then the banks o' Clyde.

The roads they were not too long for him
Nor yet too long for me.
It's on the road we used to go,
O my old horse and me.

O many's the time on a winter's night
He's stood tied to a tree
With no a bite to gie to him
And no a bite for me.

With a wee bit cover across his back
To shelter him from the snow
But I ken it's him in the morning
When on the road I have to go.

O many's the time upon the road
My horsie lost a shoe.
Up to the smiddie I would gang,
To the smiddie man I'd view.

I cannot buy a new shoe,
To the smiddie man I'd say,
O, put me on and old one,
I'm sure it'll have to dae.

Now those happy days are gone and past.
I've bought a motor car.
Sure I go driving on the road
And sure I travel far.

I drive by all those places
But I turn to you and say,
I'll never be as happy as I was
With my old horse and me. (DW)

Duncan Williamson singing
'Jock O' Monymusk', 1998. (TN)

That, of course, is my own song but I love the old ballads. I'll sing you the
ballad 'Jock of Bridleslaw – John of Monymusk'. I've been to Jock's grave up
there beneath Bennachie. This is a great ballad, this is original, this is real! This
is me.

O, Johnny, he got up one fine morning,
Cold water to wash his hands,
Said bring to me my twa grey dugs
They are bound with iron bands O,
They are bound with iron bands.

O Johnny, O Johnny, his mother she said,
To the greenwoods dinnae, dinnae gang
O Johnny, for your mother's sake,
Son, a hunting son dinnae, dinnae gang
O a hunting dinnae gang.

But Johnny busket-up his fine broad bow
And his arrows a' sae lang
And he paid nae heed tae his mother's words —
O a hunting he would gang O,
A hunting he would gang.

And there he spied a grey dun deer
Coming down through the greenwood side
And he fires on the grey dun deer
And he wounded her in her pride O,
He wounded her in her pride.

And then there comes a silly auld carl
Who comes down through the greenwood side
And he is awa' to the king's foresters
The seven foresters for to see O,
The seven foresters for to see.

What news, what news, you silly auld carl,
What news do you bring today,
What news, what news, you silly auld man,
What news do you bring to me?

He said as I cam doon through your very green woods
And through the peat and bog,
There I spied a handsome man,
He was hunting with his dogs O,
He was a hunting with his dogs.

Then up and spoke the first forester,
An elderly man was he
He said if Johnny is hunting in oor merry green wood
We'd better let him be O,
We'd better let him be.

And up and spoke the second forester
He was a man among them a'
He said if Johnny is a hunting in our merry green wood
Nae further dare we draw O
Nae further dare we draw.

And up and spake the third forester
A brother's son was he
He said if Johnny is a hunting in our merry green wood
We should gang and we'll gar him die
We should gang and we'll gar him die.

And up and spoke the fourth forester
A bright young spark was he
Gang get your bows, my brothers bold,
And come along wi' me O,
And come along wi' me.

So Johnny placed his back against an oak
And his foot against a stane
And he fired on the seven foresters
And he slew them a' but een O,
He slew them a' but een.

And then an arrow pierced him deid
Coming down through the greenwood side
And betwixt the waters and the wood
There young Johnny died O,
O there young Johnny died.

Now Johnny's great big bow lies broke
And his twa grey dugs lie slain
And his body lies in Monymusk
And his hunting days are gane O
His hunting days are gane. (Trad.)

That's a ballad from the 1600s. I learned it from my granny. The guy shot him
in the back! It was the last forester got Jock of Bridleslaw, in the back. Through
all history there's been stabbing in the back and the Travellers are used to it. My
son Willie was Scottish, European and World Kung Fu Champion. He helps
train the Territorial Army. He got a job as a doorman up at the Ice House in
Perth. Now he's in jail. For the first time in his life. He's on remand. He turned
some men out of the Ice House, it's like a club, and a few days later three of
them came to his house with baseball bats. He had to take them on – all three.
One got a broken jaw, one got a broken thigh and the other got broken ribs.
He's awaiting trial, GBH, but they don't think anybody will testify against him.
I was telling him, I was down at Norwich prison telling stories, and in walked
Ronnie Kray, a great gold chain around his neck, could buy half of London!
'Duncan,' he said before I left, 'if anybody causes you trouble just let me know.
I think your stories are great – but tell the boy to stay out of jail!' All 29 of
those prisoners lined up to shake my hand before they went back to their cells.

It was way back in 1960 that I wrote my protest song, 'They're
Closing Our Camping Grounds Down':

> *O come all ye hawkers,*
> *Ye men of the road,*
> *You hawkers who wander around.*
>
> *I'll tell you a story*
> *Will sadden your heart,*
> *They're closing our camping grounds down.*
>
> *Though we fought for our country*
> *And fought for our King*
> *And some gave their lives for this land,*
>
> *When out there in Dunkirk*
> *Many men fell and their blood*
> *Was mixed up with the sand.*
>
> *But what did they fight for*
> *And why did they die?*
> *Their freedom to wander around.*
>
> *So where can we wander?*
> *We've nowhere to go –*
> *For they've closed our camping grounds down.*

They say we're not wanted
And keep moving us on
But where can we go? We've got nowhere to go —
For they closed our camping grounds down. (DW)

I have hundreds of songs and thousands of stories. I would say I have the finest collection of stories of any human being alive today in Britain. My stories are family stories, stories of fairies, stories of witches, stories of elves, stories of goblins, stories of kings, Jack tales, sea stories, tragedy tales, tales of love, tales of sadness, tales of the seal people, the silkies — wonderful stories for the children and for the whole family. I can tell you tales of Gog and Magog, that's Satan and the Mother of Satan, about how God gave Gog the foot of a bull! But now, to finish, I'll sing one of my favourite ballads. It's called 'Hindhorn'.

In London town a babe was born
Ho li lion sae lonely O
And the name they gave him was young Hindhorn
Ho li lion sae lonely O

O he courted a lady of high degree
Ho li lion sae lonely O
And to this his father did not agree
Ho li lion sae lonely O

I'm sending you off to sea
Ho li lion...
For a sailor for to be
Ho li lion...

Hindhorn is away to his lady fair
With the rosy cheeks and the raven hair

He said, my father is sending me off to sea
For a sailor for to be

So she took a ring from her right hand
For in this ring your life must stand

If you see this ring getting dull and worn
You must leave the sea and come to the land

Hindhorn he sailed the world around
Till he saw his ring getting dull and worn

So he left the sea and he came to the land
And the first one he met was an old beggarman

What news what news you old beggarman?
What news what news you old beggarman?

He said there is a marriage in our King's toon
But the bride she won't marry her bridegroom

He said you give me your old crooked staff
And I'll give you my great broadsword

He said you give me your old ragged cloak
And I'll give you my scarlet cloak

He said you give me your old grey hair
To cover up my own sae fair

Hindhorn is awa to that Kings ha'
For to find his lady fair

Then he asked for a drink for Hindhorn's sake
And the maid his message she did take

Say my lady there's a beggar at your hall door
Like you never saw before

And he's asking for a drink for Hindhorn's sake
And the lady a drink to him did take

And he drank up the drink and he placed in the ring
The sight of it made her heart sing

Where did you get this ring this ring?
Did you get it by sea or land —
Did you take it from a drowning man?

I did not get it by sea or by land
I got it from your right hand

Then he pulled off the old grey hair
And there stood Hindhorn young and fair

And then there was a marriage in that King's toon
Ho li lion sae lonely O
And the bride was happy to marry her bridegroom
Ho li lion sae lonely O... (Trad.)

My grandmother used to sing that way back when I was a child and she used to say it was an old story-song. Today there are versions of that song in books but I don't think there's many people can sing that song as they heard it at their granny's knee. A lang sang – that's what the Travellers called a song like that, that's what they lived for. These songs were handed down father to son and mother to daughter and grandmother to grandson, to little buggers like me to remember. And I did. I keep everything hidden inside this old white head. It's a mask! Underneath I'm Duncan Ban, Duncan Ban nan Oran, Fair-haired Duncan of the Songs!

Looking west from North Uist to St Kilda. (TN)

Norman MacLean

Govan and Lochmaddy

My grandfather broke horses in the Argentine with the gauchos. His name was John MacLean and he came from Tiree. For years he was out there on the pampas and life could be wild in those days. Then he returned to Scotland to do what his ancestors had done for generations, he fished, he reared a few head of cattle, and he sang. And at the end of the summer, he would walk his beasts from Tiree to the big tryst at Falkirk. It's a long journey across difficult country – sea, loch, ford, bog, mountain – and for the men it was the highlight of the year. The big Lowland trysts would bring in drovers, dealers, tinkers, merchants, hustlers of all kinds from all over Scotland and entertainment was part of the show. Big tents were set up, there'd be missionaries, drinking, singing, boasting and story and organised competition was part of the process. As it still is at the Highland Games, at Agricultural Shows, and at the Mod. Of course my grandfather joined in and we still have the silver cup he won for his bardachd, at the Falkirk Tryst. The inscription reads 'To John MacLean, for his rendition of original Gaelic Song'. My father was very proud of that cup.

Today, the lowing of cattle is rarely heard at the National Mod of An Comunn Gaidhealtach but other than that things haven't changed at all. The Mod goes back to those free-wheeling competitions arranged at the cattle markets and those trysts were the continuance of very old gatherings. The droving life was a remnant of the heroic age, wild and very poetical. The Bard of the North, Rob Donn Calder, was a drover. He used to bring cattle down to the Lowland Trysts in the mid-18th century; it's rumoured that he met Robert

Opposite:
The Bard Norman MacLean
piping in Waterstone's Bookshop,
Sauchiehall Street, Glasgow,
1998. (TN)

Burns but the dates of the two men's lives suggest that that rumour was talk of the mart, not truth.

There is a fine description of the Falkirk Tryst of 1849 in the appendix to Haldane's *The Drove Roads of Scotland*. Readers are asked to imagine a scene

'... to which Great Britain, perhaps even the whole world, does not afford a parallel... There are three trysts held every year - the first in August, the second in September and the last and largest in October. The cattle stand in a field in the parish of Larbert at a distance of nearly three miles from Falkirk, at a place called Stenhousemuir. The field on which they assemble contains above 200 acres, well-fenced and in every way adapted for the purpose. The scene, seen from horseback, from a cart, or some erection, is particularly imposing. All is animation, bustle, business and activity; servants running about shouting to the cattle, keeping them together in their particular lots and ever and anon cudgels are at work upon the horns and rumps of the restless animals that attempt to wander in search of grass or water.

'The cattle dealers of all descriptions, chiefly on horses, are scouring the field in search of the lots they require. The Scottish drovers are for the most part mounted on small, shaggy, spirited ponies that are obviously quite at home amongst the cattle; and they carry their riders through the throngest groups with astonishing alacrity. The English dealers have, in general, large, stout horses, and they pace the ground with more caution – when they discover the cattle they want, they enquire the price. A good deal of haggling takes place, and when the parties come to an agreement, the purchaser claps a penny of arles into the hand of the stockholder, observing at the same time, 'It's a bargain.' Tar dishes are then got and, the purchaser's mark being put on the cattle, they are driven from the field.

'Besides numbers of shows, from 60 to 70 tents are erected along the field for selling spirits and provisions. The owners of these portable taverns pay 2/6 for the ground they occupy on the first tryst, and 4/6 for each of the other two. In one of these tents a few gentlemen attend from the Falkirk Bank to accommodate the dealers with the money they require. Many kindle fires at the end of their tents, over which cooking is briskly carried on. Broth is made in considerable quantities, and meets a ready sale. As most of the purchases are paid for in these tents, they are constantly filled and surrounded with a mixed multitude of cattle dealers, fishers, drovers, auctioneers, pedlars, jugglers, gamblers, itinerant fruit merchants, ballad singers and beggars. What an indescribable clamour prevails in most of these multi-coloured abodes!

'Far in the afternoon, when frequent calls have elevated the spirits and stimulated the colloquial powers of the visitors, a person hears the uncouth Cumberland jargon and the prevailing Gaelic, along with innumerable provincial dialects, in their genuine purity, mingled in one astounding roar. All seem inclined to speak and, raising their voices to command attention, all the orators are obliged to bellow as loudly as they can possibly roar. When the cattle dealers are in the way of their business, their conversation is full of animation, and their technical phrases are generally appropriate and highly amusing.'

Reading that description you'll understand how my father got on so well amongst the gauchos in Argentina – and why I became a showman! The Royal Highland Show at Ingliston still provides an irresistible draw to thousands of Highlanders. Like the Highland Games, it is a many-sided cultural event and entertainment, piping and song are still part of it. The Tiree men must have looked forward to their drives to Falkirk for many reasons, not least because it would give them a big audience for their bardachd and the inscription on the silver cup won by my grandfather makes it clear that he was not just a singer but also an original composer. John MacLean was a cowboy and a recognised bard.

There is a long tradition of bardachd and musical ability on both sides of my family. I haven't normally thought of myself as a bard because the term has become too narrowly defined and I've always done so many things besides writing poetry, but I am a bard. I'm a trouper, a troubadour in a very old tradition and there has always been something of the shaman in all that I do. Inspiration in me comes out unfettered, or not at all, and it comes from very deep down. Leaving school, I studied Celtic language and literature, then I went to work as the manager of a citrus plantation in Florida. In the sixties I taught mathematics in the East End of Glasgow. For fifteen years I made a lot of money as a stand-up comic, living on my wits, like a Fool! I like thin ice that demands speed of the skater. I'm an actor, a television performer, I've written novels and film-scripts, I've been a piper since I was a boy; I'm a chameleon so if somebody asks me, 'Are you are a bard?', I'm tempted to say, 'Bugger off!'

Above:
Niall Mor MacLean, Norman's father,
1940s. (NM)

Above right:
Peggy MacKinnon, Norman's mother,
a Glasgow dress-maker. (NM)

But I am a bard. All the Highland bards have had jobs to do besides writing poetry for at least 300 years – look at Sorley MacLean, he was a teacher, and soldier, and headmaster. Why do we think that the old bards did nothing but sit about? Not since Adam got the heave from Paradise has the bard done nothing but muse. Not till the Arts Council came by – riding a subsidised donkey!

The island of Tiree is famous for its bards and its music and it's from John MacLean that people suggest my musical abilities are inherited. But my love of language, all languages, seems to come from the MacDonalds, on my mother's side. She was a MacKinnon. They were *sgalagan* in North Uist, landless cotters, working for big landowners. In the 19th century, Lady Gordon Cathcart settled some of them on good lands in Benbecula and South Uist. They were part of what might be called 'a minor plantation' of hard-working Presbyterian families into Roman Catholic South Uist. They were storytellers who took great pleasure in the language, and as I enter my 60th year it is storytelling that is at the front of my consciousness. Life circles round. As a child, my mother told me many stories but my own creative life started with piping and bardachd – now, in my twilight years, or what will be, at best, the penultimate furlong, it is stories that I am desperate to tell. There is a symmetry about this. Music has been with me always but it is stories that impress themselves in youth and age. Hamish Henderson has a phrase, 'Youth and Age upon the face of Corrievan': say no more.

As I grow older I think a great deal of my father. He was a seaman. My mother was a dress-maker. She specialised in wedding dresses, working in Jamaica Street. Both my parents were native Gaelic speakers from the islands. My grandmother lived with us in Govan. She spoke beautiful Gaelic and had a great deal of traditional knowledge. In addition, I spent long periods on the island of Benbecula and a remote glen in Lochaber with various relations of my mother's. So, like my forbears, but unlike most Glaswegians, I was brought up speaking Gaelic in a Gaelic environment, familiar in every way with age-old community habits and values. It was when I was nine and my father got a shore-posting with the Donaldson Line that I started to live in Glasgow full time. And – crash! There was a culture shock of a very extreme kind.

On the boat from Uist I chummed up with a boy from Loch Carnan in South Uist, Iain MacGibbon. We ended up in the same street and when the two of us went out to play in the backcourt we suddenly hit a different world. A gang of Govan toe-rags came up. What football team did we support? Unable to answer, we got more than a few dunts in the face for our pains! Being a bright kid, I took an immersion course in Govanese and within ten days I was speaking exactly like them. Iain took a bit longer, in fact he was never fully accepted, and he emigrated to Australia as soon as he could. He became a gold prospector. I was lucky, I'm a leopard who can change his spots; I wasn't small, I had a temper, I was strong and soon enough I was transformed into a monoglot Scots-speaking city tough, indistinguishable from the best of them.

So I was brought up between two poles. The pubescent Glasgow cityslicker would be decanted each summer back to Uist for long holidays in a purely Gaelic environment. I remember asking my Mum, 'When am I going to become dumb?' 'What do you mean?' she asked. 'It's strange,' I said, 'I go to Uist speaking nothing but English, then when I wake up, I find myself only able to speak Gaelic. When I come back to Glasgow with Gaelic on my tongue, I wake up and find that I can't utter a word but in English! So I've been thinking, one day I'll wake up dumb – unable to utter a word in any language at all!'

Confusing it might have been but it was also very good training for a man who would one day become an entertainer. I've always had this instinct to jump in and catch the eye. I speak Spanish, Portuguese and French, as well as Scots, English and Gaelic and, like most good linguists, I can dive into and out of a language in hours. And, like any good actor, I can switch into another character, into another culture, almost without rehearsal. By nature and training I'm a man where extremes meet, like the poet Hugh MacDiarmid. Isaiah Berlin divided men into foxes and hedgehogs, those with many small interests and those with one big interest – I'm a fox as sure as God made little rabbits.

My father, Niall MacLean, was a strict sabbatarian but one December, when I was fourteen years of age, he decided to do overtime, work a Sunday, to get extra money for Christmas and the New Year. He was a big man and walking back to work after dinner break between two friends, he fell, and he died on the pavement in Govan. A massive heart-attack. I was terribly upset and his death came at a time when I'd been in rebellion against paternal authority. I felt a great guilt that I had not loved or honoured my father as he deserved and these days I'm very conscious that most of what I do is done for him. It was he who taught me the essential things in life, how to tie my shoe-laces, how to tell the time. It was he that taught me Spanish, the Spanish he had learned from his father, John MacLean, the Argentinian who went trysting in Falkirk. If I've ever done anything of value, he's the person I would most like to know. I have tried hard in my life to be worthy of him, Niall Mòr. When I play the pipes, it is often enough for him that I play. He's there in my novel *Keino*.

Someone is pounding on the door.
      'Hector – it's me, Colin.'
I do not answer. I cover my head with my pillow. All I can hear is the fast beat of my own heart.
      'Hector,' comes the voice, much fainter, 'are you all right?' Knuckles rap on the door. The door handle is tried again and again. Footsteps retreat and a door bangs.
      I draw breath. What to do? This is the first time I have wakened up with no clear idea of where I am and how I got there. But I know it will not be the last.
      I shudder and try to wake up. My heart is pounding and my limbs are paralysed. Locked in a stupor – not asleep, but not full wakefulness either – my right arm is trapped beneath my body and has no sensation in it.
      Quickly I swing my bare legs off the bed to sit up in this darkened room. I catch sight of my watch on the bedside table. Jesus Christ, it is 5:20. In the morning? Or is it night? A full

Norman MacLean with Mary MacIntyre of Bowness, Glasgow, 1998 (TN)

bottle of rum with maybe a couple of inches out of it is on the table too, along with a packet of Camel cigarettes. Camel, my father's favourite brand! A box of matches and an empty brandy glass.

To find out where I am I walk slowly over to the dressing table and pain hits me like lightning. CLAREMONT HOTEL OBAN says the key-tab.

I sit once more on the edge of the bed and try not to think about last night. Everything about Achnacarry is woozy. A series of dim images without sound.

Filling a glass with rum I place it carefully on the table.

I am on my way, coughing uncontrollably, head down, into the bathroom. While pissing, I look at my face in the mirror above the washbasin. My skin is flushed and my eyes, above the swollen nose and bruised mouth, are the eyes of a seventy-year-old inside the face of a young man. I run cold water and splash it on my face. I pour handfuls of water into my parched, damaged mouth. There is a metallic taste at the back of my

throat. I have been violently sick some time recently and there
is a dull ache in my stomach.

Back in the bedroom, my dram and the cigarettes are
waiting for me. The rum goes down well. Within half a minute
my entire body receives the welcome message. YOU ARE
GOING TO BE FINE, HECTOR.

I light a cigarette and puff deeply. I take a second swallow of
rum and sigh… A sudden memory from last night engulfs me:
voices – female voices. 'Hey Hector,' a young girl said. 'Tell us
one of your Benbecula stories.' 'No, Sandra, the poor guy's
knackered,' another female voice said. 'Here, darling – drink
this.'

Faint impressions gel into crisp images. On either side of
Hector MacPhail, grinning drunk, in the lounge of the
Claremont Hotel, two young girls were squeezed into a red
leather banquette against one of the walls. Hairs, legs, thighs,
breasts came together in the crush. I was not seriously listening
to Sandra and Lynn – were they young mothers out on the
town? Claremont staff enjoying an after hours drink? – as they
chatted across me. My eyes were closing.

'Hector, pet? Wake up,' Lynn, the tall dark-skinned one,
said. 'Hector, are you still with us? This is Lynn and Sandra here.
Hey, Hector – '
This then:

*Niall Mor is leaning across me in the bedroom of our home in
Govan. His large hand is on my shoulder and he is gently rocking me
into wakefulness. 'Wake up, lad,' he says. 'That's four o'clock. The
Mallaig train leaves at six.' It is the first day of the school holidays and
I, like hundreds of other children of my background, am being sent
'home' to Uist.*

*Within half an hour I am washed, fed and dressed in short trousers,
blazer and highly polished brogue shoes. My father picks up the battered
leather suitcase that has been standing packed for a week by the outside
door. I enter the kitchen and approach the bed where my mother and
sister lie sleeping.*

'I'm off, then,' I say.

*My mother opens her eyes, turns to face me and reaches for
something beneath her pillow. She extends an envelope. 'Here,' she
whispers, 'take this. Give it to your Auntie Seonag.'*

I accept the envelope and place it in the inside pocket of my jacket.

There is a brief silence. 'Right,' I say, 'I'm off.'

'God be round about you.'

'I'll write, Mammy.'

'Do that, Hector.'

Soon, in the pre-dawn darkness, my father and I are briskly walking along Brand Street to the tram-depot, where we board the tram that will take us into the city centre, or 'up the town' as we southsiders call it. I marvel at the ease with which Niall Mor swings the heavy suitcase in his left hand as he draws on a Camel cigarette with his right. He is a big, strong man and I would gladly give up all my so-called intelligence and the academic prizes which, I am assured by my teachers, await me, if only I could attain his stature…

At Queen Street Station, at half past five in the morning, islanders - young girls in service, merchant seamen on leave, family men in dark suits and soft hats, mothers and scores of schoolchildren — swarm through the place. It is the children, may God bless them, I remember most vividly. Clumps of baggage and parcels, guarded by women in cheap cloth coats and dark headscarves, are scattered all over the concourse. The children, all between the ages of six and thirteen, move restlessly from group to group. These are the children whose parents come from Lewis, Harris, Skye and the Uists, parents who are making sure that the Police Force, the Docks, the Clyde Navigation Trust and the Psychiatric hospitals all belong to them. The children move restlessly from one clump of baggage and parcels to another, much in the same way as they and their offspring will leave their rented tenement flats in Partick, Overnewton, Govan, Ibrox, Plantation, Kinning Park and Kingston and flee to the suburbs and beyond. These are the children who, from homes in Newton Mearns, Whitecraigs, Clarkston, Kelvinside, Bearsden and Milngavie, will make their assault on Teaching, the Law, Broadcasting, Film, Popular Music, the Theatre, Accountancy and Publishing. And while the genealogies of the blood relatives on the islands who will nurture them over the coming months trip off their lips fluently, it will not always be so…

My father speaks to a woman, bean Mhicheil Dhonnchaidh from South Uist who is accompanying her son and daughter to Lochboisdale. Roddy and Kathleen are around my own age and are near neighbours, but they are unknown to me since they attend a Roman Catholic school, St Margaret's, in Kinning Park. It is likely that he has asked her to keep an eye on me on the Lochmor, where opportunities for mishaps abound.

On the platform, Niall Mor stands apart from the little groups who babble advice in Gaelic to their excited offspring crowding round the open windows of each carriage. Eventually he steps forward, easily forcing a path through the other adults, and indicates by lifting his chin that I should approach the window.

The other children, awed perhaps by my father's height and upright, silent presence, reluctantly give way and allow me to come forward to the window. The two of us are separated by a foot and we watch each other, as if we are about to back away in different directions.

'Hector,' my father says, producing a white ten-pound note from his wallet, 'Here's some money. A man needs something to rattle in his pocket.'

I look at the hand with the note in it, as if memorising it. Finally: 'Thank you,' I say, taking the equivalent of two weeks' wages from him.

'Keep up the practice, Hector. Your uncle Angus John will let you play his pipes.'

'Uh-huh.'

'You're my son,' he says quietly, 'I want you to be the best you can be.'

'I'm NOT your son,' I silently scream behind clenched teeth, 'don't touch me!'

My father has offered me his hand, and when he sees I am not going to take it he walks away.

Tears sting the corners of my eyes as I take my seat in the corner of the carriage, but I am smiling, I am happy. Daddy? You do love me, don't you? Please don't walk away. Wait.

The MacLean family crofthouse, Lochmaddy, North Uist. (TN)

That's from my novel, *Keino*, it's fiction but it's got a powerful base in biographical fact, as has my bardachd. A good deal of my poetry deals with piping, the process and the tradition of piping. I won my two gold medals at the National Mod of An Comunn Gaidhealach when I was teaching in Glasgow and was almost obsessed with pipe music but one prize was for solo singing, the other was for an original piece of Gaelic poetry. All my bardachd comes infused with musical force: the playing of the pipes is so much part of my life that all my poetry is coloured by the rhythms and nature of pipe music, particularly the pibroch.

MAOL DONN

You were the only tree in the garden of eyes
As your nimble fingers tuned the drone of the pipe;
The hall was packed and the silent crowd held their breath
When you pushed the boat of your music from land with pride.

What I always loved around the fire was mellifluous Gaelic;
'The Man of the Habit' and new songs would come alive,
And in the cell of my memory today and yesterday were one.

At another time my spirit recognised the power of God,
With the plover falling down from the languid sky;
Silence floating gently on loch and on mountain
While the very bottom of my heart was at rest in the glen.

With care your finger left the ground behind it
And you let your horses free to go to unbridled heights —
Identical to me the brave rumbustious taorladh
And my days of freedom when I came to experience pain. (NM)

MAOL DONN

Bu tu a' chraobh leatha fhèin an lios nan sùil
'S tu gleusadh dhos na pìob' le meòirean grinn;
Bha 'n còmhlan balbh gun deò an talla dhlùth
Nuair chuir thu bàt' do chiùil le uaill bho thìr.

B' e m' annsachd riamh mun tein' a' Ghàidhlig chaomh;
Bhiodh 'Fear na h-Eabaid' 's òrain nuadh tighinn beò,
'S an cill mo chuimhn' bha 'n-diugh 's an-dè mar aon.

Uair eile dh'aithnich m' aigne cumhachd Dhè,
Bha 'n fheadag tuiteam sios on iarmailt fhann;
Bha sàmhchair 'snàmh gu ciùin air loch 's air slèibh
'S iochdar-druim mo chridh' aig fois sa ghleann.

Le curam dh'fhag do mheur an grunnd na dèidh
'S leig thu t' eich gu aonach saor gun srian —
B' ionnan leam an taorladh gàireach treun
Ri làithean m' shaorsa' san d'fhuair mi fios air pian. (NM)

AN TAORLADH

Proud was your chanter when you quickened the melody,
Swift music-smart glory-trimmed fingers were kissing it —
Taorladh upon taorladh triumphantly musical,
You threw off the yoke and unleashed your skilfulness.

As the eagle soars over moorland so lightly
Your spirit rose upon sharp cutting strokes,
Your mind was aflame and you trusted your paths,
Your eye looked divided at end and beginning.

What thoughts were you pondering on the speediest of journeys,
Borne along by your fresh clever dexterous hands?
What film from afar did your memory show you
As you confidently drew your taorladh to a close?

My shame was born in agility and eloquence,
For the city's roar and bustle attracted me —
Intense were the hunger and ambition that drove me,
And I drank my fill of the world's pleasant wine. (Aut)

AN TAORLADH

Bu phròiseil do shiunnsair nuair ghreasaich thu 'n crònan,
Bras-mheòirean ceòl-sturtail glòir-ghleust' ga phògadh —
Taorladh air taorladh gu caithreamach ceòlmhor,
Thilg thu chuing 's leig t' sheòltachd fa sgaoil.

Mar dhìreas am fireun gu h-aotrom thar mhòintich,
Dh'èirich do spiorad air buillean geur sròiceach,
Bha t' inntinn na lasair 's t' earbsa nad ròidean,
Dhearc do shùil sgaoilte air deireadh 's air tùs.

De 'n smuain bha nad inntinn air 'n turas ro shiubhlach,
Do làmhan glan innleachdach carach ga giùlan?
De 'n dealbh o chian chuir do chuimhne ro t' shùilean
Nuair ghluais thu le misneachd an taorladh gu crìch?

Rugadh mo nàire ann an lùth-chleas 's ard-agal,
Gleadhraich 's ùpraid a' bhaile gam thàladh —
Bu ghionach an t-acras 's miann rinn mo chràdhlot,
Dh'òl mi mo shàth de dh'fhìon taitneach an t-saoghail. (NM)

My poetry is personal, much more so than most Gaelic bardachd, where the tradition is to tell stories or report and respond to external events. I stand astride two worlds, the modern world of the big city slicker and the old world of the pipes and the islands and perhaps for that reason my poetry is about me rather than them, though they provide the stage.

I have a capacity for concentration of attention. I can focus on things. It is a characteristic of my family but I think it springs from the wish, the need, to get on with people, to communicate. I've always had a great need to make contact, to give pleasure, to surprise people. I've always been a shaman-like character. Because of my upbringing in two places I have always felt, I certainly could always feel, like an outsider. I was everywhere a stranger, and I still am. But also I can feel at home almost anywhere. I used to appear here and there, spotlit, like a character on a stage, from a very early age. And I must have both consciously and unconsciously developed a theatrical, an other-worldly quality, though I'm far from unworldly. It was a defence mechanism. My capacity for mimicry, for languages, for song, for playing the pipes were all part of this. I was the Fool in the gang. The Precocious Kid from the big bad city. My recall of dialogue was exceptional, my imitation of accents was a kind

of speaking in tongues. I was a freak wherever I went. The prize mad bull wherever I go.

Even today, with Gaelic experiencing this big international renaissance, I remain unique in my combination of talents and experience. I can't think of another Gaelic writer who embraces and embodies the city and the modern world as I do. They all hanker back in one way or another to the islands and the old ways of life. I'm wedded to the pulse of the city, I'm a conscientious hedonist; I like salted, fatty foods, I smoke, I don't jog, I hear the chimes of the city clocks at midnight, one after the other: I don't care a damn for the whales. But nor did the islanders! I've been tanned by the light of too many beer signs, for years I've been drifting too wide in the turns – but I haven't retreated, it's still in the city that I live and here that I find the stimulus for all that I do as an artist. The voice of the oracle is a mouth in the darkness. My first novel *Cùmhnantan* was about the greed and opportunism now rampant in the Gaelic television community. Sales have surpassed those of any Gaelic book published in the last fifty years except the Bible. It's a huge community with expense accounts! They like to read about themselves.

Of course, there is in me, as in everybody, some longing for life as a rural idyll but it has no reality to me. Reality for me is the old Glasgow tenements and the raw-boned monstrosities that respectable criminals put up in the sixties and which still bedeck the centre of Glasgow to this day. Look at that large urinal they call Scottish Television! I was a vacationer in the rural idyll

Above left:
Norman MacLean acting the villain
in one of his television stories. (TN)

Above right:
Norman MacLean, the rebel. (TN)

and I saw great poverty there on Uist but for me it appeared like unreal reality. But, having said all that, I believe that, deep down, I am in many ways more Highland than the Highlanders themselves, just as the American Irish can be more Irish than the Irish. And when I talk of the Highlanders, I mean the elitist, proud Highlanders of old – not the modern mealy-mouthed Gaels you get in the television studios spouting and blaming.

I did a BBC radio phone-in one morning. From my bedroom in Glasgow. The subject was British chocolate and EU regulations. Our chocolate does not contain the amount of cacoa that the edicts of the European Commission demand! Will UK chocolates be upgraded, phased out or relabelled? Now, I have a serious chocolate habit! It can only be sated by continental chocolate, dark and strong, so I spoke up for the deep, dark throat of European chocolate. I spoke about values, courage, strength, cacoa, about honouring your word and knowing where you stand! But all the other contributors, from Inverness and the Highlands, went on about the iniquity of EU regulations and our need to continue purchasing large amounts of third-rate tooth-rotting Cadbury's and Mars! All in a boring, pseudo-scientific jargon that was prosaic in the extreme. But from Glasgow, upspake that decadent townie, MacLean, with a poem written between rising and hearing the eight o'clock news: a poem in praise of the European Parliament's Stipulations on Chocolate. And on radio, live, I sang in praise of quality, blackness and oral satisfaction, whilst the official representatives of the Gaidhealtachd whittered on like

Norman MacLean piping al fresco,
1948. (NM)

toothless councillors on a BCCI Public Relations bender! Fortunately I'm always surprising myself as well as my audience. I have an instinctive disdain for mediocrity, pretension and institutional bullying. I like the real thing, in people and in chocolate; however, although I'm a paid-up member of the oral tradition, it's always been a fact that I need to have a pen in my hand if I'm to compose anything. Chocolate and poetry are two different things and even if you promised me a lot of money and gave me a signed photograph of Pamela Anderson, I doubt if I could compose even one quatrain unless you also gave me a pen.

That fact distinguishes me from the old non-literate bards. For them it was different, assonances and rhyme seem to have sprung from their subject, their symbols, their rhythms: everything had to be worked out and retained in their heads – but we literate poets can cheat and we have made a habit of cheating. We can set down a rhyming scheme and run our couplets and what-not around them and nothing needs to be retained in the head at all. There's a huge difference, and there are big gains and big losses. The oral tradition can gravitate too easily towards sentiment and intellectual feebleness, whereas written poetry can become dry, over-clever and masturbatory.

So there is a big difference between my poetry and the bardic tradition in the purely literary strata of poetry but, with regard to the music, I'm still at one with the old timers. When I write, I always have a particular melody in mind, a rhythm, it may be very undistinguished but it is there and the pulse is strong. The tradition of irregular rhythm that you get in much modern English poetry – T.S. Eliot, for example – is foreign to me. I'm very conservative and pre-Tony Blair when it comes to poetry. In Gaelic the rhythm is fundamental and with the stress coming on the first syllable you get a percussive beat that is very difficult to escape from. It is ancient and for me it is timeless.

And for me there is no difference between writing words for a poem and a song. Music is there in both of them. As I write, I hear music in the background, whether the piece will be there to be read, spoken or sung. We stand on a cusp in this. Most Gaelic poetry today is being written to be read; this is most true of the most arty Gaelic poetry. None of my poetry is written to be read, it is written to be heard – and of course that was true of the old tradition. There is again something paradoxical here, for whilst our young Gaelic ruralists are writing like Ezra Pound for the Edinburgh magazines, I am delighted to use every last word in technology – word-processor, Windows, video, Website, Internet, Stealth bomber. My work is spoken on screen, stage or radio, or it is damned. My verses, as seen in the pages of this book, will be seen for the first time! And like a native affeared of his image being photographed, I'm affeared for my future now. The moving finger writes and having writ moves on. I strut and fret my hour upon the stage and then come back for more! I wear a homburg with the same pride as my kilt. I have a theatrical personality and though the Gael can be dour, this showy, shamanic personality is also there in the Gael.

This persona of mine, if it is a persona, comes from my maternal grand-uncle, his name was Big James, son of Angus, son of Big John. He was my grandmother's youngest brother. It was to him that I was sent, into Lochaber, during the war. Talk about 'a poem of remote life', his was it. And his

Kenny MacDonald, a hero of the MacLean family, killed at the battle of El Alamien, 1942. (NM)

was mine. He was working for Locheil at the time, very far out. Once every two months an ambulance would be sent up the glen by the estate to take the women, keepers and shepherds down to Fort William. The women would buy foodstuffs and clothes and the men would disappear into the Imperial Hotel. That trip was the boundary stone of their lives. It happened five or six times a year and most trips were similar – but the telling of the tale was something else! When Big James reported on his trips to Fort William, he was Odysseus returned after 20 years! An English stalker met on the road, a soldier returned from the war, a drunken pub brawl, the Fort William Games, an incident at the Aluminium Smelter – these became two-hour tales that entertained the whole village for the next two months. He was a natural raconteur, but a highly polished formal structure underpinned his performance. It was 'he said' and 'I said' and 'before you could lick your moustache' , all that kind of thing. He was not a man to take a very long run for a very short slide, he could turn the shortest slide into the start of a marathon. Well, anybody who knows me as a performer should know that I learned the tricks of my trade from Big James

Norman MacLean, flautist extraordinaire, 1950. (NM)

MacDonald up there in Lochaber. I don't think Billy Connolly or Ronnie Corbett have anything Big James didn't have.

His was the only house in the village with a radio. First it would be a silent gathering, to hear news of the war. One of Big James's sons, Kenny, was with the Camerons. He was killed at El Alamein and several of the village men were away at the war, so the listening was very intense but after the news, a ceilidh, appropriate to the night, would begin. And in all this I was the small boy watching from the corner. I can still remember how vividly I wanted to be a performer like my grand-uncle, and catch the eyes of girls as those young men who played their accordions there did. How I wanted to sing and affect people, just as the women who sang affected both the young and the old. There was a magic at those ceilidhs. And I knew even then that I wanted to be a provider of this strange drug that enthused, excited and exulted everybody around that darkened fireside. The only justification of my days must be that I have done something of that over the years, in bars, in village halls, in theatres, and on television screens across the land, that I have awakened a certain delight in people's hearts.

Delight is sometimes inspired by the overcoming of fear, the wonder of a recognition that follows surprise. When my mother was just four or five, before the start of the First World War, she was very close to her Auntie Seonag. On the croft it was Seonag's job to look after the cows and the sheep, and it was she who did all the herding. Well, one morning my mother went out with Seonag to bring in the cattle. Suddenly, on the brow of a small hill, Seonag stopped and her hand went up to her mouth, 'Oh, oh,' she said, 'These ones have come.' My mother ran up, asking, 'Who has come?' 'The ceàrdan, the tinkers,' said Seonag. And those words, combined with the sight of the bow-tents set out by a burn, put a fear in my mother, 'Oh dear, oh dear – lift me, lift me,' she said. And it wasn't to see better she asked this. It was for protection. The tinkers arouse a psychic terror that must be very old. 'You're not afraid?' said Seonag. 'Are they giants?' asked my mother, 'Will they take me away?' and she clung on for dear life, unable to take her eyes off the smoking chimneys, the dogs, the tinker men emerging through the slit doors of the tents – to raise their hands – and slowly her fear turned to a strange delight that she remembers over 80 years later. Great times I've had myself with the Travellers.

Television is another thing that has separated me from the old village bards. Traditionally they worked for small, almost private, local audiences. I have always worked for a larger public, often a national audience, glued to its set. But this fact raises another paradox, there is a real sense in which the modern electronic media are once more taking us back to an oral/visual mode of communication. The printed word is now much less overwhelmingly important than it was three generations ago. We are entering a variant of the essentially oral world that existed before printing became widespread in late medieval times. And, for good or ill, I am in the van of this development as far as it affects the Gaidhealtacht. And it is noticeable that the most successful media personalities are just the kind of people who you would, in the old days, have invited into your own home, or to the village ceilidh – whether they be Cilla Black, Bruce Forsyth, Chris Evans or Norman MacLean. And I see nothing wrong with being a convivial 'mine host', whether it be in the Caledonian Bar or on ITV for £200,000 pounds an hour.

Life is full of chances. If I had been brought up in another household, I might have become a professional card player. In Benbecula I played a lot of Catch the Ten – the archetypal Gaelic card game. Is heredity chance? It is and it isn't. I've been asked whether I have an agenda. Did a Fool ever have an agenda! The shaman must be a voice, not a mouthpiece. If I have an agenda, it is to be part of, what might be called the Gaelic genius for 'communication'. Gaelic civilisation depends on the process as much as the tradition of 'cultural' communication. I have both a natural and a developed sense of communication and I have the skills to communicate. If I wish to achieve something more, it is to use my personal capacities within the wider framework of Gaelic tradition and lived life. I am not Louis XIV, I do not say 'L'état, c'est moi,' but my abilities and concerns happen to be central concerns of the Gaidhealtacht.

My poetry, my wittiness, my cleverness are tools I can use to bring people closer together, to release in them what might be joy. There is an instinct 'to grandstand', as the Americans say, in everybody, and it came easy to me but it's cheap to say everybody likes showing off and me more than most! There's more to it than that. And I think my life as a piper throws some light on this aspect of my personality. When I was a teenager, my most developed creative talent was as a piper, but I began to feel that there would always be a distance between myself, as a piper, and the audience – whereas if I was to sing, tell stories, act the goat, then that distance would disappear. That's what I wanted – immediate contact, rapport and effect. So I began to sing in public and develop my bardic and shamanic tendencies, and I enjoyed it. But I was using other people's material, other people's songs and I felt that I wasn't getting my true deserts and that the only way to get them was to create my own material, to give the audience stuff they could get only from me. Then, whatever the response of the audience was, it would be a response to my being and my creation. That's the excuse and the impulsion behind the original work of every pop group worth its salt, and at best it works. It worked for me. And even when a performance fails to please, you can still gather a certain sympathy from the audience because it knows your material is original or genuinely spontaneous. They will recognise their own selves and own incompetence in your incompetence. I like what Salvador Dali said, 'There's only one difference between me and a mad man – I am not mad!' That's true of me.

One of the strengths of our Gaelic culture is its lack of a division between the high tradition of the great poets like Duncan Ban Macintyre and Sorley MacLean and the humble village rhymester. Anyone who can make verses rhyme can be called a bard – and a great melody can elevate what might, on the page, look like doggerel into something deeply moving or grand. Education may now be eroding that tradition but I hope not. In that regard, it seems to me that the academic who delights to put bardachd into deliberately clumsy English in the name of literal meaning does a great tradition a real disservice. If a thing is worth translating, it must be worth presentation with either linguistic precision or with some kind of poetic force. Sense must be made and at best the translation will carry something of the music of the original bardachd.

And going on from there I say this: I think those of us who grew up immersed in Gaelic culture have a different consciousness from Western

Norman MacLean with Hamish Henderson filming, 'Journey to a Kingdom', 1992. (NM)

man. I hope I'm not being racist but speaking of a fact. It is a fact which involves geography, history, social structures and, above all, certain cultural norms. And culture, for the Gael, begins with the word – the word sung, the word recited and the word spoken. I think it was John Lorne Campbell of Canna who waxed most eloquent about the unrivalled memory and historical consciousness of the Hebrideans. Even in the 20th century he was finding bards and singers with a repertoire of 300 songs, songs which might average 200 lines. And many bagpipers have memories that are rivalled only by those of the great pianists, the best classical conductors, chess players and game-show freaks.

The Gael has what I call a vertical, as opposed to a horizontal consciousness. An educated Western man knows a great deal, usually superficially, about a lot but the true Gael knows a great deal only about his personal ancestry and he carries an oral and musical culture from a similarly narrow but heroic, Homeric source. There is a felt proximity of ancestors. Great battles and personal tragedies impose themselves on the living, whether they happened 50 years, 250 years or 2,000 years ago. And the high development of this kind of historical awareness and sensibility gives the Gael a different perspective of time. The single vanishing point of Brunelleschi was unlikely to have been invented by a Gael but the telescope might have been! No people telescope time like the Gael and no music carries so much that is old into the present.

Another thing that may be important – in Western countries, for many centuries, most of the poetry has been created by the young. In Gaeldom most of the poetry is carried by the old. Now few bards create great poetry in their old age but age brings creative discernment. They will have learned the best of the old tradition and they will have sifted and measured the best products of their own times (their own poetry being part of this). That which is not memorable, exalted or important gets lost. They are custodians of a highly developed form of cultural evolution and although some good things do get lost, in general the cream will rise to the top. The idea that the treasures of Gaelic oral tradition are only the remnant of a much greater tradition is largely fallacious. The commercialised pidgin Gaelic that now flows from the subsidised media is far more destructive than Old Father Time.

Increasing numbers of bards are now emerging after retirement. During busy working lives many potential bards don't have time, or reason, to give themselves to poetry. Some have a natural or religious 'reticence' and it is only age that gives them the gravitas and the impulse to collate what they have gathered in their lives. The vast majority of middle-aged Gaels would rather streak naked through the bar of the Holiday Inn in Glasgow than seriously claim, 'I am a bard'! It is a nonsense to speak about 'the last bard'! New bards are coming into their own as we speak. The fact that many are in their 60s and 70s is part of the strength of the process. I am a great believer in foundations. The walls of any old blackhouse will stand far more years than the walls of any Doran-type bungalow.

I don't want to revert to the blackhouse but I should like to see us building better things than the Doran. That served its purpose but no more. And, in education, if the Government was to bring in some kind of statute that demands that schoolchildren and university students should learn poetry by heart, no protest will be heard from this son of Govan. Things are looking good for the Gael and there are still far more citizens in the Gaidhealtacht than there were in fifth century Athens. With the advantage of MacBraynes, the motor car, the television set – it will be an outrage if we don't very quickly surpass the achievements of the Athenians – in the age of Pericles.

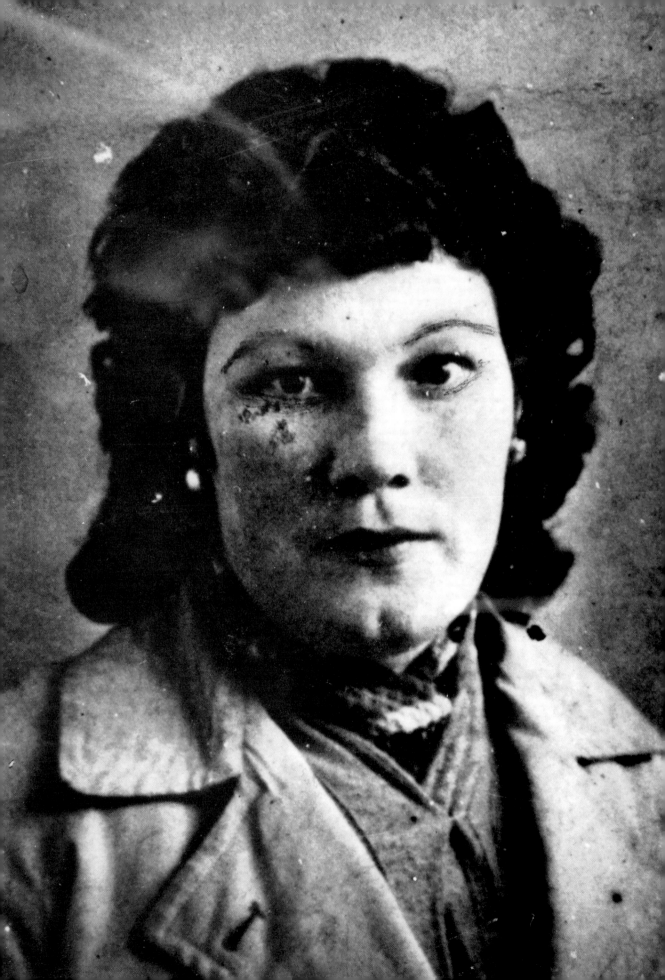

Memory:

GIVE THIS TO THE ONE YOU LOVE BEST OF ALL ONLY

All the bards represented in this book have huge repertoires of oral song/poetry, but it is those who sing who have the best memories and the largest repertoires. Why should this be? All bards need to have good memories but the very best remembrancers seem to have 'photographic-type' aural memories that are immediately triggered by the stimulus of rhythmical melodies which deliver the words onto the tongue as some kind of a chant. This is particularly true of the bardachd of Hugh MacIntosh, Murdani Mast Kennedy, Duncan Williamson, Calum Ruadh Nicolson and John Nicolson but also applies to Norman MacLean, John MacAskill and Charlotte Munro. This fact raises interesting questions, not just about Gaelic tradition, but also about the nature of poetry and the workings of the human brain.

Dramatic 'chanting' has been out of fashion among modern Western writers and literary custodians for close on a century. This has contributed to the steady 'privatisation' of most 'literary' poetry and is the prime reason why the oral memories of most contemporary poets and teachers of literature are so remarkably weak. One of the strengths of 20th century poetry has been the way in which it has integrated itself into the cinema, radio, television, pop music and folk tradition but, at its 'purer end', English poetry has become narrow, elitist and academic. Are essays, seminars, lectures and exam rooms really the places to meet poetry? Is it right that the state should subsidise the teaching and analysis of literature ten thousand times more generously than the contemporary writing, reading and hearing of literature?

One constant in the process of cultural renewal is the reappraisal of values, the values of one's own time and of history. In his book, *The Language*

Opposite:
Jeannie Robertson of Aberdeen, the traditional singer whose voice and repertoire played a major role in the International Folk Festival. c. 1940.
(LH)

of Instinct, the psychologist, Stephen Pinker, suggests that mankind has an innate 'instinct' for language and grammar. He believes this is a fundamental aspect of human being. It is a universal phenomenon and he makes the point that it is often most strongly developed where the educated mind would least expect to find it. He quotes research which suggests that there is a 'higher percentage of grammatical sentences in working-class speech than in middle-class speech' and that 'the highest percentage of ungrammatical sentences was found in the proceedings of learned academic conferences'! His own research depends heavily on the processes by which 'primitive' tribes, babies and children learn and use language. It affirms our need to give greater credence to the age-old oral tradition and to look afresh at the still relatively recent invention of writing. People who have 'libraries' of songs, poetry and lore in their heads have much to teach us and deserve recognition, and rewards.

The general neglect of Scotland's living bards is much greater than the neglect of bardic tradition as a whole. This divide has literary precedents. The Scottish universities, between them, paid the impecunious genius Hugh MacDiarmid perhaps £100 over a lifetime! Why should an intellectual and literary giant have been so treated by academics who make their livings off him? Would not students have benefited from a few more of his readings, his lectures, his tirades? Might not lecturers have benefited from such a 'laying on of hands'? Might not the universities benefit, even now, from a visit from one or two of our Highland bards? (They could be had for the tip the average professor might give the driver taking him to the airport for a tri-annual conference!) Strange 'unrealities' have established themselves in the educational marketplace, and across the world primary producers are underpaid and undervalued. False perceptions of what is really important have embedded themselves in our institutionalised consciences. (A momentary gesture by Paul Gascoigne pretending to play a flute at a football match [a sublime and naughty faun!], is condemned in the national press far more viciously than terrorist executions inside a British prison! And our political and cultural custodians complain not at all.)

Perhaps it is the fact that language is a basic human instinct, whereas writing is not, that has made the institutional elite so dismissive of tradition bearers and the unschooled poets. Pinker suggests that speech perception is mankind's sixth sense and that just as there are innate dynamics to human visual perception (clockwise rotation of vision etc.), so there are innate dynamics to the human response to speech prosody (melody, stress, timing). It has been observed that babies suck harder if they feed listening to recordings of their mother's mother tongue and that various experiential preferences are established in the womb. This 'evolutionary' knowledge and

Margaret Bennett, folklorist,
singer and bard, 1996. (TN)

emotional susceptibility may be similar to the 'folk biology' that seems to give all peoples basic intuitions about the natural 'character' of plants and animals (as opposed to there being no innate 'knowledge' about the 'character' of objects made artificially).

Traditional bards have retained direct contact with the original sources of language. They should be honoured for it. The time Coleridge spent with his 'ancient mariner' was at least as valuable to his poetic achievement as the years spent at Cambridge. 'Architecture, to be real,' wrote Charles Rennie Mackintosh 'must not be an envelope without contents.' And the same is true of poetry. Is it surprising that whilst the pursuit of knowledge becomes more and more institutionalised and diffident, the production of art becomes more and more extreme and bizarre?

The rural bardic tradition has real substance to offer the modern world. The bards are part of a disappearing continuity – of people, of work, of experience, of language, of memory. They offer connections to things that have 'worked' over millennia. They deal in memory and the phenomenon of the tongue linked to the heart.

The numinous proximity of ancestors continues to be one of the great strengths, and burdens, of Gaelic society. Interesting examples of this can be found in the work of the late 19th-century Skye poet, Iain MacLeod of Glendale, 'Iain Dubh'. He lived much of his life as a sailor. One of his best long poems is the satirical evocation of the night when a Glendale crofter, Donald Grant, felled a tree in the local graveyard. This act, against nature, moral law and ancestral being (like the evil acts of Hamlet's father and Coleridge's ancient mariner) precipitates powerful psychological consequences. The poem is called 'A Satire on Donald Grant'.

A SATIRE ON DONALD GRANT

Donald Grant was sick of guarding his cabbages;
His kale was precious as Naboth's vineyard!
His problem was simple – his wall was away –
And the sheep in his garden were cabbaging hay!

So Donald knowing that his cause was just,
Took an axe in the night to the tree of Cille Chònhghain.
He furtively chopped a branch for each gap,
Then, slinging his bundle, slunk home like a rat.

In bed much bruised with bearing his burden,
He tossed through the night till all of a sudden
A dark spectre appeared, to strike him with fear,
And all strength left his body as he broke into sweat!

The Spirit Spoke:

'Take not fright from my appearance, boy!
Though sad I was to leave the Realms of Glory
And well you know it is that I have come
Not with friendship or a welcome to your dark abode!

'Your axe brought lamentation down this night
On saints who were in bliss along with me!
That lovely shading veil has noble stood
For countless years as a beacon by yon churchyard wall!

'All light of knowledge must be long quenched in ye!
But know this — I am the son of the King of Norway!
Long buried in the graveyard of Cille Chònghain
And I was witness to your evil act this night:

'My eye never strayed as you dug through those corpses
Sleeping at rest in the silence of death — then
You slunk away home with their stain on your boots;
What madness drove you to such beastly work!

'You despoiled the tree planted on our sacred mound
By order of the Divine Creator from the Throne of Glory!
You - with your grubby, bloody paws cut down
The tree-of-memory, the tree of widows and of children;

'Its very beauty healed the grief inside their souls.
This tree that brings death to lamentation
Is the tree that brought happiness to Jonah.
The very Devil has imprinted you with poison stings!

'You thief without equal, you thief without pity!
You have no shame, no colour in your putrid skin
And you are bold enough to sleep alone!
But set down this — when strikes the morning light

'The Glendale folk will know full well what you have done
And great will their sorrow be to see their sacred tree
So loved and splendid in the blossom time
Lie broken in the graveyard of Cille Chònghain.'

Donald Grant replies:

'O, Prince of great renown, you were immortal —
Long before the skin was scoured from your bones...
After all these years buried under the sod
I never thought you'd see me chopping...

'Please, I beg you, pay attention to all I say —
My strength has deserted me and I'm not very well!
And to tell you the truth this accusation you bring
Has fairly scared me to death! Please listen, my Lord!

'Great King, your life was lived in wealth and splendour
You never knew the needs of the ordinary man
And my humble cabbages were very nice cabbages
Until they got savaged by those sheep from the township!

'So I beg of your Highness to recognise this —
It would have been crueller and much more of a sin
If I'd flung stones at their heads and chased them away
Through the gaps in the wall in the moonlight!

'That would have ensured loss of my soul and all speech!
So I promise you, Prince, if you leave me alive
And are gone, once and for all, by the morning
That I'll never, never go to the graveyard again!

'Not even if the sheep eat every cabbage in sight!
And I promise not to mend my stockade with sticks,
Till I go to the churchyard myself on bierpoles!
Nor even venture out with rope for a faggot of twigs!'

The spectre then said, as he turned from the bed,
'I've never heard so strange a confession!
But in future you'll get your fencing elsewhere,
From Hammar and Charles, in Portree, that's an order!

'And if I'm forced to this bedside once ever again,
I'll not go back to the graveyard without you!'
And the Shade sailed away through the smoke-hole —
Wishing a trembling Donald 'a very good night!'

'And the same to you,' said Donald.

AOIR DHOMHNAILL GHRANND

Nuair bha Domhnall Ghrannd ga phianadh
A' cumail dion air a' chal
A bha na shealladh cho fiachar
'S a bha 'm fion-lios aig Nabot,
Is on bha an iodhlann cho iosal
Leis na chrion dheth na ghàrradh,
Thug na caoraich de am miann dha
Na chuireadh crioch gun chus dàil air.

Ach rinn Domhnull suas inntinn
A dhol air oidhche le làmhaidh
A thoirt as craobh Chille Chòmhghain
Na chuireadh comhla 's gach beàrna:
Ghearr e nuas i na h-òrdan
Gu robh gu leòir aig' an gàdaig,
'S e deanamh earbsa le dòchas
Nach cluinneadh eòlaich an àit' e.

Nuair chaidh e chadal 's e brùite
Le bhith giùlan an eallaich,
Thainig faileas ga ionnsaigh
A sheas gu dlùth aig a leabaidh:
Nuair a chunnaic e an dealbh
A rinn dealradh na shealladh,
Dh'fhàg a fhradharc 's a lùths e
Le brùchdadh an fhallais.

Thuirt an spiorad:

"Na gabh sgeunadh ro m' iomhaigh-sa, dhuine,
Ged ghluais thu le mulad a Glòir mi,
Ach ma rainig mi t' fhàrdaich air thuras,
Chan ann le fàilte no furan gad fheòraich —
Thug do làmhadh san oidhche seo tuireadh
Do na naoimh a bha toilichte comh' rium,
Nuair a ghearr thu brat-sgaile na roilig
Bhon a mhuchadh ort solas an eòlais.

"Is mis' an spiorad aig Dil Mac Righ Lochlann
Chaidh air tùs ann an cladh Chille Chomhghain
A' toirt fianais gu fìor air an olc
Aig a' ghnìomh rinn thu nochd le do mheòirean;
Bha mo shùil ort a' bùrach nan corp
A bha sìnte nan tosd fo na bòrdan —
Ged a thàrr thu tighinn sàbhailt' air ais
Leis an uir aig mo cheap ri do bhrògan.

"Ciod e a rùpail an rùn a bh' air t' aire
Nuair a spùill thu na camain fo d' spògan
An tom-ungaidh a bhrùchd as an talamh
Bho ughdar na cathrach le òrdugh —
Craobh-chuimhne nam bantrach 's nan leanabh
Bha a h-àilleachd a' sgaradh am bròin diubh
'S a dh'fhàs a chum bàis do ar cumha
Mar an luibhe bha subhach le Ionah.

Nach b 'e 'n nàmhaid a sparr thu le ghathan
O mheirle gun choimeas gun deòn-bhaidh!
A bheil nàire no sgàth ort le athadh
No an dàna leat cadal nad ònar?
Nuair thig boillsgeadh le soillse bhon mhadainn
Bidh muinntir Ghleann Dail gu ro bhrònach
A' caoidh mun a' chraoibh bha cho maiseach
Fo bhlàth ann an Cladh Chille Chomhghain."

Fhreagair Domhnall:

"O Phrionnsa bha cliùiteach an gaisge
Mun do sgàradh am peacadh 's an fheòil dhìot,
Cha robh dùil leam gur tu dheanadh m' fhaicinn
'S an ùine bho phàisgeadh fon fhod thu;
Mas diù leat, gabh curam de m' fhacail:
Tha mo lùths, le bhith faisg ort, air fhògradh —
Thug t' iomhaigh aig beulaibh mo leapa
'S do dhàn mu mo chionta mo dheò uam.

"Bha thus', a Rìgh, làn saidhbhreis is beairteis,
Neo-fhiosraich air bochdainn mo sheorsa;
Bha mo chàl, a bha àlainn ri fhaicinn,
Aig caoraich nam bailtean ga shròiceadh;
Ar leam gum bu mhò rinn mi pheacadh
Gan ruagadh a-mach leis an dornaig
'S gan sgiursadh de m' ghrunnd ris a' ghealaich
Bhiodh daorsnail do m' anam nam chòmhradh.

"Ach ma dh'fhagas tu, Phrionnsa, mo shealladh
'S gun tàrr mi gu madainn mo bheò uat,
Bheir mise dhut m' fhacal 's mo ghealladh
Nach glac thu san roilig nas mò mi —
Ged a dh'itheadh na caoraich an iodhlainn,
Cha bhi do gheugan mu mullach ga còmhdach,
'S gu 'n teid mise don chill air na lunnan,
Cha teid mi ann tuilleadh le ròpa!"

Thuirt an Samhla 's e tionndadh on leabaidh,
Nuair a chual' e an aidmheil cho neonach,
"Gheibh thu geugan gu t' fheum ann a Hamarr
'S bheir Tearlach an gainnfhear dhut òrdugh,
Ach ma bheir thu mi rithist gu d' leabaidh,
Cha teid mi air ais gun thu comh' rium."
Sheòl an sgàile tron fharlas mar fhaileas
'S thuirt e, "Oidhche mhath leat, a Dhomhnaill."

"Mar sin leats'," arsa Domhnall. (IM)

This is village bardachd of a high order. The poem was sent to me by Johan MacLeod, a Skyewoman living at Tarbert, Harris. Composed orally, it had been handed down across four generations. Once more the question of memory arises. What combination of nature and nurture gives Gaelic tradition bearers their special skills of composition and recall? In our time, this would seem to be their most remarkable attribute. What methods do they employ to perpetuate word-perfect the impermanence of all speech?

The most outstanding living exponent of 'rhythmic/melodic recall' seems to be Duncan Williamson. He does not speak Gaelic but his background, as an Argyllshire Traveller, is deeply and thoroughly Gaelic. Where does his 'genius memory' come from? Duncan is highly intelligent but formally

completely uneducated. He reads, but not fluently. He finds writing very difficult. He doesn't like to have books in his house. The literary 'merit' of his poetic compositions is debatable but few would deny that he is a singer of great character and sensibility and that his songs are delivered with a strange and eerie magic that makes them compulsive. He gives himself utterly and innocently to his material, his imagination is vivid and fanciful, but it is the huge size and quality of his oral repertoire of song, story, riddle and anecdote that is mind-boggling. With a vice-like adherence to a number of subtly varied basic melodies and chant rhythms he can, at the age of 70, summon tens of thousands of lines of poetry and song and three thousand stories. This makes him *extraordinary* and a buried national treasure of Scotland.

It is rhythm and melody that seem to be the keys to his memory bank. This estimation is emphasised by the fact that whereas Duncan's songs, riddles and ballads are normally rendered perfectly without hesitation, his stories do carry certain hesitations, repetitions and meanderings. These may be part of a master storyteller's desire to continually 'rehook' the attention of his listeners, but it is more likely that they are proof of how aural memory is less precise when separated from the measured beat of simple rhythmic song – and

*Alexander Stewart (Ailidh Dall) of
Lairg, Sutherland, Gaelic storyteller,
singer and Presbyterian stalwart,
c. 1955. (HH)*

the pulsing flow of adrenaline that accompanies it. The swayings and chantings of oracles, rabbis, precentors, crooners and lovers are physical expressions of focused attention.

Duncan Williamson consciously memorises things but his methods are old and 'primitive'. He learned most of his repertoire around the stove and the camp fire, and in his granny's bow-tent. He was a member of a large family but part of an extremely small, archaic and rejected Traveller community. Today he is a recognised performer on the international storytelling circuit. He learns and creates new songs but he continues to use his 'campfire methodology' – not just because it is all he knows but also because it is the most effective method of verbal recall. He has a deep instinct to make songs of all poems he likes because he feels they are given their epiphany in song. He takes the plastic wrapping off any bouquet that takes his fancy and wraps it in rhythm before passing it on. And its rhythm and melody give the narrative permanence.

There may be other, genetic forces at work. The sense of 'heredity' is extremely strong amongst both the Travellers and the Gaels. Various members of Duncan Williamson's family have musical and literary

Stanley Robertson, nephew of Jeannie Robertson, renowned storyteller, bard and Mormon, 1996. (TN)

talents but he has a special gift that none of his brothers and sisters matched. Because of this he seems consciously to have taken on a 'responsibility' for his tribe's traditions. Perhaps he has inherited certain 'memory' genes; certainly his methods of presentation and recall would seem to go back to the beginnings of human culture. But his capacities are of contemporary scientific interest because they brilliantly, intuitively, make dramatically effective use of what psychologists, like Pinker, now recognise to be the basic electronic/ neurological systems by which the human brain, and digital computing, work.

Finally, the moral seriousness of most Highland bardachd cannot be ignored. A century ago the Danish philosopher, Sorn Kierkegaard, wrote, 'All moral elevation consists first and foremost in being weaned from the momentary,' and 'The evil in the daily press consists in its being calculated to make, if possible, the passing moment a thousand or ten thousand times more inflated and important than it really is.' What Kierkegaard recognised as a fact of life in his time is even more pervasive today. Does the un-newsworthy traditionalism of Scotland's Highland bards make them doubly valuable or the merely regressive remnant of a society tied to Christian fundamentalism, to sentiment and Victorian values? The great majority in contemporary urban society finds moral elevation an almost foreign, laughable concept properly undermined by modern education. Most poets of the Highlands and Islands know moral elevation as a natural and inescapable part of their lives and communal being.

A recent survey in the magazine *Nature* has revealed the crucial importance of early experience on the facilities of adult cats; visual and aural deprivation, for example, causing life-long incapacities. Researchers demonstrated how the visual world inhabited by kittens made a permanent impact on their brains. If they were allowed to see only horizontal stripes, the nerve cells primed to recognise vertical information failed to develop as they should and for the rest of their lives these 'deprived' kittens bumped into vertical objects. Human beings, like cats, are also powerful products of their experience. The childhood familiarity of the bards profiled in this book – with wild nature, with chosen words, with traditional song and story, with religious values – has obviously been crucial to their lives and their development as poets, as has the relative poverty, the work, and the elemental grandeur of the environments within which they grew up. Some of them would undoubtedly have benefited from a wider and higher education, some of their work may be aesthetically, second-rate, yet – as poets, as individuals, as citizens they are without doubt exemplary.

> *Hear the voice of the bard!*
> *Who present, past and future sees*
> *Whose ears have heard*
> *The Holy Word*
> *That walked among the ancient trees.* (W. Blake)

There is something of the sacred recurrent in the bardachd of all fourteen of our bards. They guard, as it were, one of the wells at the world's end and they keep alive traditions affirmed by the bard Columba 1,500 years ago; the saintly tradition of service, humbleness, obedience, courage, praise, and impelled visionary, peaceful utterance. A story told me by Duncan Williamson now brings this part of the book towards an appropriate close.

TELL THIS TO THE ONE YOU LOVE BEST OF ALL ONLY

Tim, I'll give you a gift of a story, to yourself, for the book: it's called 'The Golden Bowl'. In fact, it's two stories, but if I was to say, 'I'm going to make up a story,' I wouldn't be speaking the truth. I don't make stories, I tell stories, I put stories together and all my stories come down from tradition. What the good storyteller does is take a handful of beautiful words and kick them together into an even more beautiful story. I've picked them up here and there through a lifetime, but especially I got them from my grandmother, when I was just a small boy. A story is a present that you can keep for yourself, yet always share with somebody else. You can't say that about your trousers, or an apple, or a ten-pound note; you can't say that about a cigarette or a glass of beer but you can always say that about a story.

Now, it was after the death of Macbeth, in the battle up at Perth, that Malcolm became King of Scots. And Malcolm Canmore – that means 'bighead' in Gaelic – was very wise and he ruled his kingdom well. He loved hunting and minstrels and tumblers; songs and stories were told every night at his court and his people loved him. Indeed they loved him so much that when he died they wouldn't let his body go to Iona, where the bodies of nineteen kings are buried but they buried him in Dunfermline Abbey, close to the palace where he reigned for so many years. And Malcolm is still remembered by the people to this day.

Well, Malcolm's Queen was the Lady Margaret. She came from England. She was a good queen but she and Malcolm had no children and the King developed a strange obsession, the kind of obsession that many people get at Christmas time; he loved presents and he wanted more and more of them. And the people often brought him presents, sometimes out of love and sometimes in the hope of gaining a reward, and after breakfast his greatest pleasure was to go into his chamber and sit on his throne and gaze at the presents. There were so many they were stacked up around the walls. Most of them he'd never opened and he liked to wonder what he'd do with them all.

One morning he was sitting down to look at his presents when there was a knock on the door. 'You may enter,' said the King and in walked a servant with his hands behind his back. And he walked across the King's chamber and bowed before Malcolm. 'Well,' said the King, 'Can I help you?' And the servant said, 'My Lord, my Sire, my King – I have brought you another present – from an anonymous donor!' 'A present for

me!' said the King, his eyes lighting up. And the servant brought
forth a wooden box about as long as a whistle and six inches
deep, and each side was engraved with hunters and warriors,
with running deer and with hounds. The King took the box and
he turned it round and he admired it. There was no name upon
it and no indication as to from where or from whom it came.
So the King looked up and the servant backed away and went
out through the door, leaving the King once more by himself.

Malcolm sat and looked at the box and he saw it had a catch
and he opened it. And, lo and behold, there in the box was a
golden bowl, a little bowl engraved with scenes of hunting and
running deer, like those round the box. And Malcolm
wondered, 'Who could have sent this to me? This is the most
beautiful bowl I have ever seen.' And, looking inside the bowl,
he saw writing, and engraved all round inside the rim of the
bowl was a sentence in Latin, which he read: 'Give this to the
one you love most of all only.'

And the King turned the bowl in his hands and he
wondered, 'Who do I love most of all only?' And he thought of
his hound, the pride of his pack. This bowl would make a
beautiful drinking bowl for my blue and tan hound, who runs
by my side and chases the stag and the wolf. I love my hound as
true as my hand. But then he thought of Margaret, his Queen.
'Surely it is her I love most of all only? She sleeps by my side
and comforts me in my troubles. A hound can drink from the
burn or puddle and this is a bowl that is fit for a queen. Yes, I
think I must love Margaret more than my hound.' And so
Malcolm called for the Queen and she came before him and,
being the wife of the King, she said to him, 'Malcolm, you
called me, but you know how busy I am!' 'O yes,' said the King,
'But this won't take a moment. I have just received this present
and would like you to have it.' And he gave Margaret the bowl
and she, being a Latin scholar, turned the bowl in her hands and
read the inscription: 'Give this to the one you love most of all
only,' and she looked at the King and she smiled and she said,
'Thank you Malcolm, I will treasure this.' And she turned and
left the King's chamber.

Outside in the corridor, the Queen stopped and looked at
the bowl again and she wondered to herself, 'Who is it that I
love most of all only?' It was not Malcolm that she loved most

of all only – oh no. There was somebody else she loved,
somebody she admired from afar, the middle-aged captain of
the King's Guard, for she was the ageing Queen. This captain
was the man she loved most of all only. 'Yes,' she said to herself,
'I love him even more than I love Malcolm.' And she went to
the barracks and called for the captain, and the captain was
brought before the Queen; very tall and handsome he was. And
the Queen said, 'Captain, I have a present for you.' 'A present
for me, my Queen?' said the captain. And she gave the golden
bowl to the captain of the King's Guard, and he said, 'This is
very beautiful, my Queen, where does it come from?' 'From a
friend,' said the Queen, 'who wants you to have it.' And she
turned and left without adding another word.

Well, the captain of the King's Guard stood with the bowl
and he turned it round in his hands and read the inscription
inside the bowl, 'Give this to the one you love most of all only.'
And he wondered, 'Did the Queen have this beautiful bowl
made for me?' But he was a man of duty and honour, 'Who is it
that I love most of all only?' he said to himself. Well, it wasn't
the aged Queen he loved most of all, oh no. She was aged, she
was the wife of his King and he loved somebody else. Not his
wife, for she had died many years before, but their only son, a
young soldier under his own command, in the King's Guard;
the man who he hoped, one day, would take his place as
Captain. So he called his son to him and when he came, the
young man said, 'Captain, you called me?' 'Yes,' said his father. 'I
have just received this anonymous present and I would like you
to have it.' The captain passed the golden bowl to his son. And
the young man admired it and he looked at the engraved
warriors, the hunting dogs and the running deer and he asked
his father to help him translate the Latin that he saw transcribed
round the rim. 'Give this to the one you love most of all only.
Treasure it, my son.'

In the courtyard the young man stopped and looked at the
bowl shining in the light of the sun and he could think of
nothing but the one he loved best of all, a little kitchen maid
who worked in the great kitchen of the King, where she
cleaned and scrubbed the great copper pots, with her bare feet
and her ragged dress, the most beautiful little thing that he'd
ever clapped his eyes on. She was just a poor beggarmaid who

came up from the village. But he knew that he loved her and he
went down the steep steps at the back of the kitchen to find
her. When she saw him she was startled and half covered her
face with one hand with shyness and she gave a small cry. 'No,'
said the young soldier, 'Don't be afraid, little one, I come to do
you no harm. I've brought you a present!' 'A present for me,'
said the beggarmaid, 'No one ever brings me presents.' But
straight away he gave her the bowl and her eyes lighted up. 'Is it
brass?' she said. 'No, it's solid gold,' said the soldier. And the
maid turned the bowl in her hands and she saw the letters
inside the rim and, though she could not read or write, she
knew what writing was, so she asked the young man, 'Please
tell me what it says?' 'Ah,' said the boy, 'It says you must give
this to the one you love best of all only.' And she gave a small
frown and smiled, 'Thank you my Lord, I will treasure it.' And
with that the young man hurried away whilst the little
beggarmaid looked after him. And she stood in her bare feet in
the kitchen of the Royal Palace of Dunfermline with a beautiful
bowl of solid gold in her hands and she thought about the words
of the captain's son: 'You must give this to the one you love best
of all only'. And a tear rolled down her cheek. She was so
happy. She'd never been able to give anybody a real present but
now she could.

But to whom could she give it? This girl was an orphan, her
parents were dead, and she had no brothers or sisters. So she sat
by the water butt and wondered. Oh, she thought very hard.
She thought of the young soldier who had given it to her – but
she couldn't give it back to him. And suddenly she remembered
the one person who had always treated her decently. It wasn't
the cook and it wasn't the butler, it wasn't her stepmother, nor
her stepfather, nor the cobbler who wouldn't mend her shoes; it
was Malcolm, the King himself. For, of all the people in the
palace, it was always the King who treated her best, always
saying, 'Good morning, my dear.' So she thought, 'Yes, at last, I
have something fit to give to my King, something made of gold.
I shall give the golden bowl to the King.'

And so she hurried quickly along the corridors of the great
palace of Dunfermline till she came to the King's chamber and
she knocked on the door. 'You may enter,' said the King and she
opened the great door and went in with her two hands behind

her back. And the King smiled because he knew who she was. 'You've come for a visit?' said Malcolm, 'Have you come to sing to me?' and the little kitchen maid said, 'My King, I've brought you a present.' 'A present for me!' said the King. And the little girl gave him the golden bowl. And the King looked at it and he knew what it was. But not how she got it, and he said, 'Thank you, my dear, I shall treasure it all my life.' Then he asked the girl, 'Do they beat you in the kitchen?' and she burst into tears and ran from the room, closing the door behind her. 'Now why did I say a silly thing like that?' said the King to himself.

So there he was, Malcolm Canmore, silent in the great Palace of Dunfermline, and he rested his head in one hand and he lifted the golden bowl in the other, and he looked at all the presents piled high round the walls of his chamber and he knew what he would do with them. And he wondered who the anonymous person was who had given him such a beautiful bowl and how it passed to the kitchen maid who burst into tears. And he said out loud, 'Perhaps I should have given the bowl to my hound after all!'

Well, that's the first half of the story and the second half is even better! As I said at the beginning, Malcolm Canmore was a king who loved hunting and each September he would ride north into the forests of Fife with his men to hunt all the different animals that still lived in Scotland in those days — bears, wolves, deer, wild goats, even wild cattle and horses. He'd go out for days and with his huntsmen he'd live rough on the heath like the men of the olden times. Many animals would be killed and taken back to Dunfermline where they stored them in a great snow box his men dug deep in the ground. Malcolm Canmore was the man who invented the freezer.

Well, one year the hunting was not good and after a week in the forest, the King rose early and ordered his men, 'Kill everything in sight! Tonight we go back to Dunfermline.' All day they hunted till the red sun went down behind Ben Vorlich and the huntsman blew his horn and the King turned, tired and well laden with fresh meat, for home. The men were very hungry but such was the rush that morning that no food had been packed and there were only twelve oatcakes to be shared amongst all the huntsmen. Evening was falling and there was no time for the making of fires or the cooking of venison, so the

Previous pages:
Celebrations at the ninetieth birthday
party of singer and bard, Belle
Stewart, Blairgowrie, Perthshire,
July 1996. (TN)

King ordered them to stop at the next village to get food.

The long street was deserted and each little thatched house was empty, but down in a hollow, by the burn, a fire was blazing and a circle of people was cheering and laughing – so the King and his huntsmen rode up very quietly to view the celebrations. Riding on horseback they could see over the heads of the crowd and what did they see but a very small man tumbling and leaping like a one-man circus. Oh! he was very, very good and he was very, very funny and the huntsmen started laughing and they forgot their hunger and the tears were running down the cheeks of the King's face. He couldn't stop laughing! He laughed so loud that the people looked round and, when they saw it was Malcolm Canmore, the King, a great silence descended and everybody rushed to be of service to the King and his huntsmen. Food was brought and drink taken and the King asked, 'Who was that little tumbler, and is he for sale? I'd like to take a man like that back to the palace at Dunfermline. I'd pay a good price for a man like that.'

Well, it was a local merchant who owned the little fellow, and there and then the captain of the King's Guard bought him for 40 pieces of silver. And the little tumbler was brought before the King and the King leaned down from his horse and lifted him up by one hand. To the King he seemed to weigh no more than a feather and he said, 'Don't be afraid little one, no one is going to hurt you and Margaret, my Queen, will be delighted to meet you. We need somebody like you now age comes upon us.' And the little fellow smiled and said, 'I am honoured to serve a man with such a big head!' And the King roared with laughter and spurred on his horse and before the moon had set over the mountains, the little tumbler was asleep in his own little room, high in the palace in Dunfermline town. But Malcolm was still up and telling his Queen about the new friend she would meet in the morning 'He's a dwarf! But you should see the things that he does, hear the things that he says, hear the songs that he sings!' And they both went off to sleep as though they were young once again.

The Queen, of course, had no family of her own and she instantly took a liking to the little fellow and 'From this day on,' she said, 'You will be known as the King's Little Fool.' At first she hoped he would grow but the years passed and he never

Traveller humour captured on camera.
Big Willie Cameron pretends to arrest
his uncle, Duncan Cameron, as a
drunken piper, Perth, 1920s. (WM)

grew any taller. 'I was born to be small, that is my secret!' the
little fellow would say and each evening he would make the
King laugh and the Queen laugh and the court and the King's
visitors laugh till the tears ran down their cheeks.

The King's Little Fool had a special place at the King's table,
and he served the King's wine, and he walked with the Queen
in the palace gardens, and the King's purse he carried round his
waist. No one would guess the tricks he got up to but from his
mouth it was only the truth that came out. When he told the
King his hair had turned white, the King smiled. When he told
the Queen there were crow's feet around her eyes, she said it

was because he made her laugh too much. And the years passed and the King took very ill and in a fever he lay in his bed. The quack doctors were brought and they listened to his heart and they got leeches to bleed him and said he must rest. Then they went to the Queen and told her that the King would die. And with that the Queen went to Malcolm and told him the news and she said, 'No one else must know this! I will tell the people the King has taken a cold in the nose.' Well, when the Little Fool heard that the King was ill, he became very sad and he went to his room and he wouldn't come out.

And now Malcolm decided this was the moment to do something with the presents! And he asked that they be brought to him and heaped up on his bed. But there were too many presents and his servants had to stack them in four rooms and two stables and move out the horses. 'It is given that everybody must die,' said the King. 'My people have given me many presents, now it is time for me to give back.' And he ordered the presents to be distributed, still wrapped, to all the poor people in Scotland and all those who had done him service over the years. Many wonderful presents were opened. The jailer, the gardener, the kennel man who looked after the King's hounds, the huntsman, the son of the captain of the King's Guard – everybody who was somebody received something, but for the Little Fool, who was shut away in his room by himself, forgotten.

For twelve nights the palace stood silent and dark, then the King called for his Queen to say goodbye for the last time. And as Margaret passed the door of the Little Fool's room she heard a small voice singing and she listened and what she heard was the Little Fool saying his prayers. And on she hurried.

'Well,' the King told her, 'You have been a good queen and a good wife. I have received many gifts and given them away. I have asked to be forgiven my trespasses and forgotten no one and now I say my last good night.' And the King lay back and closed his eyes and the Queen thought of the Little Fool and suddenly she said, 'Malcolm, there is just one person you did forget, your Little Fool!' And the King started and he opened his eyes, 'Oh! Why did I forget my Little Fool and why did no one bring him before me? Now I have nothing left to give him! Send him to me at once.' And the Little Fool came and he

climbed up onto the King's bed. He had wrinkles on his
forehead but he was still no bigger than the day the King first
saw him, and from the corner of the King's eye a tear rolled
down. 'I'm sorry, my Little Fool,' said the King and the Fool
said, 'Sorry my King! Why are you sorry? I'm so pleased to be
here at your side, I'll dance on the bed and make you laugh till
you cry!'

'Oh no!' said the King, 'There will be no more laughter and
no more tears, I'm going away on a very long journey. I've said
goodbye and given all my presents away but, to my shame,
given you nothing, nothing at all.' 'Given me nothing, my King!'
said the Little Fool. 'I shall get angry! You have given me
everything – my home, my happiness, my life, you have been
like a father to me and the Queen has been like a mother. I sit
at your table, I pour out your wine, I carry your purse, I see
you don't spend all your money. I have my own room with a
painted wall and you say you have given me nothing!' And the
King said, 'No, no, no, I don't mean that, I mean a real present,
like the ones I gave to the chancellor, to the gardener, to the
children down on the shore…' Suddenly the King remembered
that at the head of his bed was an ivory staff, given him by his
father. 'One moment,' he said and he reached back behind his
head for the staff. It was a hand-carved rod from the tusk of an
African elephant and two snakes were twined round it with red
ruby eyes. And the King laid the staff across the bed before him.
'Little one,' he said, 'Perhaps, I didn't forget after all, for here is
the staff of my fathers!'

But the Little Fool knew that the staff was a royal staff and
no stick for a Fool and he said, 'My Sire, my King, I cannot, I
will not take the staff of your forefathers!' And he put it back
on the bed. But the King insisted, and he said, 'Little Fool, I am
your King, you will take this staff and you must promise me
you will never give it away till you meet somebody more
foolish than you are!' And with that the little fellow gave
Malcolm his promise and he picked up the ivory staff and
looked at the four red ruby eyes. 'This staff,' he said, 'will be
most helpful when we set off on this long journey you've talked
of.' 'We!' said the King, 'We are not going on a journey! This is
a very long journey and I have to go on my own. I will travel
without Queen, without huntsman, without food, without

crown; it is the River of Life I must cross and there's no coming back.'

And the Little Fool made a terrible face; he was baffled and puzzled. He looked at the King and he said, 'You are going on a very long journey without your Queen, without food, without drink, without a tailor to mend your clothes, with no purse for the poor, without hawk and no hounds, without guardsman, tumblers and singers, or me? You are a fool!' And the Little Fool leapt up and down on the bed and he thumped his staff on the floor. 'Here, take your staff back! I gave you my promise and I give you the staff – for you are more foolish than I!' And the Little Fool thrust the staff back into the hand of the King, saying, 'You are the Fool, not I!' And he jumped from the bed and pretended to hurt his foot. 'Oh! Oh!' he cried, 'Life's full of pain!'

And the King smiled and he said, 'My Little Fool, you are not a fool, you are the wisest man in my kingdom!' And the little fellow poured the old King a glass of water and the King sipped the cool water and, and this is the strangest thing in the story, Malcolm Canmore began to recover and he lived for many years. Years of happiness, peace and of war, and when the news came that Malcolm had been killed in battle, Queen Margaret asked that the Little Fool come to her room and from her throne she spoke, 'Before the King left for war, he said, "If it should be that I should die, I ask you to give this box to the Little Fool, who I forgot." ' and the Queen went to her cupboard and brought out a wooden box as long as a whistle and about six inches deep, carved all round with hunting hawks, with hounds and running deer. And the Little Fool thanked the Queen and he took the box and he opened it and inside there was nothing – but a beautiful Golden Bowl.

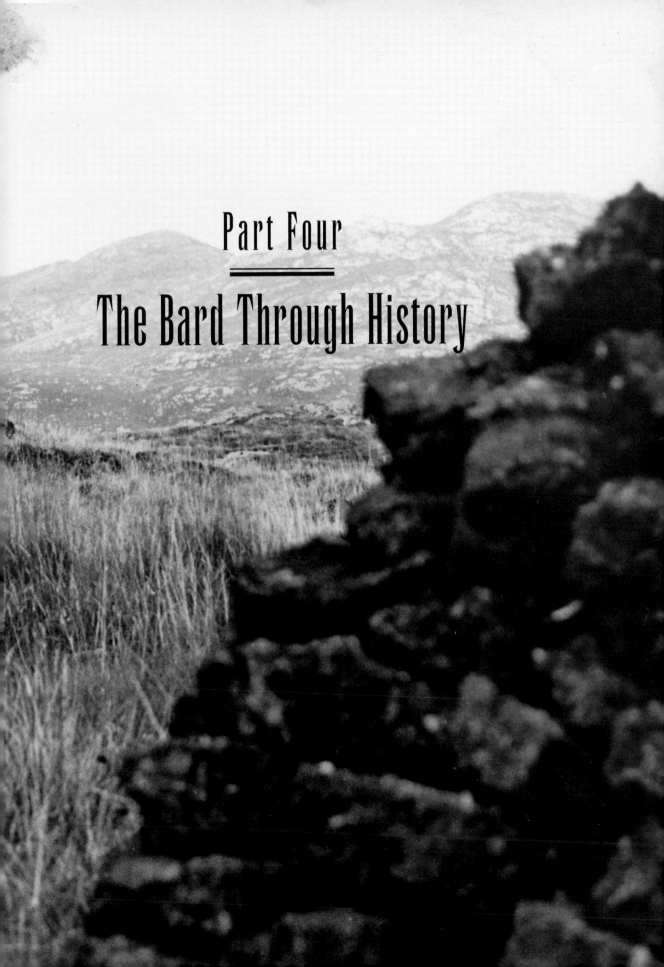

Part Four

The Bard Through History

The Bard Through History

JOHN MACINNES

The word 'bard' in Scottish Gaelic means 'poet'. It was not always so, however, for in earlier times 'bard' was a technical term, and only one among many such terms for makers of verse; and its development, in which it becomes the generic word for poet in the Gaelic of Scotland, requires to be examined.

There is evidence also for the existence of poets who were known by the name 'bard' (or one of its cognates) in places beyond the Gaelic lands, beginning with the Celts of Continental Europe. Even if the status and function of the bard has varied considerably from place to place and from age to age, the word itself is highly conspicuous in descriptions of Celtic societies throughout history. From a Common·Celtic 'bardos' are derived Irish, Scottish and Manx 'bard', Welsh 'bardd', Cornish 'barth' and Breton 'barz'. The word is thus represented in all the Celtic languages.

Classical writers tell us of Celtic 'bardoi' (Greek) and 'bardi' (Latin). Greek commentators also mention 'ouateis', cognate with Latin 'vates'; both of these corresponding to early Gaelic 'fáith', singular; fátha plural. The Gaelic word, which still survives in slightly different form, is normally translated as 'prophet', though now with biblical rather than pagan connotations. These 'vates', prophets and seers, of early Gaelic society, according to the same Classical sources, were either identical with the druids or had closely related functions, one of which was poetic composition. But more conspicuous as composers of poetry, in contrast to prophecy and divination, were the bards. They were, according to one source, makers of odes and poems and specifically, according to another, makers of praise-poetry.

These bardic panegyrics might have been addressed to people of relatively low degree in society but, if so, we do not hear about them. What we do know is that kings could be praised in the songs of the bards. A well-known story in Greek tells how the Gaulish King Lovernios (c.100 BC) held a feast at which a bard, who had arrived too late for the banquet, ran after the royal chariot, chanting a poem in praise of the king, while making apologies for his own late arrival. The king threw him a bag of gold whereupon the bard declaimed the words 'The track of your chariot on the ground brings gold and profit to men,' and that sentiment has been noted as being very similar to that which can be found, centuries later, in Gaelic praise-poetry.

In another Greek source, of the mid first century AD, bards are described as 'lyric poets… they compose praise for some and satires for others and chant them to the accompaniment of a kind of lyre'.

This role of praise-singer (with its concomitant of dispraise) may have always been the defining role of the bard in Celtic society and sixteen centuries later Gaelic poets are described in the words 'Some made panegyricks onlie, others made onlie satyrs.' But there are early sources from Continental Europe at this early period which suggest the bard might act in other capacities also, such as those of shaman or seer – functions that are more generally ascribed to the vates or prophets. Perhaps, indeed, the latter might from time to time adopt the bardic role of the praise-poet in what for them, the seer-poets, would be a secondary capacity.

The earliest evidence for the role and status of Gaelic bards comes from Ireland. Here we have two main categories of verse-makers. The first is the 'fili', plural 'filidh', whose name is connected with a verb 'to see'. According to Irish tradition of the ninth century, the 'fili' could achieve mystic vision and engage in divination. The other category is that of 'bard', plural 'baird'. Juristic descriptions, which establish a variety of grades within each of the categories of 'bard' and 'fili' (so that we have, for example, 'free bards' and 'unfree bards', each of these containing eight sub-classes) are absolutely clear in making bards the lower of the two.

According to tenth century juristic tradition, for example, the honour-price of a bard was only half that of a 'fili'. 'A bard can claim nothing on the grounds of being a man of learning, but must be satisfied with whatever his native wit may win him.' In the Medieval Irish *Book of Rights*, it is stated that 'Knowledge about kings and their privileges is proper to the 'fili' rather than the bard.' In the early 13th century, a bard's poem is described as 'camdhuan', 'a crooked lay', while 'barduigheacht', 'the work of a bard' came finally to mean 'vulgar abuse'. In a Cornish vocabulary of around 1100 AD, the word 'barth', 'a bard', is glossed in Latin 'mimus vel scurra', 'a mime or buffoon'. And in Scottish Gaelic dictionaries we may still find entries such as 'bardalachd' with secondary meanings of 'unseemly language' and the like. Clearly these are linked with the bard's capacity to produce not only praise but dispraise and satire as well.

It is worth noting that in Wales the 'bardd teulua', 'household bard', had a lower status than the 'pencerdd', who held land in freehold and had the right to sit next to the king. Although Gaelic bards, 'as long as they existed as a recognised social class and as far back as our sources permit us to go', occupied a similar relatively low position, various metres characteristic of bardic work were also used by the higher-class filidh. More than that: from the early Middle Ages onwards, almost all those metres that the filidh used come from this category of bardic metres. This apparent contradiction is resolved by arguing that the filidh took over the essentially bardic function of making praise-poetry – and took over the bard's metres as well.

This theory may well be valid but there is sufficient evidence to suggest that filidh from at least as early as the ninth century might act as panegyrists even if that were not their primary function. Certainly, from later Medieval times, roughly from the end of the twelfth century, panegyric poetry became the dominant mode within the entire field of Gaelic verse. An interest in the high mythological and historical lore once characteristic of the filidh gave way to a taste for straightforward praise poetry. The generally accepted theory is that this shift in fashion was caused by the Norman invasion of Ireland. In that process, the great centres of patronage were destroyed or lost their importance. In those reduced circumstances, the order of the filidh took over what had hitherto been the definitive role of the bard. But in Gaelic they did not call themselves baird. They still clung to their proud name of filidh. Indeed, to the present day the Irish Gaelic term for a poet is 'file', plural 'fili'. 'Bard' there has simply disappeared from colloquial use, while in Scotland it has become the all-embracing term.

But one family of Irish bards rose in the poetic hierarchy. These were the Wards, in Irish 'Clann a' Bhaird' – the Clann of the Bard. This kindred is listed among the leading families of poets, along with O Higgins and O Dalys and others, and carried on their profession on hereditary principles, from generation to generation, acting as poets to particular families, but honoured and rewarded also by any patron on whom they called while making their circuits from one great house to another. This highly privileged caste survived in Ireland until the 17th century and in Scotland until the middle of the 18th. Their verse craft was not oral. They wrote their poetry and had it preserved in manuscript. Yet, as we shall see, certain vestiges of an ancient oral tradition remained attached to practices of composition.

In English language usage, these learned poets are frequently referred to as 'bards' and their poetry as 'bardic' poetry. Understandably, this

has been the source of immense confusion. Some scholars have declared that
'from the 13th century onwards, if not somewhat earlier, the bards were the
chief intellectual force in the country [of Ireland]'. Others have asserted 'it is
clear that at no time in Ireland was there confusion between the class known
respectively as baird and filidh, and that at no time were the baird looked upon
as the leading intellectual class.' The contradiction is in reality in the
nomenclature, as the foregoing description will have made clear.

Yet the English use of 'bard' to denote the 'filidh' of the late
Middle Ages is not merely a modern convention. English commentators of the
16th century who describe the verse-makers of Ireland not only call them
bards but use that word as if it were a native English term. Thomas Smyth, for
instance, refers to the 'filidh' under the term 'Aosdan' ('Aos-dana', a collective
name, 'folk of poetry, the learned') and proceeds to define them: 'Which is to
say in English, the bards, or the riming septs...' Smyth also refers to them as
'Fillis, which is to say in English, a poet. These men have great store of cattle
and use all the trades of the others, with an addition of prophecies. These are
great maintainers of witches and other vile matters, to the great blasphemy of
God and to the great impoverishing of the Commonwealth.'

The references to prophecies and witches reflects some
knowledge of the 'filidh' and divination but his remarks are no more than crude
propaganda, for Smyth was a violently partisan agent of the English interest in
Ireland. With regard to his phrase 'great blasphemy', it is worth pointing out
that the 'bardic verse' of the 'filidh' contains a very considerable corpus of
religious poetry, some of it of a very high order indeed. As David Greene puts
it, those poets 'were very far from being medicine men or shamans inciting
barbarian chieftains to murder, as Thomas Smyth would have us believe; on the
contrary, they were highly educated professional men'.

As their stock in trade was praise of the leaders of their society,
who in turn rewarded them for their support, they obviously had a stake in the
survival of that society and its values. Greene goes on: 'Their weakness was that
they were, by the very nature of their calling, as much the paid propagandists
of the existing order of things as any writer east of the Iron Curtain; when that
order vanished, they vanished with it. They had no interest in the common
people, who can hardly have understood their archaic and ornamental style...'

The difference between the Gaelic of the bardic poets and that of
the common people is frequently commented upon and sometimes
exaggerated. Around the end of the twelfth century writers and scholars had
created a standard language which we call Classical Gaelic. For some five
centuries this remained the standard for the whole of Gaelic-speaking Ireland
and Scotland together, coming to an end in Scotland only in the middle of the

18th century. Its uses in Protestant translations of the Bible in Ireland, which were modified for use in Scotland, brought a valuable dimension to Scottish Gaelic writing and beyond that to the oral tradition, particularly in the abundant field of religious verse.

It is, however, true that as centuries passed and dialects continued to develop, from the high to the late Middle Ages, the gap between Classical and Vernacular must have widened, but stylistically both prose and poetry in Classical Gaelic can vary from 'archaic and ornamental' to relative simplicity. Even if, as Kenneth Jackson expresses it, 'a stanza of an Irish or Scottish bardic poem is a marvel of compression and elegance', some vernacular poets must have been able to unravel their sense. For in Scotland, in the 17th century, some of these had already succeeded in drawing upon the formulas and images of their Classical brethren, and this in itself provides at least a partial answer to the argument that the learned language was completely unintelligible to the common people.

Nevertheless, the bardic poets we are now considering were indeed a privileged caste of formidable erudition. Even the English poet Edmund Spenser, hostile to the whole Gaelic civilisation of Ireland as he was, has to admit they were not uninstructed, even though what to him was 'natural device' is in fact the product of much labour. 'I have caused divers of their poems,' he writes, 'to be translated unto me and surely they savoured of sweete wit and good invention, but skilled not of the goodly ornaments of poetry; yet they were sprinkled with some pretty flowers of their own natural device, which gave good grace and comeliness unto them...'

It is said that the bardic poets' courses of training covered seven years. From these courses of instruction, a remarkable amount of teaching materials has survived. Anyone who thinks of 'bards' as 'singing their native wood-notes wild' will certainly be impressed, by the discussion of grammatical, syntactical and metrical usages that the Gaelic bards' textbooks contain, It is obvious that the Bardic Schools had a severe academic discipline. Of the typical product of these schools, it has been said: 'He was, in fact, a professor of literature and a man of letters, highly trained in the use of a polished literary medium, belonging to a hereditary caste in the aristocratic society, holding an official position therein by virtue of his training, his learning, his knowledge of the history and tradition of his country and his clan. He discharged... the function of the modern journalist. He was not a song writer. He was often a public figure, a chronicler, a political essayist, a keen and satirical observer of his fellow countrymen. At an earlier period he had been regarded as a dealer in magic, a weaver of spells and incantations, who could blast his enemies by the venom of his verse, and there are traces down to the

most recent times of a lingering belief, which was not, of course, confined to
Ireland, in the efficacy of a well-turned malediction. He might be a poet too if,
in addition to his training, he was gifted with the indefinable power, the true
magic, of poetry. But whether he was a poet in the higher sense or not, he
always composed in verse.'

    So said the great Irish scholar, Osborn Bergin, writing in 1912.
And the English Celticist, Robin Flower, has this to add about the Gaelic bardic
poets: 'They correspond in a way to the University men, but their fixed place
in society was higher than any that his attainments alone have ever been able to
secure for the University man in England. They were, indeed, until the fall of
the old Irish order, an intellectual aristocracy, with all the privileges and, no
doubt, many of the prejudices of a caste. They held their position by virtue of
their birth and the practice of their art.'

    What now of the 'schools' in which the bards received their
instruction? The word in Gaelic is 'scol'/'sgol' (later 'sgoil') from Latin
'schola', and it can be used collectively to mean 'the learned' as well as the
place of learning. The most famous description of a bardic school is to be found
in the 'Memoirs of the Marquis of Clanricarde' (published in 1722).

> Concerning the poetical Seminary or School, from which I was
> carried away to clear other things that fell in my way, it was
> open only to such as were descended from Poets and reputed
> within their tribes. And so was it of all the Schools of that kind
> in the nation, being equal to the number of Families that
> followed the said calling. But some more or less frequented for
> the difference of Professors, Conveniency, with other Reasons,
> and seldom any come from remote parts, to be at a distance
> from Relations and other Acquaintances that might interrupt his
> Study. The Qualifications first required were reading well,
> writing the Mother-tongue, and a strong Memory. It was
> likewise necessary the Place should be in the solitary Recess of
> a Garden or within a Seat or Enclosure far out of reach of any
> Noise, which an Intercourse of People might otherwise
> occasion. The Structure was a snug low Hut, and beds in it at
> convenient Distances, each within a small Apartment without
> much Furniture of any kind, save only a Table, some Seats, and a
> Conveniency for cloathes to hang upon. No Windows to let in
> the Day, nor any Light at all us'd but that of Candles, and these
> brought in at a proper season only. The Students upon thorough
> Examination being first divided into Classes, wherein a regard

was had for everyone's Age, Genius and the Schooling had
before or otherwise. The professors (one or more as was the
occasion) gave a Subject suitable for the Capacity of each Class,
determining the number of Rhimes, and clearing what was to
be chiefly observed therein of Syllables, Quartans, Concord,
Correspondence, Termination and Union, each of which was
restrain'd by peculiar Rules. The said Subject (either one or
more as foresaid) having been given over Night, they worked it
apart each by himself upon his own Bed, the whole next Day in
the Dark, till at a certain Hour in the Night, Lights being
brought in, they committed it to writing. Being afterwards
dress'd and come together in a large Room, where the Masters
waited, each Scholar gave in his Performance, which being
corrected or approv'd of (according as it requir'd) either the
same or fresh subjects were given against the next Day. This
part being over, the Students went to their Meal, which was
then serv'd up; and so, after some time spent in Conversation
and other Diversions, each retir'd to his rest, to be ready for the
business of the next Morning. Every Saturday and on the Eaves
of Festival Days they broke up and dispers'd themselves among
the Gentlemen and rich Farmers of the Country, by whom they
were very well entertain'd and much made of, till they thought
fit to take their leaves, in order to re-assume their Study. Nor
was the people satisfied with affording this Hospitality alone;
they sent in by turns every Week from far and near Liquors and
all manners of Provision towards the Sustenance of the
Academy, so that the chief Poet was at little or no Charges, but,
on the contrary, got very well by it, besides the Presents made
him by the Students on their first coming, which was always at
Michaelmas, and from thence till 25th March, during the cold
season of the Year only, did that close Study last. At that time
the Scholars broke up, and repair'd each to his own Country,
with an Attestation of his Behaviour and Capacity and from the
chief Professor to those that had sent him.

The reason of laying the Study aforesaid in the Dark was
doubtless to avoid the Distraction which Light and the variety
of Objects represented commonly occasions. This being
prevented, the Faculties of the Soul occupied themselves solely
upon the Subject in hand, and the Theme given; so that it was
soon brought to some Perfection according to the Notions or

Capacities of the Students. Yet the course was long and tedious, as we find, and it was six or seven Years before a Mastery of the Last Degree was conferred, which you'll doubtless admire upon considering the great Difficulty of the Art, the many kinds of their Poems, the Exactness and Nicety to be observed in each, which was necessary to render their Numbers soft, and the Harmony agreeable, and pleasing to the Ear.

As every Professor, or chief Poet, depended on some Prince or great Lord, that had endowed his Tribe, he was under strict ties to him and Family, as to record in good Metre his Marriages, Births, Deaths, Acquisitions made in War and Peace, Exploits, and other remarkable things relating to the Same. He was likewise bound to offer an Elegy on the Decease of the said Lord, his consort, or any of his children, and a Marriage Song when there should be Occasion...

The last Part to be done, which was the ACTION and PRONUNCIATION of the Poem in Presence of the Maecenas, or the principle Person it related to, was perform'd with a great deal of Ceremony in a Consort of Vocal and Instrumental Musick. The Poet himself said nothing, but directed and took care that everbody else did his Part right. The Bards having first had the Composition from him, got it well by Heart, and now pronounc'd it orderly, keeping even Pace with a Harp, touched upon that Occasion; no other musical Instrument being allowed for the said Purpose than this alone, as being Masculin, much sweeter and fuller than any other.

We know from other sources that the reciter of the poem was termed 'reacaire' and how the bard, member of the lower poetic order, acts the part of 'reacaire' to the 'fili'. The significance of this is easily overlooked, viz. that the bard must have been literate also and have possessed a reasonable knowledge of Classical Gaelic.

In Scotland Martin Martin has an account which adds some details to that of Clanricarde:

The Orators, in their Language called Is-Dane [Aos-dana] were in high esteem in these islands and the Continent [Scottish mainland, esp. the Gàidhealtachd], until within these forty years they sat always among the Nobles and Chiefs of Families in the Streah or Circle. Their Houses and little Villages were

Sanctuaries, as well as Churches, and they took place before
Doctors of Physic. The Orators, after the Druids were extinct,
were brought in to preserve the Genealogy of Families and to
repeat the same at every succession of a Chief; and upon the
occasion of Marriages and Births they made Epithalamiums and
Panegyricks, which the Poet or Bard pronounc'd. The Orators
by the force of their Eloquence had a powerful ascendant over
the greatest men in their time; for if any Orator did but ask the
Habit, Arms, Horse, or any other thing belonging to the
greatest Man in these Islands, it was readily granted to them,
sometimes out of respect, and sometimes for fear of being
exclaimed against by a Satire, which in those days was reckon'd
a great dishonour; but these Gentlemen becoming insolent, lost
ever since both the Profit and Esteem which was formerly due
to their Character; for neither their Panegyricks nor Satires are
regarded to what they have been, and they are now allowed but
a small salary. I must not omit to relate their way of Study,
which is very singular. They shut their Doors and Windows for a
Day's time, and lie on their backs with a Stone upon their Belly,
and Plads about their Heads, and their Eyes being cover'd they
pump their Brains for Rhetorical Encomium or Panegyrick; and
indeed they furnish such a style from this Dark Cell as is
understood by very few; and if they purchase a couple of
Horses as the reward of their Meditation, they think they have
done a great Matter...

Martin, writing in his native Isle of Skye in the closing years of the 17th
century, is an important witness. For one thing he would have known a number
of these 'Orators', the learned poets, personally. His remarks on their loss of
status and influence in the second half of the century accords with what we
know from other sources: that this was the era in which outstanding poets
composing orally, in vernacular Gaelic, came into prominence. But it is not
absolutely clear whether his 'Poet' or 'Bard' is an alternative designation or
whether he is referring to two individuals. Elsewhere he seems to use Poet and
Bard as mere variants. If this is his intention, he is calling a poet of the schools
a 'bard' and here, the performance, as Martin knew it, differed, perhaps only
in the Isle of Skye, from what the Marquis of Clanricarde tells us about Ireland.

    It has been suggested that while the convention of composing in
the dark helped concentration, the origin of the practice was something
different. Bergin says: 'It looks very like the relic of a rite or ceremony of

divination handed down from pagan times, long after its original purpose had
been forgotten. We know that in early times the functions of the poet and
Druid or Magician were very similar, and both practised magic.'

Just about the time that Martin Martin published his description
of the Islands, the Rev. John Fraser (c.1701–02) supplied the following
information in his correspondence with Robert Wodrow:

> 'They had Bardi, poetici... peculiaire to every family... the
> bard's office was to rehearse what was compiled by the Poets;
> the poets versified with admirable art, and in such a high and
> lofty style, and such exact measures, and variety of measure...
> The Bards were sometimes allowed to compose some rhythmi
> but not to meddle any higher...'

> From J L Campbell and D S Thomson *Edward Lhuyd in the
> Scottish Highlands* (Oxford, 1963)

Fraser's Poetici and Bardi (simply the Latin forms for Poets and Bards) are
obviously the higher and lower orders with which we are familiar. And
'rehearse' which means here 'to repeat or recite aloud in a formal manner'
(OED.) corroborates the Irish Clanricarde account admirably. The distinction
between 'measures' and 'rhythmi' is that between the metres of the bardic
poets, in which lines are regulated by an exact syllable count, in contrast to
those metres in vernacular Gaelic where the regulating principle is not equal
numbers of syllables in corresponding lines, but equal numbers of stresses. The
Heroic Ballads, on which James MacPherson loosely based his 'Ossian' in the
18th century were, for the most part, originally composed in these 'syllabic'
metres and in Classical Gaelic. But in course of time they were drawn into the
vernacular repertoires and in the process usually lost their precise syllabic
measures.

It is obvious that the bard-as-reciter was in a particularly
advantageous position to act as an intermediary between the traditions of
Classical and Vernacular Gaelic. His metier was the vernacular, but he would
be sufficiently conversant with Classical poetry to draw upon its resources and
use them in his own craft. And this in fact is what we find in Scottish Gaelic. By
the 16th century and, no doubt, earlier, perhaps much earlier, vernacular poets
were using 'filidh'-derived metres with subtlety and ease. That added major
dimensions of rhythmic variety to their successors' work.

There is still another, and very illuminating, account of bards in
the 17th century. This is Professor James Garden of King's College Aberdeen's

reply to John Aubrey, the Diarist, in 1692. Aubrey had written to Garden to ask for information about stone circles in North-East Scotland, Highland customs, second sight, and other matters in which he was interested. One of these was the bards. 'Common Irish' in the account means no more than 'ordinary Gaelic', 'Irish' having for some two centuries been used to denote the Gaelic of Scotland. Garden's informant is described as 'by profession a student of Divinity, and by birth a gentleman's son from Strathspey'. This 'account of the bards such as they are at present in these parts, and such as they were within the memory of my informer's father (who is an aged man of ninetie seven years)' may, because of the time-span involved, contain facts which relate to bards in the early 17th century. (In what follows, conventional Gaelic spellings are substituted for Garden's orthography.)

'A Bard in common Irish signifies a little poet or a rhymer, they use to travel throw countries and coming into ane house, salute it with a rhym called [Beannachadh Baird: 'Bard's Blessing'], ie the Bard's salutation qch is only a short verse or rhym touching the praise of the master and mistress of the house. The inferior sort of them are counted amongst the beggars and the rhym wherewith they salute each house is called [Dan nan Ulag: Meal-Rhyme], ie a verse and a handful or such little quantitie of meal. This inferior sort, otherwise called beggars, makes few or no rhyms of their own, but onlie makes use of such hath been composed by others... He that's extraordinarie sharp of these bards is named 'fili', ie an excellent poet, these frequent onlie the company of persons of qualitie and each of them has some particular person whom he owns his own master. When anie of these travels abroad and comes to a house he tells whose 'fili' he is & then is welcomed & treated according to the qualitie of his master.

These bards in former times used to travel in companies, sometimes 40, 50, 60, persons between men, wives and children...

The whol caball was called [Cliar Sheanchan], ie a companie... These haunted onlie great men's houses, and coming near anie town, sent one of there sharpest to salute the house with a new made rhym in praise of the familie, whereupon there quarters were assigned and provision sent them and during there abod (which would sometimes be 2 or 3 months) one or two of them came in each-night to the familie to make good companie by telling stories, making rhyms and such drolleries. The day they were to remove, the Laird of the place either came to their quarters or els called them to some other room, where being gathered and silence commanded the sharpest [fili] amongst them started up and repeated such verses and lines as they had composed since they came there touching the praise of the Laird and Ladie of the place, there descent, heroic acts and deeds of there predecessors… and so haveing ended they receaved wages according to the Laird's degree and quality and then marcht…

The first point to note about this account is that 'bard' is used in the opening sentence as a technical term meaning 'little poet or rhymer' but later it is used as a generic for all grades of poet. Garden's informant may be using 'bard' first in its older Gaelic sense and later in its English sense. Or his usage may indicate that while at the beginning of the 17th century the word 'bard' in Gaelic still retained its restricted technical meaning, by the end of the century it had been given something like its meaning today.

Garden's tantalisingly brief sketch allows us a unique glimpse of the bards as travelling artists. This 'circuit' from place to place, from patron to patron, was a recognised perquisite of poets of whatever grade and known in Gaelic as 'cuairt' (the nearest modern equivalent is no doubt the poetry reading).

A 17th-century poem of uncertain authorship shows a bard going to visit 'one of the great men's houses ', equipped 'with a new made rhym in praise of the familie…' The recipient is the chief of the MacKinnons of Strath in the Isle of Skye; the poet is possibly Iain Lom MacDonald of Keppoch or a MacGregor bard. At any rate he is arriving from the central or Southern Highlands.

'Distant and long have I waited without going to visit you, O Lachlan from the northern airt.

The snow of the cairns came down with every stream, and every mountain lost her gloom.

If the moorland grew dark and the sun would bend down it were time for me to go on a round of visiting.

It is not the plains of the Saxons (Lowlanders) that I would make for, but the braes of the glens up yonder,

And the hall of the generous one, the destination of hundreds of travellers, Kilmaree under the wing of the bay.

Bear this greeting over the Kyle, since they cannot hear my cry, to the company which is without surliness or gloom.

… In the time of the sun's going under, the sound of the harpstrings was heard about your ear.

Your young men would be drinking, full stoups on the table, and horns of silver going around in their fists…

You got a gift from Clan Leod of the banners of satin, of the cups, of the horns, of the goblets.

You took the white pebble for wife, she of the level regard. Lovely is your wife by your side, and courteous,

Sweet mouth to raise the song, side like the swan of the waves, thin brow that will not bend with gloom!'

Translation from Hugh MacDiarmid *The Golden Treasury of Scottish Poetry* pp 97-99

This poem uses all the basic conventional formulas of praise of a patron's household. Some bardic poems pay greater attention than others to the drinking and music and board games in the chief's hall. Others develop with greater sophistication the domestic scene and the less warlike aspects of the hero who is being addressed. These poems will focus on the hall with its silver and gold cups and plate, its music of violins and harps and pipes, red wine in abundance, white waxen candles blazing, bardic contests, dispensing of gold to poets and musicians, and minstrels gathered from all corners of the Gaelic world.

In bardic tradition the individual exists in a network of relationships. A patron will therefore be praised not only as an individual, isolated figure but in a context of family, ancestors and allies. And not a few poems, like this one to MacKinnon, contain a complimentary reference to the subject's wife also. Normally, as above, the reference comes near the close of the poem: a touch of urbanity and a gracious compliment to the bard's hostess.

We cannot say from Garden's letter to Aubrey whether the top grade bards are those who wrote in Classical Gaelic or whether they belong to the top ranks of vernacular composers. As regards the designation 'filidh' (the normal, though unhistorical spelling of the singular in Scottish Gaelic; plural 'filidhean'), Scottish usage does not confine it to the former, ie to the learned poets of the Schools. And this usage may have been established for a long time.

At all events, we do not hear in modern Gaelic tradition that high-caste poets, whether composing in Classical or Vernacular Gaelic, were included in this 'whol caball', the 'Cliar Sheanchan'. 'Cliar' is a collective noun for poets and bards in general; 'Seanchan' is the name of the poet who is said to have been the leading, most learned poet of Ireland in the seventh century. But in modern oral tradition (going back, where this can be checked, to the mid-19th century), the 'Cliar Sheanchan' are depicted as a motley crew of strolling bards and usually not so much composers of song and poetry as impudent, masterful cadgers who would quarter themselves on reluctant hosts and then proceed to eat them out of house and home. Tradition endorses the description of them as 'such as proponed enigmaes and othere difficult questions... intimating one that delights to invade others with subtilities and ambiguous questions.' Only if the host or his representative could defeat those unwelcome visitors at their own verbal games, or turn the themes of their satirical verses and sayings against themselves, could the household be rid of them. They were in this manner protected by the sanctions of Gaelic society.

Modern tradition has therefore focused on the lower orders of the travelling bards who are occasionally grouped in anecdotes with other travelling craftsmen. It is likely in fact that there was a very significant link between such travelling craftspeople and travelling bards, minstrels and storytellers.

Although Medieval and later Gaelic society was stratified in terms of economic wealth and social status, poor or deprived people had an immemorial right to ask for sustenance from those placed in more favourable circumstances. In 1792 the minister of Fortingall in Perthshire says 'The begging poor have a share of everything the tenants can afford; meal, wool, milk etc... It would be deemed impious to refuse an alms or a night's quarters to a poor person.'

Obviously, much the same priveleges were extended to poets and, in addition, the person of a poet was sacred. Ironically, perhaps, higher-grade poets themselves were not immune to visits by lower order poets or what an Act of the Scots Parliament calls 'siclike ither rinners aboot'. In the following poem from around 1500, a poet complains of these exactions, though whether his visitors were actually travelling bards or not is unclear. At any rate, the description is vivid and reminiscent of the complaints that tradition has preserved, though in much less detailed form, about the depredations of the wandering poet bands. The author ends his poem by promising to go to his own patron, MacDonald, since it was MacDonald's people who despoiled him, confident that his chief will, in turn, be obliged to make restitution.

'To answer the demands for aid that come in turn is a great
effort for those on whom they come hugely from every side...
They are courteous, friendly, kindly, as is meet; and when

they are bidden stay for friendship's sake, which of them fails to understand?

They take a fit of displeasure, rough ill-humour, and of peevishness; they bend and gather their eyebrows one after another. "Never," they say, "will we be friends to you in a dispute."

Understand well the style of the folk I have in mind. Bad or good though the morning be, once it is light they go forth quickly, all too quickly, King of grace!...

Then I go forth for shame's sake – it is a regular bondage – and I give them a handful of my means...

Some little of their style I will set forth: they are Roving-eye-sons, Fly-by-night-sons while yet afar off.

They are Early-rising-sons, who on a summer's day demand more sun; Spyer-sons, Greedy-sons are they all...'

Translation from W G Watson *Scottish Verse from the Book of the Dean of Lismore*

In addition to the benefits enjoyed by going on circuit, bards held lands in freehold by virtue of their office. The lands held by the MacVurichs in South Uist, for example, was known as 'Baile nam Bàrd' (not, interestingly, 'na filidh', though they were a learned literary dynasty). 'Achadh nam Bàrd' in Skye was the land held by lower-caste poets.

The 17th century witnessed revolutionary developments in Gaelic poetry. They are associated with one woman and two men: Mairi nighean Alasdair Ruaidh (c.1615–1707) of the MacLeods of Harris and Skye; Eachann Bacach (c.1600–post 1651), the Lame One, of the MacLeans; and Iain Lom (c.1625–post 1707) of the MacDonalds of Keppoch. All three had an aristocratic background and the men, by the same token, were of the warrior caste of Gaelic society. Iain Lom was apparently a somewhat reluctant warrior but Eachann was active in the wars and severely wounded – hence his sobriquet – at the Battle of Inverkeithing in 1651. Although it is possible to connect the art of such poets with the panegyrics of earlier and humbler bards, it is very difficult to class men like Iain Lom and Eachan Bacach only with little poets and rhymers. But, as praise singers, they could possibly accept that they were bards, though of a higher order. That itself would raise the status of the term 'bard' in Gaelic society.

In terms of metrical specialisation or innovation, these are noted for their use of declamatory 'strophic' metres. Their verse forms can be linked to earlier Gaelic metrical structures but nothing of such rhetorical power or amplitude has survived in Vernacular Gaelic from before their time.

Eachann Bacach is one of the four or five poets of this age who were given the honorific of 'Aos-dàna' ('Men of Art'). This is a curious title, since it is a collective. It may be explained by the fact that the precise meaning of the term had been lost, leaving it to be applied to poets who held a position of some importance in a chief's household around the end of the 17th century and the beginning of the eighteenth. The surviving work of the men who bear the title of 'Aosdàna' indicates that, whilst they were poets who composed in the Vernacular, not Classical, Gaelic, their status was that of a superior grade of demotic composer. But there is no evidence that they were classed with the literate order of 'filidh'. And two of them, the Mac Shithich poet who composed a powerful elegy for Archibald, Earl of Argyll, who was beheaded in 1685 for his leadership of an attempted rebellion, and the Mac Mhathain (c.1670–1757), who was poet to William, 5th Earl of Seaforth, bear the title of 'bard' as well. Until 1719 Mac Mhathain held lands from Seaforth and Eachann is said to have had 'a small annuity' from MacLean of Duart. All this indicates that, although such bards were not professionals in the sense that the learned poets of the Schools were professionals, it is none the less clear that their status as poets, especially panegyric poets, brought them at least some economic benefit.

The next century, the 18th, witnesses the final demise of Classical Gaelic poetry. A fascinating example of the bridging of the two literary worlds is seen in the poetry of Niall Mac Mhuirich (or MacVurich), 1637–1726. Here is a Classical Gaelic professional poet who in his old age produced two poems in Vernacular Gaelic.

This is the century which is often regarded as an age of individual achievement. Alasdair mac Mhaighstir Alasdair (a MacDonald), Gaelic nationalist and Jacobite – he was an officer in Prince Charles Edward Stuart's army in 1745–46 – was the first person to have a volume of secular poetry published, in 1751. MacDonald was a university man, aware of the wider political and literary issues of the age, and he deliberately extended the scope of Gaelic poetry. His innovations were rapidly assimilated by his contemporaries and successors, some of them illiterate but so sophisticated in their craft that Alasdair's formal learning (in Classical Gaelic as well as Latin and Greek) gives him little or no advantage over non-literate poets like Duncan Ban Macintyre (1724–1812), whose masterpiece 'The Praise of Ben Doran' is a praise-poem to a mountain and a visual documentary invented before the invention of the camera. Duncan Ban had his own poems taken down to dictation and published. He is remembered in Gaelic tradition as an invariably genial, easy-going man. He was a member of the city guard of Edinburgh and is buried in the churchyard of Greyfriars there. Tradition also preserves, perhaps as a counterweight, the memory of William Ross (1726–91) as the poet who became so anguished and obsessed with love that he wasted away physically to the dimensions of a child. Ross was a schoolmaster. Rob Donn in Sutherland was a drover and a hunter of deer, among other things: he, too, learned from Alasdair. Finally in the 18th century, Dugald Buchanan of Perthshire is regarded as the 'sublime' poet of the Presbyterian Evangelical Revival. He is certainly the most powerful religious poet of that age. His 'hero' is not the traditional subject of panegyric – the glorified warrior – but the true follower of Christ.

All these poets give their own unmistakable individual impress to their themes but their concerns – praise of men and events, nature, love, religion – are a recreation of topics that were age-old in Gaelic literature and are still manifest in the poetry and song of our own time. None of them earned their living by their verse: they are 'bards' in the modern generic sense. The last bard to enjoy specific patronage was John MacLean of Tiree (1787–1848), bard to the Laird of Coll, before he emigrated to Nova Scotia.

Here is a continuity of literacy in Gaelic from the sixth century to the present day. Literacy in Vernacular Gaelic does not begin in the 18th century but that is the age in which it begins to impinge on the lives of ordinary people. The state, incidentally, gave no help in this respect. Literacy came largely through translation of the Bible and the efforts of the Presbyterian schools. By the 19th century, more and more poets, even if they worked in what was still essentially an oral tradition and drew upon its conventions and its formulas, came to consider publication of their poetry as a worthy goal. And so, some of those who did not themselves achieve full literacy none the less had their verse taken down by others. In Gaelic society the authority of the written word has for centuries commanded respect and the publication of a poem or a book of poetry does confer a certain kudos on a bard. Nevertheless, publication in itself is seen as no more than an extension into the dimension of print of the reality of the spoken or sung word. What makes a poem acceptable to the 'traditional' Gaelic public, generally speaking, is its quality as song. Thus, contemporary Gaelic verse which is not sung, nor is capable of being fitted to any traditional melody, has a limited following.

The designation 'bard baile', 'poet of a township', is now used more frequently than in the past and with a rather different denotation. Traditionally, the phrase described verse and rhyme-makers whose reputation was never likely to extend beyond the bounds of their own townships. It now seems to designate all versifiers who live in the Gaelic-speaking areas or whose outlook is said to be, somewhat imprecisely, restricted to the 'traditional'. This is a broad category and the term can easily become vague.

In Gaelic society there is still a palpable respect for the poet. Whether he or she is called a village poet, a township poet, or classified in some other way by scholarly commentators, the Gaelic public accords the man or woman who makes poetry a particular esteem.

The bard, technically speaking, was a praise-poet from the beginning; so too, could he or she articulate criticism and utter dispraise in the 'aoir', plural 'aoirean'; a word conventionally translated 'satire(s)'. The power of such compositions, however, was far greater than the English word 'satire' often conveys. The 'aoir' had a physical as well as a psychological effect. Even as late as the 19th century, it was believed to be capable of actually dealing death to its victim. Bards were thus naturally approached with some circumspection. While they remained, as they did in most of the Gaelic communities, spokespersons for their society, their potential as satirists was genuinely feared. Now that the media have taken over as the agents that censure aberrant behaviour, the bard's role has accordingly diminished in proportion. But positive respect remains.

The 'traditional outlook' referred to above is perhaps difficult to encapsulate in a single descriptive formula. There is a framework of praise versus dispraise, clearly a legacy from a very distant past. In our times this is modified by a variety of influences, internal and external, for now all Gaelic communities are bilingual and bicultural.

One strange belief is still subscribed to: that is, that a bard cannot be sued for libel uttered in his or her poetry, provided the poet's name is in the 'Book of the Bards', 'Leabhar nam Bàrd'. Yet this term has no denotation. There is no such book in existence. The idea is that the bard must have been officially recognised as a poet. For example, if he or she had been charged with some crime or cited to appear in a court of law or some other public place, and proclaimed as Poet by profession, then he or she would from then on enjoy a kind of diplomatic immunity. There are numerous anecdotes told in connection with this, always involving the composition of satires. One of these stories relates how a bard from the Isle of Mull, hearing that he was about to be served with a summons, walked to Edinburgh and proclaimed himself publicly at the Mercat Cross as a poet. He thereupon walked back to Mull, confident in the belief that he was now immune from prosecution. And, the anecdote tells, as soon as the news reached Mull, the case was dropped.*

---

* This notion is probably the last reflection in Scottish oral tradition of the ancient privileges of the poets.

THE TRADITION IN SKYE

The Isle of Skye has for centuries been notable for its poets, named and unnamed. Writing in the 1690s, Martin Martin, graduate of Edinburgh and Leiden, tells us that the people of his native island have a 'genius for poetry' and are 'lovers of music'. He continues, 'Several of both sexes have a quick vein of poesy, and in their language (which is very emphatic) they compose rhyme and verse, both which powerfully affect the fancy. And in my judgement (which is not singular in this matter) with as great force as that of any ancient or modern poet I ever yet read.'

The distinction between 'verse' and 'rhyme' is one which other writers of this age make as well. 'Rhyme' is the song-poetry of the oral poets, composed in Vernacular Gaelic. 'Verse' has a wider denotation and includes the written poetry of the formally trained poets. By Martin Martin's time, it was entering its last phase in Scotland. This learned verse is, as he puts it, in 'such a style… as is understood by very few'. Martin would have been personally acquainted with some of the leading practitioners of this poetry, for he had been a tutor to the MacDonalds and MacLeods who were their patrons, and classical poems associated with Dunvegan Castle still survive in manuscripts of this period.

The disjunction between 'verse' and 'rhyme', between the learned literary tradition and oral song-poetry, is, none the less, not absolute. One of the most important mediators between Classical and vernacular is Mairi nighean Alasdair Ruaidh ('Mary MacLeod', c.1615–c.1707), herself also associated with the MacLeods at Dunvegan. Composed in vernacular Gaelic, Mairi's songs present us with a model of the mandatory commonplaces of Gaelic praise-poetry. Her manner of handling these could be said to represent the norm of vernacular high-style panegyric. It is essentially formal court poetry, almost entirely confined to the affairs and personages of Clan MacLeod and uses a repertoire of images based on that of classical Gaelic verse, although she herself was non-literate. From that time onwards, such imagery continues to develop, and the songs of later poets, oral and literate alike, continue to draw upon it.

Màiri is the senior member of a group of women in different parts of the country whose poetry spanned the period from the first half of the 17th century to beyond the middle of the 18th. A much younger member of the group is Sileas of Keppoch, one of whose most popular poems is the 'Elegy for Alasdair Dubh (Black Alasdair) of Glengarry', who died in 1721. It is composed in a metre, not attested before her time, which may derive from the metres used in Classical Gaelic. At any rate, whatever its origins, it came to be used by a large number of poets and survived in the Isle of Skye until quite recently.

In the 19th and early 20th centuries there were two poets whose names, and some of their songs, were known to almost everybody. One was Màiri Mhòr nan Oran, Mary MacPherson, 'Big Mary of the Songs', the other Neil MacLeod. Both had books published, thus giving Gaelic readers access to their poetry far beyond the bounds of their native island. Màiri Mhòr's reputation now stands a good deal higher than that of Neil MacLeod but one critic has described him, with much justification, as 'the most popular Gaelic poet of the 19th century'.

Màiri Mhòr was born in Skeabost, Skye, in March 1821. Her parents had spent the first twelve years of their married life in Glasgow where they settled after rejecting an offer made to groups of Skye crofters and others at that time to emigrate to Canada. They had apparently discovered that this scheme, with assisted passages, promised rather more than it was going to deliver. That realisation contributed to Màiri's view of the exploitation of the common tenantry and the entire history of the Highland Clearances. The parents returned to Skye before Màiri and one of the brothers was born.

In 1848 Màiri married Isaac MacPherson in Inverness; in 1871 she was left a widow with four children. At that juncture, having become a domestic servant, she was falsely accused of stealing a pound note from her employer, taken to court, found guilty and imprisoned. That experience provides the central and essential fact of her artistic biography. Màiri, at the age of 50, never hitherto conscious of her great creative powers, suddenly became a poet. But, as with many a similar cataclysmic conversion, there had been a long process of preparation for the moment. She knew the events of her parents' life and knew the events of Highland life on which they acted as a focus. Now she had direct experience of judicial bias and public humiliation. This is the point at which her attitude to those set in authority crystallised.

Her love of poetry and song from an early age was intense. According to Dr. Alexander MacBain, one of the foremost Gaelic scholars of his age, Màiri carried in her memory something between 20,000 and 30,000 lines of Gaelic verse. In his introduction to her book, MacBain has this to say: 'Though she can read her own poetry in print, she cannot write it. All the following poems were taken down from her own recitation within the last twelve months by the well-known Gaelic authority, Mr John Whyte. Between 8000 and 9000 lines from memory! And she has at least half as much more of her own, and twice as much which she is able to repeat of floating, unpublished poetry, mainly that of Skye and of the western Isles.' No doubt a good deal of this would have been local verse, now irretrievably lost.

Allowing for some exaggeration, Màiri Mhòr clearly possessed astonishing powers of memory, perhaps rarely equalled even in a society where a knowledge of hundreds of songs was not exceptional. But it is necessary to point out that only a few of Màiri's own songs became common currency in the repertoires of Gaelic singers, and the same is true of scores of other oral poets.

Dr MacBain was the first to link her firmly with the movement for land reform. Before placing her in popular esteem as the poet 'who seemed destined to fill among female bards the position which Duncan Ban [Macintyre 1724–1812 – still the most highly honoured poet in Gaelic tradition] holds among the men', MacBain tells us, 'Mrs MacPherson came first into prominence in the contested election in Inverness Burghs in 1874, between Mr Aeneas Mackintosh of Raigmore and Mr Fraser Mackintosh of Drummond [the Liberal pro-crofter candidate]. She composed several songs during the contest and afterwards in favour of the latter, who was the successful candidate. Throughout the whole of the Highland land law reform agitation, Mrs MacPherson gave herself wholeheartedly to the people's cause, and her songs largely contributed to the victory of the popular candidates all over the Highlands in 1885 and 1886. Indeed she might very properly be described as the bard of the movement, for with the exception of her fellow Skyeman, Neil MacLeod, we are not aware that any of her contemporaries has written anything which has given voice to the aspirations of her countrymen during these eventful years.'

Now there is another important dimension to the life of the Gaels during those same years: the Presbyterian Evangelical Revival.

The cultural and psychological chaos that the break-up of any traditional society produces was intensified beyond endurance in the bewilderment of a people under attack by those whom they had hitherto looked to as their own natural leaders. This broken community eagerly accepted the demands of a passionate and uncompromising faith. Many who were not converted in the religious sense nevertheless grasped the implications of a movement that was full of non-conformist zeal and intellectual tumult. This was a new dialectic in Gaelic society, powerful enough to replace the deep loyalties of the traditional order, in which not religion but genealogy had been the opiate of the people. Social protest now becomes closely bound up with religion. But because Evangelicalism was other-worldly in its focus, essentially reclusive although practised in open society, it could hardly yield an adequate artistic strategy that drew upon anything like the full spectrum of human experience.

Amongst all the poets of her troubled times, Màiri Mhòr nan Oran is unique in having come nearest to achieving a unified sensibility. She was not conventionally pious. Yet in the climate of that period she could hardly escape conscience searching. But she had come to terms with herself and elected to remain robustly of this world, albeit with a strong religious sense of ultimate justice. Màiri's introspection borrows from religion but never turns morbid.

Her harrowing experience of unjust conviction is, she says, 'what brought my poetry into being', and the anguish of it remained ardent in her until the end of her life. But that also gave direct authority to her words of comfort to the Skye crofters who were imprisoned in Edinburgh in 1883: 'A good college is prison – I learned that myself, long ago.'

Equally passionate was her affection for her native language and her own people. It emerges powerfully in her celebrations of place and place-names, the fertility of the earth, the food it produced, the flocks and herds it supported, and all the vivacity of communication in the communal life of her youth.

All these elements combine in her work, resolved and integrated and given a major dimension by being set in the context of 19th century Radicalism.

Màri Mhòr's criticisms of the role of the clergy at the time of the land agitation are sometimes cited in a rather simplistic fashion. On the one hand, she is the most eloquent opponent of those who remained aloof. 'Preachers have so little concern / Seeing the plight of my people – / As dumb on the subject in the pulpit / As though their listeners were of the brute creation.'

But no one could be more celebratory of the Calvinist ministers who did support the movement, especially the Rev. Donald MacCallum of the Established Church, who was arrested for 'inciting the lieges to violence and class hatred', and the aristocratic Maighstir Ruairi, the Rev. Roderick MacLeod, who joined the Free Church of Scotland at the Disruption of 1843. Mgr. Ruari was one of the most fearless and tireless champions of the crofters' cause. He was also an intensely austere and ascetic Christian. Yet he never adopted the Pharisaic attitudes that Mairi and some other poets detested.

In a mock flyting, 'The Civil War', composed after the floodtide of the Evangelical Revival had reached Skye and all the pleasures of this world were at best vanity, Mairi makes her woman friend declare: 'The people have become so strange / That sorrow to them is wheat, / And if you won't go into a whelk-shell for them, / You cannot stay alive.' Her own reply is incisive and peremptory: 'We will not go into a whelk-shell for them / And we will stay alive, / Although we will not put on long faces / Nor wear a look of gloom / With groans and plaintive sighings / With no substance in them but vapour, / So that the world may believe / That a change has come on us.'

The poem ends with a moving rejection of certain Evangelical attitudes to the 'vanities' of earthly life. 'But because vanity is a plant that satisfies the flesh, / It clings to me as firmly / As the thong does to the shoe.'

Màiri Mhòr is representative of many traditional strains of Gaelic poetry and song, and sometimes limited by their conventions, but her best work gives the sharp feel of immediate experience while at the same time conveying the pressure of contemporary events. Because she possesses such abundant emotional vitality and because she is not a self-conscious analyst of historical processes, the Gaelic world of the late 19th century, with its varied and sometimes antipathetic movements, is more vividly and intimately realised in her poetry than in that of any other poet of the age.

Neil MacLeod, as Alexander MacBain wrote, also had 'given voice to the aspirations of [his] countrymen'. But Neil was temperamentally very different indeed from Màiri and lived his life in very different circumstances too.

He was the son of Donald MacLeod, Dòmhnall nan Oran, 'Donald of the Songs' (c.1786-1873), a native of Glendale. Donald composed personal poetry and songs on topics of local interest but saw himself also in the role of poet to Clan MacLeod. In this capacity he took up a convention used by Alexander MacDonald and John MacCodrum in the 18th century, announcing himself to be 'The Mavis of the MacLeods' in order to sing the praises of his clan. In 1811 he published an anthology which contains some of his own poems; others were printed in 1871, including a satire on the elders of the parish. Donald had the reputation of being a notable seanchaidh, indeed one of the most consummate storytellers on Skye; he had, in fact, an interest in the entire range of Gaelic oral tradition and he was also highly literate. From him came the version of the Fairywoman's Lullaby for the heir of MacLeod in Dunvegan, taken down from the singing of his son Neil in 1908 by Francis Tolmie and printed in her collection of Gaelic songs in 1911. After spending four years in America (1829–33), Donald returned a merchant. At the age of 60 he married a girl of 19; they had ten children and two of their four sons became poets.

Those two brothers, Neil and John MacLeod, were inheritors of a rich family tradition as sons of a noted poet and seanchaidh: a father who had collected and published poetry, and enjoyed respect as a man of letters. But, of course, they also drew upon an inheritance that went deeper and wider than the confines of a family circle: they had their father's library and the lore of the island at their disposal, including the songs of local bards.

The poetry of the 19th century is not at all dull or trivial throughout, but it does bear the evidence of being the unsettled complex of a transitional age. It is sometimes nostalgic and anachronistic, still limited by the stereotypes of the praise-singers. It is prone to go off in false directions that could lead to nothing but sentimentality, as when it borrows from English or Lowland Scots and reproduces weak and prettified aspects of Romanticism without its strengths. Yet it is still instinct with the old splendid craftsmanship and there is a palpable widening and deepening of human sympathy, partly due to the influence of Christian teaching, partly due to that of Romantic sensibility itself. There are contrasts and opposites almost at every turn, and they serve to remind us that we are dealing not with one simple strand but with what is still the art of a nation, no matter how attenuated.

One vivid contrast, one that might be made a symbol of that age, is illustrated in the poetry and lives of these two MacLeod brothers in the Isle of Skye.

At the age of 22 Neil moved to Edinburgh and remained there for the rest of his life, employed by a firm of tea merchants whose senior partner was his cousin. He became, in effect, a modestly prosperous middle-class gentleman and a respected member of society. He by no means lost interest in his native island, to which he made periodic visits and regular business trips, but he ceased to be involved directly in the life of the island. Neil was a quiet, somewhat diffident, abstemious man, according to those who knew him. He was a fine craftsman whose verse is never less than competent, at its best exquisitely polished. Most of his poems were made, in the traditional manner, to be sung, and became enormously popular. But they frequently tended towards the pretty and sentimental and, when he commented on the life of Skye at a time when the great dominating issues were social and political, his focus is not on the struggle but on an arcadian past. His sympathies are profoundly with his own people but the characteristic expression of them is elegiac. His book, *Clàrsach an Doire* (*The Harp of the Grove*) was first published in 1883 and subsequently reprinted a number of times, most recently in 1975.

Neil's brother John was Iain Dubh – 'Black John'. Iain Dubh went off to sea in his teens and was, it is said, at least as well acquainted with New York and Sydney and Calcutta as he was with Glendale. He was remembered in Skye as a thickset, handsome man, somewhat swarthy and black haired, with intense, humorous eyes. And some said 'He was black in hair and black in heart.' Those who knew him in the Lowland ports and elsewhere gave him the sobriquet of 'The Wizard of the North'. The fact is that Iain Dubh is as well remembered as a bohemian trickster and practitioner of magic as he is as a poet. He may have himself possessed hypnotic powers; but according to the late Donald Sinclair in Tiree, a sailor, too, in his youth, Iain Dubh became friendly during his voyages with a certain 'Professor' Anderson (1812-74), one of the leading professional magicians of the day. Interestingly enough, he was a Scot who called himself 'The Great Wizard of the North'.

It is scarcely surprising that Iain's older contemporaries believed him to be in league with the devil and asserted that he had learned his 'Sgoil Dubh' – 'the Black Art' – in the 'Black School' in Italy, that being one of the centres of magic and devilry in Gaelic legends as in those of other Western European languages.

Iain Dubh was no doubt literate in Gaelic, given his family background. But he never wrote down his songs nor had them collected for publication and now there are, for the most part, only fragments to be heard. He was essentially a composer in the oral tradition, a wanderer all his life, a poet of strong, realistic poetry, the polarities of which are rooted in Skye and the brutality of life on the sailing ships. But there are really too few of his compositions extant to assess him in the round. Probably the two best preserved of his compositions are 'A Satire on Donald Grant' (presented on pages 296 of chapter 14) and a song that tells what life at sea was like in those days. One evening a group of boys was questioning him and Iain is supposed to have said, 'I'll put in poetry every good and bad I learned in a seaman's life. Listen to this!' Then he sang his song.

> Sturdy young lads who are growing up in Glendale,
> Some of you are keen to make your livelihood at sea.
> Listen to the song MacLeod made who was really there
> And if you sail the ocean you'll remember it for the rest of your lives
>
> When you are young and uninstructed out on the ship of sails,
> Everything is so new and strange to you until you learn each rope.
> Oh, often will you be cursed and damned to the devil
> Until you're able to go into her masts as lightly as do birds.

A less well-known song ends:

> You who reflect and ask who made the rhyme
> Tell them it was a MacLeod who sailed the seven seas
> And who'll be up at her helm when the waves are turning green —
> Fortunate are you, Finlay, that you learned to sow and reap.

Until perhaps the middle of the 20th century, the people of Skye were unanimous in their opinion that in spite of Neil MacLeod's virtues and the vices of Iain Dubh, Iain was the better poet. And, furthermore, there was a rumour Neil had actually stolen some of Iain's poems and published them under his own name. There is actually no evidence for this, stylistic or otherwise, but amongst the older generation the belief still persists.

Since Neil MacLeod's poetry is now regarded by most critics as rather facile, whereas Mairi Mhor nan Oran has become something of an icon, it must be emphasised that critical opinion was not always divided along those lines. Alexander Nicolson in his *History of Skye* (1930; revised edition 1995) is worth quoting if only for the fervour and the uncompromising nature of his literary judgements.

To Neil MacLeod, he asserts, 'has been revealed, in a manner vouchsafed to few, the secret of the problem of life'. MacLeod is a moralist and didactic but never a prude. His satires and humorous pieces are free from 'personal bitterness and those crudities of expression, tainted with obscenity, that too often mar the works of other bards.' 'His "Tigh a' Mhisgeir" ["The Drunkard's House"] is a faithful exposure of the evils of intemperance… Throughout his work there glows a love of home that borders close on piety.' MacLeod's nature poetry is admittedly lacking in power; on the other hand, he raised the love-lyric 'to a plane far higher than was customary… in the past'. In one of them 'the poet's art has touched a level seldom attained by the master minds of any clime or age'. In another, MacLeod 'kindles our sympathy for the island Ophelia even more powerfully than does Shakespeare himself.'

In contrast to that fulsome praise we have a fierce denunciation of Màiri Mhòr. 'Few of her productions are worthy of preservation. She was incapable of sustained effort, her imagery was too fleeting and superficial, and we tire of her pleonastic and rambling treatment of her subject…

'Màiri Mhòr was a welcome guest at the "gatherings" of her isles-folk in particular, and of Highlanders generally, in Glasgow and in Greenock. In celebration of these functions she often composed, and sang, songs that evoked a large amount of enthusiasm at the time; but now that the scenes have changed, and the personalities have passed away, one is forced to admit that the great majority of these effusions have no permanent value.'

In one 'of her most popular pieces, "Soraidh le Eilean a Cheo" ["Farewell to the Island of Mist"], she depicts beautiful vignettes of scenes in her native island; but displays them in such rapid succession, and in such a haphazard manner, that the mind wearies in following her, so that the whole production resolves itself into a glorified tourist guide… At that time (1882) the land troubles were agitating the islands and she championed the peoples' cause in speech and song. Many of her poems were then composed, though few of them possess any poetic value. She composed a large number of elegies; but in these, as in her political songs, she betrays the shallowness of her genius.'

In tone and attitude, this is at the far end of the gamut from Dr Alexander MacBain's judgement that Màiri Mhòr seemed destined to be the equal of Duncan Ban Macintyre in popular esteem and that 'her poetry is a well of pure Gaelic undefiled'. Subsequent critics have endorsed MacBain's views and developed his succinct appraisal. The first writer to do so (in Gaelic) was Murdo Murray, in a well-balanced, responsible critique in the *Transactions of the Gaelic Society of Inverness* in 1936. There Murray takes Nicolson to task for his extraordinary denigration. But although no one has equalled Nicolson in his virulence, it is necessary and salutary to recognise that there was a spectrum of critical appraisement of all this poetry, in the past as in the present, amongst those who listened to it sung as well as those who read it on the printed page. This will be seen presently, from a contemporary bard's point of view, in the comments made by John Nicolson.

In the second half of this century a small group of Skye bards has become known to a wider audience. The group includes three who are now dead, Malcolm Nicolson of Braes, Angus Fletcher of Bernisdale and John Nicolson of Cuidreach. These men can be seen as representatives of the continuing 'quick vein of poesy' of the people of Skye. John Nicolson, 'the Skipper', was recorded by Professor Derick Thomson, poet and critic, as early as 1950 for the then embryonic School of Scottish Studies of the University of Edinburgh. But it was not until Catriona Montgomery, herself a poet in a modernist style, published some of his songs along with those of Angus Fletcher (1980, cassette and booklet) that he began to attract general attention. Recently a detailed study of Nicolson with a cassette of selected songs, sung by himself, has been published: Dr Thomas A McKean's *Hebridean Song-Maker*.'

Malcolm Nicolson (1902–78) was known locally as Calum Ruadh ('red haired'). His maternal grandfather, a MacLeod of Raasay stock, was a township bard almost all of whose songs appear to be lost but Calum Ruadh is now seen as a 'classic' representative of Scottish bardic composition in the 20th century.

Two musicologists, the late Donia Etherington and Thorkild Knudsen, a Danish folklorist, working under the aegis of the School of Scottish Studies, were told about Calum Ruadh and became interested in his use of melody and the link between text and music in the process of composition. In his own neighbourhood Calum was not regarded as a singer, although from time to time he might be asked to sing his own songs in an informal setting. Those who were recognised singers and musicians asserted that Calum either sang all his songs to the same basic melody, with capricious variations, or that he muddled his tunes.

In reality Calum Ruadh used three or four melodies, drawn from older songs, and moved more or less at will among them. But he could cope perfectly adequately with the tunes of traditional songs, of which he had a good repertoire.

Donia Etherington soon came to the conclusion that further musicological research was not necessary and the project, which was to be undertaken in conjunction with textual analysis, was dropped. Knudsen, however, took a different view, viz., that oral poets throughout Europe (from

Romania to Iceland) used a technique of composition similar to Calum Ruadh's, and he seemed to imply that Calum was the sole surviving representative of it in the whole of the United Kingdom and Ireland. By superimposing recordings of the poet chanting his own songs, taken at irregular intervals, Knudsen was able to let listeners hear this exotic weave of melody. It is obvious, however, that all Gaelic oral poets relate words and melody, sometimes regarding them as inextricably related. In that, Calum was in no way exceptional.

The fact of the matter is that Calum Ruadh employed as one of his dominant melodies the tune of the elegy (mentioned above) by Sileas of Keppoch to Alasdair Dubh of Glengarry in 1721. In metre and in melody it may be derived from the work of Classical Gaelic poets but that has never been proved beyond doubt. Calum himself had not heard the elegy but he had heard variants of its chant-like tune, of which there are a number, for it was adopted after 1721 by many bards. Given all these provisos, and put in that perspective, it may be that an archaic technique is involved. At all events, Calum Ruadh was a fine dramatic performer of his own songs, giving prominence to each syllable in the line, whether it was stressed or unstressed. The chant and metre and stanzaic pattern of Sileas' elegy gave ample scope for that.

Rather like Iain Dubh's poem 'A Satire on Donald Grant', and perhaps suggested by it, Calum Ruadh's 'Fairy Song' purports to describe a vision. It begins: 'One night when I was asleep…' (This and translations are to be found in the booklet, *Scottish Tradition 7*).

John Nicolson, 'the Skipper', who is now in his late nineties, and vigorous for his age, has always felt that he is himself essentially a maker of songs rather than a maker of poems (*bardachd*). His insistence on the difference is unusual but it enables him to display fierce critical assessment of the work of his fellow poets, present and past. Màiri Mhòr nan Oran: 'I wouldn't say she was anything like Uilleam Ros (C18) or Neil MacLeod – she didn't make anything like Neil MacLeod – and his brother Black-haired John was much better than him.' Of Murdo MacFarlane of Lewis: 'Not one line rhyming with the other!' Of Calum Ruadh's poems: 'No, I didn't approve of them at all – they're not poetic at all; they don't rhyme or anything. Mind you, he was probably making a bardachd of it, but there's no songs at all… Of course it was this "Gairm" that was going about, that did the publishing for them and of course they will be likely glad to get anything, but I wouldn't say they're with Màiri Mhòr or Neil MacLeod. Màiri Mhòr was more popular than any of them.' [Quotations from T. A. MacKean *Hebridean Song-Maker*, pp158–61].

PATRONAGE AND CONTINUANCE

While the old order lasted, the privileges of the poets were real enough. An anecdote from the mid-17th century illustrates this. At the Battle of Inverlochy in 1645, the MacDonalds, under the leadership of the great warrior Alasdair Mac Colla, inflicted an overwhelming defeat on the Campbells. Before the battle, Iain Lom, the bard of Keppoch, is supposed to have said to his fellow MacDonalds: 'You fight and I will tell.' He did so in a powerful celebration of the victory but his poem, 'The Battle of Inverlochy' is probably the most savage paean, exulting in the utter rout of Clan Campbell, ever to have been composed by a Gaelic bard.

When the Campbells heard this and other satirical invectives, the Earl of Argyll, head of Clan Campbell, put a price on the poet's head. Iain Lom, secure in the knowledge that Gaels everywhere regarded the person of a poet as inviolable, decided to make his way to Inveraray Castle to meet the Earl and claim the reward himself. Not only did the Campbell Earl show no hostility, he is even said to have been amused and invited the poet to stay for a week as a guest in the castle. Iain Lom, however, did not feel it necessary to moderate either his attitudes or his language in return for this act of hospitality.

(A phrase in the translation of the dialogue that follows requires to be explained with reference to a still common Gaelic expression. 'To make a black-cock' of someone is to fell a man or knock him out.)

As the Earl showed Iain Lom round the castle, he pointed out various trophies of the hunt, among them a collection of heads of these game birds. 'Iain,' said the Earl, 'have you ever seen so many black-cocks in one place?' 'Yes, I have,' said the poet, 'at Inverlochy.' 'Iain, Iain,' said the Earl, 'will you never stop gnawing at the Campbells?' 'What troubles me,' said Iain Lom, 'is that I cannot swallow them.' Although this legend may well be apocryphal, it was accepted in all its details throughout the Campbell and MacDonald lands, and farther afield, as a token of what was perfectly proper in the circumstances.

This social order, with its well-defined sets of obligations and responsibilities between temporary or permanent patron on the one hand and a visiting or resident bard on the other, survived into the 18th century. The abolition of the clan chief's powers after the defeat of the Jacobite campaign of 1745-46 had no doubt some bearing on the relationship between poets and their patrons. But although the Battle of Culloden is important in military and political affairs, it has hardly the same significance in cultural matters. For one thing, changes in the status of professional poets and musicians had begun much earlier. It is said, for example, that the MacLeod chief who died in 1693 was the last patron who maintained a full complement of artists: bard, harper, piper, violinist and jester.

But as late as 1763, the erudite Sir James MacDonald of Sleat (who spoke Gaelic from early childhood and took up the serious study of it after graduating from Oxford) appointed John MacCodrum in North Uist (1693-1779) to the office of bard. For his services MacCodrum was given a small farm free of rent, yearly supplies of meal and cheese and an annuity of two pounds and five shillings sterling. After Sir James's untimely death at the age of 25, his brother Sir Alexander (later Lord MacDonald), though a man of quite different temperament and interests, continued these allowances.

John MacLean (Iain mac Ailein) of Tiree (1787–1854) held the honorific position of bard to MacLean of Coll and is often referred to in Gaelic as 'Bard Thighearna Chola' – the Laird of Coll's bard. He emigrated to Nova Scotia in 1819. Around 1788, Sir Hector MacKenzie of Gairloch made Alasdair Buidhe (yellow-haired) MacIver (1767–1843) his family bard. It is told at a banquet held about 1790, where Alasdair Buidhe was present, the chief of the Nicolsons of Scorrybreck in Skye observed, 'The bards have gone.' 'Not so,' said Alasdair Buidhe, 'but those who supported them have gone.'

None the less, poets and poetry remained. The poet-patron relationship is only one aspect of a complex cultural process. It is clear, indeed, that for many centuries there were amateurs of poetry – but 'amateur' only in the sense that they were not restricted by the demands of professional service – at every level of Gaelic society.

For the past two centuries and a half this is the tradition of Gaelic poetry. Throughout that time it has continued to grow and develop, with its own innovations, into a mainstream of numerous cross-currents. The well-known resurgence of Gaelic poetry in the 20th naturally shows some continuity with the past. In other respects, it is a transformation, veering sharply away from song and chant, gaining and losing in the process. One consequence of this is that most of the other kinds of poetry tend to be classed together, uniformly, under the label of 'traditional'. This is seriously misleading and obscures the variety. Yet it is also true that the native Gaelic community, as represented by its tradition bearers, has a fairly consistent view of Gaelic poetry. All makers of poetry and song are 'bàird' and 'bana-bhàird': poets and poetesses, whether they are of the past or the present, professionals or amateurs, writers or oral poets. In that view there is no secure or uncontested boundary between 'major' and 'minor' bards, even if all agree there is a spectrum of excellence that places, say, Alexander MacDonald of the Forty-five or Duncan Ban Macintyre at one end and most 'township bards' at the other.

Potentially any Gaelic bard is the inheritor of all that has gone before, just as in any other literary tradition. For Gaelic, this includes the village poets no less than those who are far-famed, and comprises what had survived in books, manuscripts, and oral tradition, with countless anonymous songs and those of named authors. In such sources every part of Gaelic is represented, from Arran to Sutherland, from Aberdeenshire to Nova Scotia.

But of course few contemporary bards, living in areas remote from libraries, can have access to much of this very considerable corpus of verse and must depend on their own local, oral tradition. On the other hand, some bards nowadays read as widely as they can. Makers of religious poetry, generally well versed in that abundant tradition, published and unpublished, habitual readers of scripture who draw upon a theology that takes the world as its parish, may in spite of all that do little more than versify sections of Holy Writ or compose edifying moralistic poems. Their learning in their chosen field does not inevitably make them less parochial. Others again have wide spiritual horizons and address issues of genuine religious concern. One of these is the late Donald John MacDonald of South Uist. As in the field of secular poetry, the excellence of the product depends on the individual creative genius.

Considering all these issues, it is fair to say that while 'village' or 'township verse' may serve as a convenient enough label, it is difficult to isolate the poetry categorically and establish a precise definition.

As the bard at the highest level of society was a spokesperson who articulated the aspirations of the leaders of that society, so, at lower social levels, the poet of a district or a parish was, and still is, a commentator on local events. He or she composes songs on anything that might be of interest to the community at large in order to amuse, to ridicule, to mourn, or to celebrate. There is celebration of places and persons; love-songs, many of them composed by sailors remembering the girls they left behind them; a large corpus of religious verse; some didactic poetry; and, within a still secure framework of panegyric, a convention of composing elegies. The verse is centred linguistically on the poet's local dialect, giving it a rich idiomatic flavour. But borrowing from beyond that linguistic compass can occur also, particularly where the poet is literate in Gaelic. The poetry of Donald MacIntyre (1889–1964) of South Uist and Paisley provides a good example of this. The basic diction is the Gaelic of Uist but MacIntyre deliberately extended his vocabulary by drawing on the works of the major 18th- century poets and others.

The bard Rob Donn is usually singled out as a precursor of our contemporary village poets although with the qualification that Rob Donn had wider interests and worked on a larger scale. As a native of north Sutherland, Rob lived on the periphery of the Gaelic world that for centuries had been dominated by the warrior-aristocrats of the Lordship of the Isles and their bardic panegyrists. In addition, the poet's clan territory had experienced the force of an early form of Evangelicalism which questioned both the Established

Presbyterian church and the ideals of a heroic society. All this would encourage the development of a naturally satirical talent away from simple dichotomies of praise versus dispraise towards the much subtler and truer social criticism that characterises Rob Donn's poetry. It is equally true, however, that other poets, among them John MacCodrum, who lived in an area where the bardic praise-singer flourished, could compose poetry which is focused on local events and is primarily of local interest. As Professor Derick Thomson has put it: 'It may sometimes be difficult to decide questions of demarcation between village and other poetry.' There are gradations everywhere.

With the growth of literacy in Gaelic, and particularly from the 19th century onwards, and the concurrent development of Gaelic publishing, more and more poetry became widely accessible. Drawing on these published sources and supplementing them with sound recordings from the second half of the 20th century, it would be possible to take almost any area of the Gaelic speaking Highlands and Islands to represent a fair spectrum of the work of Gaelic bards. And an in-depth study would demonstrate that, whether bards are described as 'national' or 'local', composers of 'literary' or 'folk' poetry, they are all inheritors of an ancient tradition that is still vital.